Cultural Mobility

Cultural Mobility is a blueprint and a model for understanding the patterns of meaning that human societies create. Drawn from a wide range of disciplines, the essays collected here under the distinguished editorial guidance of Stephen Greenblatt share the conviction that cultures, even traditional cultures, are rarely stable or fixed. Radical mobility is not a phenomenon of the twenty-first century alone, but is a key constituent element of human life in virtually all periods. Yet academic accounts of culture tend to operate on exactly the opposite assumption and to celebrate what they imagine to be rooted or whole or undamaged. To grasp the shaping power of colonization, exile, emigration, wandering, contamination, and unexpected, random events, along with the fierce compulsions of greed, longing, and restlessness, cultural analysis needs to operate with a new set of principles. An international group of authors spells out these principles and puts them into practice. *Cultural Mobility* sets out a powerful intellectual agenda with which scholars across the humanities and social sciences will need to engage.

STEPHEN GREENBLATT is Cogan University Professor of the Humanities at Harvard University. The author most recently of *Will in the World* (2004), Professor Greenblatt is one of the most distinguished and influential literary and cultural critics at work today, as well as the general editor of *The Norton Anthology of English Literature*. His team of collaborators on *Cultural Mobility* all worked together at the Wissenschaftskolleg in Berlin under Professor Greenblatt's overall direction, and represent a suggestive and unique range of voices and approaches.

CULTURAL MOBILITY:
A MANIFESTO

Stephen Greenblatt, with Ines G. Županov,
Reinhard Meyer-Kalkus, Heike Paul, Pál Nyíri,
and Friederike Pannewick

CAMBRIDGE
UNIVERSITY PRESS

CAMBRIDGE UNIVERSITY PRESS
Cambridge, New York, Melbourne, Madrid, Cape Town,
Singapore, São Paulo, Delhi, Mexico City

Cambridge University Press
The Edinburgh Building, Cambridge CB2 8RU, UK

Published in the United States of America by Cambridge University Press, New York

www.cambridge.org
Information on this title: www.cambridge.org/9780521682206

First published 2010

A catalogue record for this publication is available from the British Library

Library of Congress Cataloguing in Publication data
Cultural mobility : a manifesto / Stephen Greenblatt ... [et al.].
    p. cm.
ISBN 978-0-521-86356-8 (hardback)
1. Culture. 2. Social change. I. Greenblatt, Stephen, 1943– II. Title
HM621.C85344   2009
306.01–dc22
                                                2009035491

ISBN 978-0-521-86356-8 Hardback
ISBN 978-0-521-68220-6 Paperback

CONTENTS

CONTENTS

vi

AUTHORS

STEPHEN GREENBLATT
Harvard University

INES G. ŽUPANOV
Centre national de la recherche scientifique, Paris

REINHARD MEYER-KALKUS
Wissenschaftskolleg zu Berlin

HEIKE PAUL
Friedrich-Alexander-Universität Erlangen-Nürnberg

PÁL NYÍRI
Macquarie University

FRIEDERIKE PANNEWICK
University of Oslo

ILLUSTRATIONS

ACKNOWLEDGMENTS

The authors are deeply indebted to the Institute of Advanced Study in Berlin (Wissenschaftskolleg zu Berlin), where the seeds of this project were sown and nurtured. We are grateful both for the generous fellowship support that the Institute provided and for the unflaggingly energetic, attentive, and resourceful help of the justly celebrated administration and staff. The executive secretary of the Kolleg, Joachim Nettelbeck, was particularly instrumental in forming the focus group on cultural mobility. Many of those who were in residence with us as fellows for the year, along with others who visited for shorter periods of time or were in fruitful long-distance contact with us, contributed to our thinking: among them, we would like to mention Homi Bhabha, Horst Bredekamp, Giovanni Carreri, Charlotte de Castelnau-de l'Estoile, Stefan Epstein, Pierre-Antoine Fabre, Egon Flaig, Marie Fourcade, Rossitza Guentcheva, Peter Hall, Ulrich Herbert, Carla Hesse, Christoph Horn, Ronnie Po-Chia Hsia, Susan James, Bernhard Jussen, Ousmane Kane, Joseph Koerner, Thomas Laqueur, Wolf Lepenies, Stefan Litwin, Klaus Lösch, Peter Mason, Kenneth Mills, Ashis Nandy, Dominique Pestre, Robert Pippin, Christof Rapp, Amnon Raz-Krakozkin, Beate Roessler, Carlo Severi, Quentin Skinner, Ramie Targoff, Rosemary Taylor, Denise Vidal, Rudolf Wagner, Stefan Wild, and Ângela Barreto Xavier. This is a dauntingly long list, but it is by no means complete: at a bare minimum

ix

it should also include our families and many others. For help in pulling together our manuscript, with its contributors spread across vast distances of space, we owe special thanks to Emily Peterson and to the editorial staff of Cambridge University Press.

1

Cultural mobility: an introduction

STEPHEN GREENBLATT

In the latter half of the twentieth century many in the social sciences and humanities gleefully proclaimed the demise of a set of traditional assumptions about cultural identity. Notions of wholeness, teleological development, evolutionary progress, and ethnic authenticity were said to have been dismantled forever. A few lamented their passing, but most scholars energetically grappled with brave new theories of hybridity, network theory, and the complex "flows" of people, goods, money, and information across endlessly shifting social landscapes. But as the new century unfolds, it has become increasingly clear that the bodies of the deceased have refused to stay buried: those who thought to have bid farewell once and for all to the heavily guarded borders of the nation-state and to the atavistic passions of religious and ethnic identity find themselves confronting a global political landscape in which neither nationalism nor identity politics shows any intention of disappearing. While the older conceptions of rootedness and autochthony seem intellectually bankrupt, the heady theories of creative metissage have run aground upon the rocks of contemporary reality.

There is an urgent need to rethink fundamental assumptions about the fate of culture in an age of global mobility, a need to formulate, both for scholars and for the larger public, new ways to understand the vitally important dialectic of cultural persistence and change. This dialectic is not only a function of triumphant capitalism, free trade, and globalization; it is, as we hope to show, a much older phenomenon. The essays in *Cultural Mobility* aim to reorient traditional understanding and to serve as a framework for new research in many fields.

There is no going back to the fantasy that once upon a time there were settled, coherent, and perfectly integrated national or ethnic communities. To write convincing and accurate cultural analyses – not only of the troubled present but of centuries past – requires, to paraphrase *Hamlet*, more a chronicle of carnal, bloody, and unnatural acts than a story of inevitable progress from traceable origins.[1] We need to understand colonization, exile, emigration, wandering, contamination, and unintended consequences, along with the fierce compulsions of greed, longing, and restlessness, for it is these disruptive forces that principally shape the history and diffusion of identity and language, and not a rooted sense of cultural legitimacy. At the same time, we need to account for the persistence, over very long time periods and in the face of radical disruption, of cultural identities for which substantial numbers of people are willing to make extreme sacrifices, including life itself.

Beyond the recognition of this dialectic, there is an urgent need to address what we might call the rigid

---

[1] For an elaboration of these views, see my essay "Racial Memory and Literary History," *PMLA* 116 (2001), pp. 48–63.

compartmentalization of mobility. Although in the past twenty years or so many academic disciplines have formally embraced ideas of "cultural mobility," they have for the most part operated with tunnel vision: the times and places in which they see significant mobility occurring remain strictly limited; in all other contexts, they remain focused on fixity. The fact, to cite a single example, that some of the prisoners at Guantánamo Bay are citizens of Western states simply has no place in a dominant understanding heavily influenced by ideas about the "clash of cultures." The complicated trajectory that led these prisoners from Europe to the Middle East or Central Asia and then to the no-man's-land on Cuba falls outside the available analytical framework, as does their tangled inner experience of alienation and adherence to various national, ethnic, and religious communities.

The problem is that the established analytical tools have taken for granted the stability of cultures, or at least have assumed that in their original or natural state, before they are disrupted or contaminated, cultures are properly rooted in the rich soil of blood and land and that they are virtually motionless. Particular cultures are routinely celebrated for their depth, authenticity, and wholeness, while others are criticized for shallowness, disorientation, and incoherence. A sense of "at-homeness" is often claimed to be the necessary condition for a robust cultural identity.

Everyone recognizes, of course, that the global economy has drastically altered the picture, but the pervasiveness and power of contemporary developments have paradoxically only reinforced the assumption that the originary condition was one of fixity and coherence. Academic departments are

3

routinely organized as if the division between English and, for example, French were stable and timeless, or as if the Muslim and Christian worlds had existed in hermetic isolation from one another, or as if the history of ideas were somehow entirely independent of the history of exile, migration, and economic exchange. The phenomenon of mobility is acknowledged in passing, of course, but as the exception to the rule or as its more or less violent disruption. Literary and historical research has tended to ignore the extent to which, with very few exceptions, in matters of culture the local has always been irradiated, as it were, by the larger world.

"Perhaps people will soon be persuaded," Goethe wrote in 1826, toward the end of his long life, "that there is no patriotic art and no patriotic science. Both belong, like everything good, to the whole world and can be promoted only through general, free interaction among all who live at the same time." These words lie at the heart of what Goethe called *Weltliteratur*, world literature, which he conceived of as a ceaseless process of exchange across the borders of nations and cultures. As Reinhart Meyer-Kalkus' essay shows, Goethe dreamed that "the general, free interaction among all who live at the same time" would liberate human genius from the vicious parochialism of competing communities, cultures, and nation states. If this prophetic dream by now seems shopworn and almost absurd – its optimism spectacularly disproved by almost two centuries of fathomless hatred and bloodshed – it was nonetheless based upon a canny insight into the restless process through which texts, images, artifacts, and ideas are moved, disguised, translated, transformed, adapted, and reimagined in the ceaseless, resourceful work of culture.

This process obviously long preceded the internet or Apex fares or the spread of English on the wings of international capitalism. Such recent developments are, to be sure, significant factors in enabling us to effect a return to world literature and, more broadly, to world culture, for the digitization of library resources, the ease with which we can access newspapers and reviews from every continent, the rise of international discussion groups in multiple languages all pull away from national and ethnic exclusivity. But world culture does not depend on recent events or on a transient wave of American triumphalism or on recent technological innovations.

The apparent fixity and stability of cultures is, in Montaigne's words, "nothing but a more languid motion."[2] Even in places that at first glance are characterized more by homogeneity and stasis than by pluralism and change, cultural circuits facilitating motion are at work. This is not only true of trade, religious proselytizing, and education, where the circuitry is obvious. Tourism, for example, often depends on a commodification of rootedness: cultures that appear to have strikingly unmixed and local forms of behavior become the objects of pilgrimage and are themselves fungible as mobile signifiers. That is, not only do people from very diverse backgrounds travel great distances to view them, but they themselves are frequently broken into smaller units and, like the bands of Andean musicians on the streets of European and American cities, set in motion.

---

[2] Michel de Montaigne, "Of Repentance," in *The Complete Works of Montaigne*, tr. Donald M. Frame (Stanford: Stanford University Press, 1948), p. 610.

As Walter Burkert observed in his study of Near Eastern influence on Greek culture in the Early Archaic Age, the adoption of Phoenician script by the Greeks and its skillful adaptation to Greek phonetics, some time around the eighth century BCE, sparked an unprecedented intellectual, religious, and literary mobility.[3] This cultural mobility, facilitated by traders, craftsmen, and troops of mercenaries, is obviously uneven and at certain times and places has been sharply restricted. But once launched, it has proved unstoppable.

A vital global cultural discourse then is quite ancient; only the increasingly settled and bureaucratized nature of academic institutions in the nineteenth and early twentieth centuries, conjoined with an ugly intensification of ethnocentrism, racism, and nationalism, produced the temporary illusion of sedentary, indigenous literary cultures making sporadic and half-hearted ventures toward the margins. The reality, for most of the past as once again for the present, is more about nomads than natives.

Enhanced cultural mobility, Goethe ardently hoped, would foster a new cosmopolitanism, an unregulated free trade in expression and feeling, an epoch of global respect founded on the conviction that "poetry is the common possession of humanity and that it emerges everywhere and at all times in hundreds and hundreds of people." The actual effect, of course, has been far less reassuring. Mobility can indeed lead to heightened tolerance of difference and an intensified

---

[3] Walter Burkert, *The Orientalizing Revolution: Near Eastern Influence on Greek Culture in the Early Archaic Age*, tr. Walter Burkert and Margaret E. Pinder (Cambridge, Mass.: Harvard University Press, 1992).

awareness of the mingled inheritances that constitute even the most tradition-bound cultural stance, but it can also lead to an anxious, defensive, and on occasion violent policing of the boundaries. The crucial first task for scholars is simply to recognize and to track the movements that provoke both intense pleasure and intense anxiety.

When it comes to the past, the enterprise of tracking the restless and often unpredictable movements of texts, ideas, and whole cultures is still at a very early stage. There are, to be sure, two powerful traditional models for understanding cultural mobility. The first is the account that historians and ideologues developed for describing the *translatio imperii*, the "translation" of power and authority from the Persians to the Greeks, from Greece to Rome, and then from imperial Rome to a succession of ambitious regimes in nascent nation states. The second is the account that theologians developed for describing the ways that Christianity "fulfilled" the Hebrew Scriptures and hence transformed the Torah into the "Old Testament." Each model possesses rich resources for grasping the mechanisms through which one cultural system is taken over or reshaped by another.

Hence, to consider the first, the symbols, regalia, and other literal trappings of Roman imperial power were physically carried, when the empire was no longer able to defend itself, from the ancient capital of the world to a succession of new sites of global ambition. In this displacement, of course, the conquerors were merely doing to Rome what Rome itself had long done to those it had subdued: appropriating the tangible emblems of authority, including the gods, of the conquered peoples, along with the treasure, grain reserves,

7

commodities, arms, slaves, and other worldly goods that it was able to seize. The urbane Propertius prays in one of his elegies for "the day on which I see Caesar's chariot laden with spoil and captured chieftains sitting beneath their arms, shafts from cavalry in retreat and bows of trousered soldiery, the horses oft halting at the people's cheers, and leaning on the bosom of my sweetheart I begin to watch and read on placards the names of captured cities!" (III.4).

The Roman custom of forcing captive leaders to sit on floats beneath their weapons or to march in chains behind the triumphal chariot of the conquering emperor or general is the most vivid instance of this appropriation: not only is the abjection of the defeated ruler displayed to the cheering populace, but with each shuffling step he takes that ruler's former power further swells the pomp of the victor. Mobility is not incidental here: physically displacing conquered chieftains, compelling them to parade through the streets, exposing them to the gaze of strangers are all key elements in what it means for the Romans to make a much larger cultural field available for transfer to themselves.

By the time Rome was vulnerable enough to have its own cultural field appropriated by others, it had developed complex institutions and traditions of such prestige, density, and symbolic force that no simple act of plunder, however greedy, could easily set in motion the process of translation. The fierce tribes of Germany and Scythia under the leadership of Alaric, who sacked Rome for six days in 410, hauled away on their heavy wagons massive chests of gold and jewels, costly vases, wardrobes of silk, precious statues of gods and heroes, barrels of the finest wine, and all the other portable wealth of a population long accustomed to luxury. But rapine, even on a huge scale, is not the same as cultural mobility, and indeed there are indications that Rome's first conquerors, the Goths, were uninterested in (or incapable of) setting Rome's culture, as distinct from its riches, in motion.

Alaric, who died relatively soon after the sack of Rome, was interred in a sepulchre adorned with Rome's spoils, but he had not seized for himself the cultural authority of the empire he had brought low. Indeed his successor, his brother-in-law Adolphus, is said to have formally acknowledged the impossibility of doing so, at least for the Goths. "In the full confidence of valour and victory," Adolphus reputedly declared, "I once aspired to change the face of the universe; to obliterate the name of Rome; to erect on its ruins the dominion of the Goths; and to acquire, like Augustus, the immortal fame of the founder of a new empire. By repeated experiments I was gradually convinced that laws are essentially necessary to maintain and regulate a well-constituted state; and that the fierce untractable humour of the Goths was incapable of bearing the salutary yoke of law and civil government. From that moment I proposed to myself a different object of glory and ambition; and it is now my sincere wish that the gratitude of future ages should acknowledge the merit of a stranger, who employed the sword of the Goths, not to subvert, but to restore and maintain, the prosperity of the Roman empire."[4]

---

[4] Orosius, 1.vii.c.43, pp. 584–5, cited in Edward Gibbon, *The Decline and Fall of the Roman Empire* (New York: Alfred Knopf, 1910), 3:301.

Such a comforting declaration, or anything resembling it, seems exceedingly unlikely, given the dubious chain of transmission: Adolphus supposedly shared his views with a leading citizen of Narbonne who subsequently went on a pilgrimage to the Holy Land, where he told the story to St. Jerome in the presence of the historian Orosius. It nonetheless reflects two important early perceptions about cultural mobility. First, the sheer brute fact of conquest does not necessarily set a culture, whether that of the victor or of the vanquished, in motion. And second, though material goods may at moments have powerful symbolic importance, at other moments those goods may carry very little cultural charge, and cultural mobility may lie elsewhere. Adolphus, or at least the historian Orosius imagining Adolphus, believed that in the case of Rome, law and civil government counted for more than treasure. To transfer masses of wealth was relatively simple, even if it involved stripping whole buildings of their fabric; to transfer a cultural system was a far greater challenge.

The true cultural mobility of the Roman Empire was sometimes said to reside in the person of the emperor himself: "Where the emperor is, there is Rome." But this piece of extravagant flattery lightly concealed the fact that the emperor was a transient, all-too-human place holder in an elaborate network of offices, laws, duties, titles, definitions, mutual understandings, and, above all, tax codes. This network was ultimately upheld by the power of the state to direct its violence against those who did not submit to it, but, though the guarantor of the whole system, violence by itself was not the "real" meaning of Roman culture. The medieval lawyer who wrote of the fiscal system of the state that *Ubi est fiscus, ibi est imperium* – "Where the fisc is, there is the empire" – was appropriating something more essentially Roman than anything seized by the Gothic armies rampaging through the streets of Rome.[5]

It was this mobility of Roman codes, structures, and definitions – what we might call categorical mobility – that enabled the massive transfers of prestigious cultural norms from the ancient capital to a series of would-be heirs and successors. The rulers of the Eastern Empire in Constantinople first made the strong claim that the essence of Rome had migrated to the banks of the Bosphorus and that all that remained on the Tiber were mere bricks, stones, and rubble. The Byzantine claim was challenged by the Ottonian princes in the west, who claimed that Rome was to be found in in Aachen. And after the fall of Constantinople to the Turks in 1453, the imperial claimants moved further and further to the west: Paris, Madrid, Lisbon, London. Each city was declared by its adherents to be the new Rome; each professed to be the site to which the imperial capital, the aspiring ruler of the known world, had been "translated." Lawyers steeped in law worked out the precise mechanisms through which codes that had been developed in the very special circumstances of Rome or Constantinople could be accommodated to the peculiar needs of the local elites; administrators helped to organize the court and the chain of command; rulers dressed themselves in robes that conjured up the illustrious imperial

---

[5] Baldus, cited in Ernst Kantorowicz, *The King's Two Bodies: A Study in Mediaeval Political Theology* (Princeton: Princeton University Press, 1957), p. 204.

predecessors; intellectuals worked out the historical processes that had inevitably and providentially led to this glorious outcome; and artists, architects, musicians, and writers provided the imagery that confirmed in the imagination of both the rulers and the ruled the successful transfer of cultural authority.

The lines of transmission, of course, are far more complex than this brief sketch can suggest. In the early centuries of the Catholic Church, for example, prelates often adapted political terms and ceremonies from the Roman state. These terms and ceremonies were in turn adapted by jurists formulating the principles of the secular state. Something of the empire survives then and is handed down, but only by passing through the prism of the papacy – a passage Hobbes described with mordant wit when he remarked that the pope is "no other than the ghost of the deceased Roman Empire, sitting crowned upon the grave thereof."[6] What is fascinating about this ecclesiastical medium of transformation is the riddle that obsessed Gibbon: the immense difficulty of deciding whether the Church was the fatal enemy of the Roman empire or the agent that saved much that would otherwise have been forever lost.

Something of the same intertwining of destruction and mediated transmission is conveyed by the second great traditional model for cultural mobility. For centuries the concept of *figura* served Christian theologians – and artists and writers – as an extremely subtle and flexible tool both for

---

[6] Thomas Hobbes, *Leviathan*, ch. 47, in *English Works*, ed. William Molesworth (London: J. Bohn, 1839–45), 3:697–8.

appropriating prophetic signs and for reconceiving figures and events as living anticipations of the Redeemer. Abel was Abel, but he was also, in his goodness, in his piety, and in his death at the hands of the wicked Cain, a prefiguration of Jesus. Indeed Abel's full significance, his deeper meaning, could only be understood through the Christian story.

Mobility was facilitated through a wholesale reinterpretation of history, a change in its valence, so that Moses could be understood (and represented) at once as a significant person in the history of Israel and as a type or prefiguration of Christ. The cunning of this form of interepretation was that it left things standing in place and at the same time emptied them out, in order to claim that a full actualization of the precious cultural resource – in this case, the religion of Israel – could only be realized in the religion that had come to displace and triumph over it. Things – historical individuals, narratives, symbols, and ceremonies – that had once claimed an independent and substantial existence were revealed to be shadows. Conversely, shadowy metaphors and similes in the Hebrew Bible, meant to illuminate and intensify the narratives, were developed into substantial historical truths only disclosed to the world in the life of the Messiah.

What is most striking perhaps about the concept of *figura* is its blend of homage and aggression, a phenomenon that extends far beyond this particular instance of cultural mobility but that here achieves one of its most resonant forms. Thus the elaborations of the Passion story in the narratives and art of the fourteenth and fifteenth centuries – a story notably spare and austere in the Gospels – almost all depend upon the appropriation of figures and imagery from the Hebrew Bible. Not only are individuals – Jacob, for example, or Moses, or Job – revealed to be anticipations of the Redeemer, who gives them their true meaning by enacting, now in what is claimed to be a final and definitive form, their stories, but the enactment, the historical realization, is constructed out of imagistic fragments borrowed from scriptural texts. "He gave his back to the smiter," from Isaiah, thus becomes a whole full-staged scene of vicious flagellation. And the perpetrators of the torment and murder of the Lord are, of course, the Jews from whose sacred books the narrative hints have been taken. The clerical storytellers elaborate the Passion story by setting in motion and appropriating the sacred materials of the Jews and then use that story to call for Jews' destruction.

Cultural mobility then can take the form of attempted cultural (and, of course, actual) murder. The murder in this case stopped short of total extermination both because the Hebrew scriptures, though superseded, had to retain their sacredness in order to serve as a prophetic anticipation of the Redeemer and because an impoverished, immiserated and despised Jewish remnant could serve as a perpetual reminder to the faithful of the long-term consequences of rejecting the Messiah. Hence in response to repeated calls, especially from itinerant friars, for the final elimination of the Jews, a succession of popes ruled that it was in the interest of Christianity, in the time before the end of time, for some small number of Jews to survive and to eke out their lives in misery. A surviving remnant and a text transformed into a shadow became key elements in the symbolic transfer and transformation of sacredness.

For all of their interpretative richness, both of these models, the "translation of empire" and *"figura,"* are severely constrained by the teleological triumphalism that helped to launch them. Outside the circles of the faithful, they are now generally approached with justifiable wariness, irony, and historical distance. Pieces can be isolated and savored: the triumphal chariot of the Roman emperor, for example, was revived by Renaissance princes and adapted to grand funerary processions. There it served as a symbolic affirmation of the continuity, the immortality even, of the *imperium*, however mortal and transitory the individual emperor. Its use, practical and symbolic, was not restricted to kings: the corpse of the Duke of Wellington was carried in such a chariot, and, with suitable democratizing modification, it helps to explain the black Cadillac hearse and the long procession of cars that accompanies it to the cemetery.[7] But this and comparable histories of literal and symbolic mobility no longer reinforce or confirm the grand narrative. When, in a singularly misguided moment, Richard Nixon chose to have the White House guards dressed in neo-imperial uniforms, the immediate outburst of ridicule compelled a quick change of costume.

We have more a sense of fragments than a set of coherent histories: Latin grammar arose when a Greek diplomat, Crates of Mallus, broke his leg in a sewer-hole in Rome and whiled away the time of his recuperation by giving lectures on language; Leone Ebreo fled from Spain into Italy, in the wake of the Expulsion of the Jews in 1492, encountered

---

[7] Leopold Ettlinger, "The Duke of Wellington's Funeral Car," in *Warburg Journal* 3 (1939–40), cited in Kantorowicz, *The King's Two Bodies*, pp. 427ff.

Florentine neo-Platonism, itself a recent Greek import, and was inspired to write his great dialogues on love; Giordano Bruno lectured at Oxford, where he almost certainly encountered and influenced Sir Philip Sidney, before returning to Italy and meeting his end at the pyre in the Campo dei Fiori.

Mobility studies, as these fragments suggest, are essentially about what medieval theologians called *contingentia*, the sense that the world as we know it is not necessary: the point is not only that the world will pass away, but also that it could all have been otherwise. This *contingentia* is precisely the opposite of the theory of divinely or historically ordained destiny that drove the imperial and figural models of mobility. And yet, to be fully convincing, mobility studies also need to account for the intense illusion that mobility in one particular direction or another is predestined. They need to account as well for the fact that cultures are experienced again and again – in the face of overwhelming contrary evidence – not as contingent at all but as fixed, inevitable, and strangely enduring.

How is it possible to convey a sense of *contingentia* (and its counterbalancing illusion of fixity) in practice? The answer in large part lies in the patient charting of specific instances of cultural mobility, that is, not in an attempt to construct new grand narratives (in the manner of the translation of empire or of *figura*) but in detailed, intellectually vital engagements with specific cases. "I cannot keep my subject still," Montaigne wrote in "Of Repentance." "It goes along befuddled and staggering, with a natural drunkenness"(610).

These words can serve perhaps as the motto of the essays assembled in *Cultural Mobility*. Montaigne's response was not to try to construct an abstract system but to try to describe a single object in motion, himself. Our projects are less resolutely autobiographical, but they are comparably peculiar, particular, and local. The case studies in this volume – microhistories of "displaced" things and persons – represent cultural connections between unexpected times and places. A resonant emblem of such a connection is the moment, discussed by Reinhart Meyer-Kalkus, when Goethe read a Chinese novel and dreamed of "world culture." So too, as Heike Paul demonstrates, Harriet Beecher Stowe's novel *Uncle Tom's Cabin* (1852) not only inspired a mass American audience to oppose slavery but also, in a series of encounters entirely unimagined by Stowe herself, inspired the rhetoric of mid-nineteenth-century German feminists to demand equal rights for women, of Russian peasants to call for the abolition of indenture, and of English maids to rebel against domestic abuse. The novel is paired in Paul's essay with a less easily adaptable signifier of the institution, namely a slave's iron collar traveling from the American South to England in 1849 in the luggage of the fugitive slave William Wells Brown. This circulation and the European reactions to both sentimental novel and iron collar demonstrate, as Paul observes, that American slavery and its critique have repeatedly served as blueprints for political empowerment far beyond America's borders.

These optimistic visions of cultural mobility are set against the more ambiguous story told by Ines Županov, who looks closely at the contrasting works of two Portuguese contemporaries in late sixteenth-century Goa. One, the humanist physician Garcia da Orta, wrote a book that manifested a remarkable openness to, and curiosity about, the unfamiliar Asian world in which he found himself; the other, Archbishop

Gaspar de Leão Pereira, wrote a book in which he attempted to shore up the faith of the Christians against the subtle temptations and the satanic errors of unbelievers. To Orta's proferred healing, using the precious medicines of the Indies, Dom Gaspar opposes what he insists is a salutary fear. "Fear," he writes, "is the origin of wisdom." The two positions represent sharply opposed responses to the exceptional mobility which the Portuguese in India directly experienced, and there is no reason to believe that the more hopeful vision ever gained the upper hand. In 1580, twelve years after Orta died, his bones were dug up by order of the Inquisition, burned, and scattered. Dom Gaspar's bones, Županov notes, are preserved even today in the cathedral of Goa.

Pál Nyíri's "Struggling for mobility: migration, tourism, and cultural authority in contemporary China" is a comparably sobering challenge to any utopian vision of cultural mobility, that is, any account that would see cosmopolitanism, tolerance, critical intelligence, or political democratization as the inevitable or even likely consequences of ventures into unfamiliar territories. In the Chinese domestic tourist industry, mass mobility is encouraged and controlled by a project, at once nationalist and racist, designed to keep power in the hands of the party apparatus. And, apart from the isolated experiences of independent backpackers, there seem to be very few cracks in the walls carefully constructed to channel the experience of other cultures.

None of these case studies can be adequately summed up by the simple contrast between optimistic and pessimistic visions of cultural mobility. The heart of the matter lies in the surprise of movement, the sense of not quite knowing where the journey will end or even where it began. The theater is said to be a Western art form, alien to the Islamic world, but, as Friederike Pannewick shows, powerful Islamic traditions of performativity can be traced back for centuries. This performativity can be mobilized, transformed, politicized, and deployed in ways that at once adapt to and challenge both traditional and newer forms of theatrical artistry. It becomes difficult, perhaps impossible, to say any longer which elements are native and which are imported from elsewhere.

What is most striking perhaps about the essays collected here is their diversity and range, from colonial Goa to mid-nineteenth-century America to contemporary China, from Goethe's theoretical reflections to the theatrical experiments of a contemporary Syrian playwright. Together, they explore the more or less conspicuous "unhomeliness" of objects, practices, and people in the places they inhabit and trace the itineraries that lie behind them, as well as the intellectual and material investments that have been conferred upon them in the process of circulation. Their places and their out-of-placeness – two sides of the same coin – are described and analyzed in a way that puts the management of movement (its restriction, its amplification and, above all, its diffusion) at the center. What are the mechanisms at work when movement encounters structures of stability and control? How do local actors accommodate, resist or adjust to challenges posed by outside movement? What are the cultural mechanisms of interaction between states and mobile individuals? What happens to cultural products that travel through time or space to emerge and be enshrined in new contexts and configurations? How do they set in motion – imaginatively as well as geographically – people who encounter them and, in turn, are set loose themselves?

Along with these shared questions, the authors of these diverse essays share certain basic principles, which I will outline at the end of this volume. They also have in common a single biographical fact: an association with a project on cultural mobility initiated at Berlin's Institute for Advanced Study. That Institute is one of the great contemporary agents of intellectual mobility and exchange: brilliantly run, supremely well organized, at once congenial and contentious, it uses its situation in a brooding, scarred, immensely vital city at the heart of Europe to bring together scholars from all over the world. The constitution of the initial cultural mobility group – a Croatian who works on the Jesuits of Goa, a Hungarian who works on Chinese overseas migration, a German who works on American slavery, a Bulgarian who works on Communist business travel, an American who works on Shakespeare – only reflects the Institute's larger vision of intellectual exchange across multiple borders. And, despite occasional bitter setbacks, that exchange, fostered not only by this remarkable institution but also by thousands of universities and research centers and think tanks, is one of the sources of hope in the contemporary world.

Further Reading

Appadurai, Arjun. 2003. *Modernity at Large: Cultural Dimensions of Globalization*. Minneapolis: University of Minnesota Press.

Auerbach, Erich. 1984 "Figura." In *Scenes from the Drama of European Literature*. Minneapolis: University of Minnesota Press.

Benjamin. Walter. 1999. *The Arcades Project*. Trans. Howard Eiland, and Kevin McLaughlin. Cambridge, MA: Harvard University Press.

Bhabha, Homi. 1994 *The Location of Culture*. London: Routledge.

Bourdieu, Pierre. 1977. *Outline of a Theory of Practice*. Trans. Richard Nice. Cambridge and New York: Cambridge University Press.

Bourne, Randolph. 1916. "Trans-National America." *Atlantic Monthly* 118 (July): 86–97.

Breinig, Helmbrecht and Klaus Lösch. 2006. "Transdifference." *Journal for the Study of British Cultures* 13 (2): 105–22.

Calvino, Italo. 1974 [1972]. *Invisible Cities*. New York: Harcourt, Brace, Jovanovich.

Carrasco, David. 1999. *City of Sacrifice: The Aztec Empire and the Role of Violence in Civilization*. Boston: Beacon Press.

Certeau, Michel de. 1988. *The Writing of History*. Trans. Tom Conley. New York: Columbia University Press.

1984. *The Practice of Everyday Life*. Trans. Steven F. Rendall. Berkeley: University of California Press.

Clendinnen, Inga. 2003. *Ambivalent Conquests: Maya and Spaniard in Yucatan, 1517–1570*. Cambridge and New York: Cambridge University Press.

Clifford, James. 1988. *The Predicament of Culture: Twentieth-Century Ethnography, Literature, and Art*. Cambridge, MA: Harvard University Press.

1997. *Routes: Travel and Translation in the Late Twentieth Century*. Cambridge: Harvard University Press.

Cohen, Margaret and Carolyn Dever, eds. 2002. *The Literary Channel: The Inter-National Invention of the Novel*. Princeton, NJ: Princeton University Press.

Conley, Tom. 1996. *The Self-Made Map: Cartographic Writing in Early Modern France*. Minneapolis: University of Minnesota Press.

Dening, Greg. 1980. *Islands and Beaches: Discourses on a Silent Land: Marquesas, 1774–1880*. Carlton: Melbourne University Press.

Elliott, Emory. 2007. "Diversity in the United States and Abroad: What Does it Mean When American Studies Is Transnational?" *American Quarterly* 59 (1): 1–22.

Foucault, Michel. 1998 [1971]. "Nietzsche, Genealogy, History." In *Aesthetics, Method, and Epistemology*. Ed. James D. Faubion. *Essential Works of Foucault, 1954–1984*, vol. II. New York: New Press.

Geertz, Clifford. 1973. *The Interpretation of Cultures: Selected Essays*. New York: Basic Books.

Giles, Paul. 2002. *Virtual Americas: Transnational Fictions and the Transatlantic Imaginary*. Durham, NC: Duke University Press.

Greenblatt, Stephen. 1991. *Marvelous Possessions: The Wonder of the New World*. Chicago: University of Chicago Press.

Greene, Thomas M. 1982. *The Light in Troy: Imitation and Discovery in Renaissance Poetry*. New Haven, CT: Yale University Press.

Gregory, Derek. 1994. *Geographical Imaginations*. Cambridge, MA: Blackwell.

Helms, Mary W. 1988. *Ulysses' Sail: An Ethnographic Odyssey of Power, Knowledge, and Geographical Distance*. Princeton, NJ: Princeton University Press.

Isaac, Rhys. 1982. *The Transformation of Virginia, 1740–1790*. Institute of Early American History and Culture, Williamsburg, VA. Chapel Hill: University of North Carolina Press.

Kaplan, Caren. 1996. *Questions of Travel: Postmodern Poetics of Displacement*. Durham, NC: Duke University Press.

Latour, Bruno. 1993. *We Have Never Been Modern*. Trans. Catherine Porter. Cambridge, MA: Harvard University Press.

Lévi-Strauss, Claude. 1992 [1955]. *Tristes Tropiques*. Trans. John and Doreen Weightman. New York: Penguin.

Löfgren, Orvar. 1999. *On Holiday: A History of Vacationing*. Berkeley and London: University of California Press.

Massey, Doreen. 2005. *For Space*. London: Sage.

Ong, Aihwa. 1999. *Flexible Citizenship: The Cultural Logic of Transnationality*. Durham, NC: Duke University Press.

Pratt, Mary Louise. 1992. *Imperial Eyes: Travel Writing and Transculturation*. London: Routledge.

Presner, Todd Samuel. 2007. *Mobile Modernity: Germans, Jews, Trains*. New York: Columbia University Press.

Todorov, Tzvetan. 1999. *The Conquest of America: The Question of the Other*. Trans. Richard Howard. Norman: University of Oklahoma Press.

Urry, John. 2007. *Mobilities*. Cambridge: Polity.

Vertovec, Steven and Robin Lohen. 2002. "Introduction." In *Conceiving Cosmopolitanism*. Ed. Steven Vertovec and Robin Lohen. Oxford: Oxford University Press.

Werner, Michael and Bénédicte Zummermann. 2002. "Vergleich, Transfer, Verflectung: Der Ansatz der Histoire Croisée und die Herausforderung des Transnationalen." In *Geschichte und Gesellschaft* 28.

2

"The Wheel of Torments": mobility and redemption in Portuguese colonial India (sixteenth century)

INES G. ŽUPANOV

Garcia da Orta wrote in his *Colóquios dos Simples e Drogas he Cousas Medicinais da India* that "the Portuguese who sail through many parts of the world, wherever they go do not look for knowledge but only how to dispose of their merchandise ... They are not curious to know about things that exist in those countries."[1] In 1563, when the book was printed in Goa, the capital of the Portuguese colonial empire in Asia, trade and profit-making were routinely branded as sinful from the pulpits and as unlawful when taxes and bribes were not paid to the royal officials. A sense of decay, decadence, and loss of spiritual and moral nerve was pervasive in contemporary Portuguese correspondence and in the treatises reflecting on the *Estado da Índia* that stretched along the coasts of the southern seas from Africa to Asia. Fifty years after the successful military conquest of Goa in 1510 and the self-declared possession of the oriental "Indias," those first two decades

[1] Garcia da Orta, *Colóquios dos Simples e Drogas he Cousas Medicinais da India* (Goa, 1563), ed. Conde de Ficalho, facsimile of the 1891 edition (Lisbon: Imprensa Nacional-Casa da Moeda, 1987), vol. I, p. 151. Hereafter "Orta." There exists also a facsimile edition of the original edition published in Lisbon by the Academia das Ciências de Lisboa in 1963.

appeared to the late sixteenth-century Portuguese in India as a "golden" age, *idade dourada*, after which everything went downhill. Though the accumulation and consumption of goods, riches, and capital had created euphoria and fantastic mercantile *élan*, they also provoked anxiety and profound soul searching. Complaints about the economic and moral crisis that started in that period may have been widely exaggerated, but these complaints engendered a new genre of colonial writing and historiography that focused specifically on the *decadência* of the Portuguese empire.[2]

Given that the Portuguese held on to Goa for another four centuries, until 1961, the doomsday scenarios of the colony in the 1560s were obviously premature. Leaving aside the question of whether there actually was a severe social crisis and financial crunch at this particular moment, what is of interest to us is the fact that prominent intellectuals and administrators in late sixteenth-century Goa experienced the world of the Portuguese colonies as trapped in a deranging and painful state of permanent mobility – mobility that would lead to disaster and loss of cultural, political, and religious community, unless some sort of framework or boundary were contrived to legitimize their hastily acquired Asian *dominium*.

---

[2] See Sanjay Subrahmanyam, *The Portuguese Empire in Asia: A Political and Economic History* (London and New York: Longman, 1993), pp. 80–106, and "The Trading World of the Western Indian Ocean, 1546–1565: A Political Interpretation," in *A carreira da Índia e as rotas dos estreitos*, eds. Arturo Teodoro de Matos and Luís Filipe F. R. Thomaz (Angra: O Seminario, 1998), pp. 207–27; Luís Filipe F. R. Thomaz, "A crise de 1565–1575 na história do Estado da Índia," *Mare Liberum*, 9 (1995).

Poetic licence, literary genius, and the desire for royal gratification made Luís Vaz de Camões rhapsodize in his epic *Os Lusíadas* about the courageous Lusitanians at the door of Asia.[3] Refashioning a small, unruly band of sailors and soldiers, led by Vasco da Gama, into the valiant successors of the conquering Roman legionnaires, supported in their actions by the Roman gods themselves, Camões consecrated all present and future Portuguese Asian conquests as a "new" *imperium Romanum*. This poetic vision was in fact all-pervasive in sixteenth-century Portugal, and it coexisted with the darker side of Portuguese imperial ambition. A fear of geographical overextension, combined with an inability to consolidate and control "possessions," presented a permanent source of anxiety. Already in 1540, João de Barros, a grammarian and historian of Portuguese Asia who believed in the spiritual, social, and linguistic future of the empire – he envisaged Indians speaking Portuguese in their temples – was having doubts about "material" survival: "Portuguese arms and memorial stones [*padrões*], planted in Africa and in Asia, and on thousands of islands beyond the three parts of the world, are material and time might spoil them, but it will not spoil the doctrine, customs and language that the Portuguese have left in those parts."[4]

The fantasy of successful *translatio imperii* that the Portuguese shared in the sixteenth century with the Spanish

[3] Luis Vaz de Camões, *The Lusiads* (London: Penguin, 1987 [1952]).

[4] João de Barros, *Gramática da Língua Portuguesa: Cartinha, Gramática, Diálogo em Louvor da Nossa Linguagem e Diálogo da Viciosa Vergonha*, ed. Maria Leonor Carvalhão Buescu (Lisbon: Faculdade de Letras da Universidade de Lisboa, 1971), p. 405.

monarchy, with which they had stood "united" from 1580 to 1640, acquired an eschatological streak in the later seventeenth century, due to António Viera's belief that the re-established Portuguese royal dynasty was predestined to rule the fifth and last earthly empire before the advent of the Judgment Day.[5] As Anthony Pagden has convincingly argued, the European political imagination developed over time an image of the Roman empire as "the object of successive 'renovations.'"[6] It was precisely moments of crisis that had signalled, invited, and enabled movements of "re-foundation." Rather than view the middle of the sixteenth century as a period of decline for the Portuguese empire in Asia, Ângela Barreto Xavier has recently argued that the reign of João III (1521–57) was not a fall into the trap of bigotry and the Jesuit Counter-Reformation, but was instead a re-foundation of a state apparatus capable of supporting the burden of the global imperial project.[7] Ecclesiastical hierarchy and religious order were constitutive elements of the construction of the Joanine administrative state. Behind and below this overarching political design, colonial actors such as Garcia da Orta, a doctor, botanist and merchant in precious stones, and Gaspar de Leão Pereira, a theologian and archbishop of Goa,

---

[5] Thomas Cohen, *The Fire of the Tongues: António Vieira and the Missionary Church in Brazil and Portugal* (Stanford: Stanford University Press, 1989).

[6] Anthony Pagden, *Lords of the World: Ideologies of Empire in Spain, Britain and France, c.1500–c.1800* (New Haven and London: Yale University Press, 1995), p. 27.

[7] Ângela Barreto Xavier, *A Invenção de Goa: Poder Imperial e Conversões Culturais nos Séculos XVI e XVII* (Lisbon: Imprensa de Ciências Sociais, 2008).

seized the moment to propose their own respective visions of cultural mobility and political legitimation.

First, they had to identify the immediate source and cause of the corruption. Orta's humanist indignation at the lack of Portuguese interest in the natural sciences, geography, and history was a minor item on the list of complaints levelled against degraded colonial society in India. Louder, stronger, and more ominous voices than Orta's were heard expressing aversion to what was perceived as unprecedented zeal for the acquisition of material riches. The first two archbishops of Goa, Dom Gaspar de Leão Pereira and Dom Jorge Temudo, thundered warnings directed at the lost souls of their contemporaries.[8] They were echoing the charismatic voice of the famous Jesuit Francis Xavier, who a decade or two earlier had repeatedly asked the question, "For what is a man profited, if he shall gain the whole world, and lose his own soul."[9]

The heart of the problem for sixteenth-century Portuguese colonial society in Asia was that it was being pulled in contrary directions – it was caught between an expectation of and desire for unlimited movement, and a longing sense, a still famous *saudade,* of belonging and at-homeness. In their two colossal books printed in Goa, Orta's *Colóquios* of 1563 and Dom Gaspar's *Desengano de perdidos* of

---

[8] José Wicki, "Duas relacões ... 1568 e 1569," *Studia,* 8 (1961), pp. 123–221.

[9] In a letter to João III, the king of Portugal in 1548, St. Francis Xavier advised the king to meditate on Matthew 16:26 – "Quid potest homini si universum mundum lucretur animae vero suae detrimentum patiatur" – a quarter of an hour every day. José Wicki, "La Sagrada Escritura en las cartas e insturcciones de Francisco Xavier," *Manresa,* vol. 24 (1952), pp. 259–64.

1573, both men took movement and mobility as their starting point. Their separate tropical paths, however, would lead them to different conclusions. Grounded in his personal experience as a physician, pharmacist, and botanist, Orta found mutability and change to be a permanent feature of the natural world, to which human beings had to adjust, as individuals and through society.[10] In response to the corrupting exterior powers presented by the tropics, this New Christian doctor proposed local drugs, plants, and potions for the purposes of rejuvenation and cure. The reinvigoration and acclimatization of the body were the only means of fighting, if only temporarily, the merciless forces of natural decay.[11]

For Dom Gaspar de Leão Pereira, the transience and frailty of the human condition had nothing to do with nature. It was rather about the sinful soul travelling through terrestrial zones of agony and temptation. The struggle between the soul and the flesh was a universal war with only two possible outcomes: ascent to heavenly Paradise, or descent into the fires of Hell. For Dom Gaspar, no amount of investment in the human body, something advocated by Orta, could restore health to the soul. The worst of all evils to befall the soul, he

---

[10] Orta celebrated movement in a way that reminds us of Montaigne's statement that "being consists in movement and action." Antonio José Maraval, *Culture of the Baroque: Analysis of a Historical Structure*, (Minneapolis: University of Minnesota Press, 1986 [1975]), p. 175. Hereafter "Maraval."

[11] Ines G. Županov, "Drugs, Health, Bodies and Souls in the Tropics: Medical Experiments in Sixteenth-century Portuguese India," *The Indian Economic and Social History Review*, 39, 1 (2002), pp. 1–43. See also Ines G. Županov, *Missionary Tropics: The Catholic Frontier in India (16th–17th Centuries)* (Ann Arbor: University of Michigan Press, 2005).

insisted, was for it to become carnal. "Sensualists ... do not have soul because they have converted it into flesh."[12] It is worth following the movement mapped by these two conflicting and yet, as we will see, in many ways complementary manuals for survival in the Portuguese colonial tropics – not just the geographical tropics but also the tropics of the soul or, as Ronaldo Vainfas put it in the case of Brazil, "the tropics of sin."[13] Orta's *Colóquios* and Dom Gaspar's *Desengano de perdidos* are products of a culture in need of guidance, advice (*aviso*) and counsel (*conselho*).[14] Captains, pilots, and sailors were being invited to write *Roteiros* to facilitate travel to India; spiritual directors were flooding the market with *Guías* and *Spiritual Exercises*; viceroys and state administrators were writing *Pareceres* (opinions) on how to govern the *Estado da Índia*. Within this plurality of viewpoints and judgments, it was not a question of where one stood, but rather of where one was moving to, or what one aspired to get. The opening of a myriad of capillary tubes and the dramatically enhanced porosity of the communal tissue caused social relations and individual desires to become so densely opaque that reality became almost surreal in its complexity. The problem of knowing how to situate oneself in this labyrinth of possibilities could bring an individual to the point of doubting his own existence. For a Jesuit,

---

[12] D. Gaspar de Leão [Pereira], *Desengano de Perdidos* (Goa, 1573), ed. Eugenio Asensio, (Coimbra: Por ordem da Universidade, 1958), p. 146. Hereafter "*Desengano*." In translation, the *Desengano de Perdidos* may be rendered imperfectly as *Disillusioning the Lost*.

[13] Ronaldo Vainfas, *Trópico dos Pecados: Moral, Sexualidade e Inquisição no Brasil* (Rio de Janeiro: Nova Fronteira, 1997).

[14] Maraval, pp. 57–78.

Baltasar de Gracián y Morales, human existence could not itself "exist without a human being who knows."[15] How one might know that one knows was also in question. As that sage in Bordeaux, Montaigne, bluntly asked: "What if knowledge, trying to arm us with new defences against natural mishaps, has imprinted in our fancy their magnitude and weight, more than her reasons and subtleties to protect us from them?"[16]

At one point or another between 1560, the year that Dom Gaspar arrived in Goa, and 1568, when Orta died, the physician and the archbishop must have met. Since the prelate did not oppose the publication of the *Colóquios* in the press, which was mostly under his wing, we can safely say that he did not find the book offensive, subversive, or contrary to his own very different pedagogical program. What this program was is more than apparent from a book printed in Goa in 1565, *Tratado que fez mestre Hieronimo, medico do papa Benedicto 13 contra os judeus: em que prova o Mesias da ley ser vindo*, prefaced by Dom Gaspar's *Carta do primeiro Arcebispo de Goa a povo de Isreal, seguidor ainda da ley de Moises, & do talmud, por engano & malicia dos seus Rabis*.[17] According to the

---

[15] Maraval, p. 61. See also Baltasar de Gracián y Morales, *El Discreto*, in *El Héroe. El Político. El Discreto. Oráculo manual y arte de prudencia*, ed. Arturo del Hoyo (Barcelona: Clásicos Plaza y Janés, 1986), p. 92. *El Discreto* (1645) is a portrayal of the typical courtier.

[16] Michel de Montaigne, *The Complete Essays of Montaigne*, trans. Donald M. Frame (Stanford: Stanford University Press, 1965), p. 795.

[17] *Tratado que fez mestre Hieronimo, medico do papa Benedicto 13 contra os judeus: em que prova o Mesias da ley ser vindo*, prefaced by Dom Gaspar's *Carta do primeiro Arcebispo de Goa a povo de Israel, seguidor ainda da ley de Moises, & do talmud, por engano & malicia dos seus Rabis*. Biblioteca Nacional, Lisbon, Reservados, 411.

archbishop, Judaism was an illness, one that lasted 2,000 years and claimed 2,000 million souls, and had come about because the Jews had originally refused remedy from the hand of the ultimate *médico*, Jesus Christ.

We cannot know just how Orta felt about this "medical" text. As a *cristão novo*, a New Christian, whose family had converted from Judaism around the turn of the century, he must have grasped the menace of the newly established Inquisition, transplanted into Goa in 1560.[18] Significantly, the armada of that year brought to Goa both the archbishop Dom Gaspar as well as the first inquisitor, Aleixo Dias Falcão. That the threat was real was confirmed in 1580, four years after Dom Gaspar's death, when Orta himself was posthumously tried by the Inquisition and sentenced to be burned at the stake; his bones were dug out, burned and scattered in the Mandovi river. Dom Gaspar's bones are preserved even today in a tomb near the altar of St. Joseph in Goa Cathedral. In the 1560s, however, the two learned men were still busy pushing for their different programs, both of them sure that they knew how to deal with the fantastically dynamic and disturbingly transitive Portuguese colonial order.

Orta, who placed his confidence in empirical observation, viewed mobility through a horizontal "spyglass." His gaze was fixed on the here and now, flatly spread across the surface of the phenomenal world. Likened to a garden (*orta*) by Luís Vaz de Camões, an admirer of his who was versed in rhetorical ruses and puns, Orta would not only map, pin

---

[18] "New Christian" was a term used to designate converts from Judaism.

down, and describe his objects but also watch them grow, change, and travel from one place to another.[19]

Of concern in this essay is the translation into language of what Orta perceived as the horizontal mobility of plants, drugs, spices, animals, and people in Portuguese colonial India. Our hope and conviction is that we will glimpse social relations and cultural practices through this language. Orta's ingenious power of display should not blind us to the fact that he is consciously intent on blurring the distinction between reality and representation. To do so persuasively was for him, as we will insist, a matter of life and death.

Matters of life and death were always on Dom Gaspar's mind, and before his eyes. The archbishop was acutely aware of the material world in movement, which enabled and facilitated phenomenal colonial expansion. Given his roots in the mystical Iberian spirituality of the early sixteenth century, however, his spiritual astrolabe was pointed elsewhere. To his audience in Goa, Dom Gaspar proposed that the eyes be averted from the flesh, and that the eyes of the spirit be opened. Instead of a horizontal mobility of things, he put forward an interior vision, one that would reveal an even richer world, such as the one painted by Hieronymus Bosch, perhaps, in which creatures and things move up and down the ladder of salvation. To drive his message home to stumbling Christian souls, in his *Desengano de perdidos* Dom Gaspar conjured up the *figura* of the mermaid. This monstrous creature, known to classical European literature, whose serpentine form was also sculpted

---

[19] Orta, vol. I, pp. 7–8.

on the walls of the "pagan" temples of India, became a heuristic device for acquiring knowledge. In Dom Gaspar's text, mermaids came to personify the five senses and were, as such, pronounced guilty of misleading spiritually directionless Christians. While it certainly seems that Dom Gaspar specifically chose mermaids to fashion a persuasive allegory of errant human perception, it appears also that he, in turn, was chosen and "possessed" by them. These were a special kind of "local" mermaids and mermen, the *nagini* and *naga*; they had survived a long series of idol-smashing campaigns, and were eventually assigned a particular role in the Christian economy of visibility and subalternity.

If the *figura* of the mermaid enabled the archbishop to deliver his pious homily against sensual knowledge of the world, it may also have opened a passageway to the messages that Indian "alterity" strove to imprint on the body of the tropical *Christianitas*. As they passed through the factory of cultural translation, the mermaids blended with local, autochthonous divine creatures (the *nagini* and the *yakshi*), assimilating strands of imported European imagination and refurbishing their traditional purpose and meaning. The forces behind these fantastic catalysts of cultural migration were, even before the arrival of the Portuguese, associated with gender, fertility, and rootedness in the soil.[20] Unwittingly initiated by Dom Gaspar de Leão Pereira, this assimilation,

---

[20] Ines G. Županov, "Conversion, Illness and Possession. Catholic Missionary Healing in Early Modern South Asia," in Ines G. Županov and Caterina Guenzi (eds.), *Divins remèdes: Médecine et religion en Asie du Sud*, *Purusartha* 27 (Paris, 2008).

enabling mermaids and *nagini* to become incarnations of each other, was not at all what he had had in mind. It fact, he desired just the opposite.

Both the *Colóquios dos Simples e Drogas he Cousas Medicinais da India* and the *Desengano de perdidos*, in spite of their celebration of movement and mobility, deal with the acquisition of stability in a rapidly expanding early modern world. They are both rhetorical *tours de force*, spectacularly boastful linguistic constructs that orbit the same burning question of how to shore up imperial Portuguese acquisitions in Asia.

"From long roads, long lies"

The first point of encounter between the physician and the archbishop is the choice of literary genre: a dialogue. At first glance, it does not appear an original choice: this is one of the privileged literary genres of the Renaissance. Manuals for self-fashioning, such as Baldassare Castiglione's *Il Cortegiano*, and religious works of catechetical nature, often seized upon this older classical form, grafting onto it new and urgent messages and lessons. As a verbal construct, dialogue is inherently peripatetic. It follows the pace of an intellectual promenade, with stopovers, occasional *double entendres*, witticisms, surprises, confessions, and conversions. The first crucial difference between *Desengano de perdidos* and *Colóquios* is the choice of ending. The former offers a customary conclusion with the triumph of revealed knowledge. The second does not really end at all: it stops abruptly, with an additional chapter left behind due to the author's "forgetfulness." Orta, who plays the part of himself in the dialogue, apologizes to his interlocutor Ruano: "I thought that the lecture on *betre* [betel] was already completed, but, alas, my memory is so weak that you must pardon this instance of forgetfulness, as well as many other that may have occurred."[21] Oblivion, whether due to old age or to the incapacity to encompass the multitude of things to be uncovered, observed and studied, emerges as the limit of the individual quest for knowledge.

Dom Gaspar, on the other hand, brings his two inter-locutors, a Christian/Teacher and a Turk/Disciple, to the gates of Heaven.

> We will reach this stage, & all [things] from this place [earth] have to remain, & only love can accompany us, & we'll acquire reason, & understand ourselves armed with divine love, & we will begin to be like those we want to find at the moment of the dreadful and horrendous Death: Horrendous I say to the Mundane for whom all the good ends with its [death's] arrival, & but not to Christians, if they spent their life in patience, & and in desire of Death, then it [death] is a Door through which they enter to enjoy God the supreme good, praised forever and glorified. Amen.[22]

The use of the future tense in this passage is an estab-lished strategy for inducing certainty and rendering as complete

---

[21] I translate *prática do betre* as "lecture on betel" in order to render the translation smooth. That he calls his explanation *prática* rather than lecture comes from the fact that he clearly distances himself from the academic, that is non-empirical, type of lecture still in vogue at this point in Europe. Orta, vol. II, p. 389.

[22] *Desengano*, p. 353.

events that may never occur. It also triggers an act of volition: what I will do is what I want to do. Throughout its text, the *Desengano de perdidos* exemplifies numerous acts of will that play a part in the Christian theatre of hope. The dismissal of illusions and of the spiritual errors that cause the loss of the soul requires a teacher or director, in both the theatrical and the pedagogical sense, who is capable of guiding the volition along the path of perfection. Dom Gaspar sets up his didactic theatre as a journey to the heart of Islam, and then out of it into the gates of Heaven. The only two interlocutors, a Christian and a Turk, meet on the road between Suez and Cairo and converse all the way to Constantinople.[23] As they travel through the countryside, which is under the control of the Ottoman empire, the Christian wears local "Muslim" dress, so as not to betray his origin and religion. When Dom Gaspar wrote his text, this kind of strategic disguise was being introduced in India as a particular, official Jesuit method of conversion called *accommodatio*.[24] The technique came into being officially after the arrival of Alessandro Valignano in 1575, and it was applied mostly in the territories outside and away from the Goan capital.

The archbishop never completely trusted his Jesuit subordinates in Goa. Profoundly touched by Franciscan spirituality, he was suspicious of both *accommodatio* as well as the Jesuit concept of contemplation in action. Between *vita activa* and *vita contemplativa*, his choice was easy and

---

[23] *Desengano*, p. 55.

[24] There was nothing exceptional about adopting local dress code when engaged in travel, commerce and intelligence work. What the Jesuits did, is turning the practice of disguise and passing for a "native" into cultural theory.

unequivocal. He went even further and renounced his office between 1567 and 1574, and established a convent of Madre de Deos for the Franciscan Friar Minors in Daugim, east of the Goan capital. It is during this time of retreat and spiritual leisure that he completed most of his literary works. After the death of Dom Jorge Temudo, the archbishop he had appointed in his place, and an order from Lisbon, Dom Gaspar reluctantly resumed his ecclesiastical duty for just short two years before he died in 1576.

The opening conversation of the *Desengano de perdidos* is posted with (deceptive) signs of equality between the two pilgrims. The Christian has a crippled hand and the Turk a limping leg. Both acquired their infirmities while fighting in wars; both have renounced military life. When they meet, one is on his way from India to the Holy Land, the other to his native town, Constantinople. During the first leg of the journey, it is the Turk who knows the way, and he prods the Christian to increase his pace. Soon, however, the Turk begins to lag behind, not, according to the Christian, because of his crippled leg, but "because you are more lame inside than outside."[25] Little by little, through question and answer, the Turk becomes more and more "persuaded" and thus dependent on the guidance of the Christian, and an initially horizontal relationship turns into a vertical, hierarchical bond.

The erosion of the Turk's confidence is not solely the work of a single Christian. It is also the work of the Catholic League, Dom Gaspar insists, which defeated the Turkish armada at Lepanto (1573). In Constantinople, when the

---

[25] *Desengano*, p. 44.

conversation reaches its apogee (and the book its midpoint), the Turk is converted.[26] From then on, the roles of the two protagonists slightly change, at least in name. The Christian instantly decides that "it does not conform to reason, when there is such a big change to allow to remain the infamous name of Turk; and I'll call you a Disciple, & you call me a Teacher, so that we are all disciples of the Lord Jesus"[27]. At the moment of conversion, the Disciple loses all vestiges of the autonomy and ethnicity he possessed as an "infidel."

Orta and his invented character Ruano converse on an equal footing as two expert physicians. The difference between them, one which Orta periodically underscores, is their nationality. The Spanish Ruano often refers to "your Portuguese," and Orta likewise affirms with "our Portuguese." Orta moreover expresses the common Portuguese rancour directed at imperial Spanish pretensions concerning the Molucca islands.[28] This open and frequent expression of Portuguese national pride possibly presents a way for Orta to soften and obscure his New Christian and Spanish origins.[29] There are, however, real

---

[26] *Desengano*, p. 173.   [27] *Desengano*, p. 179.   [28] Orta, vol. I, pp. 361–2.

[29] His father, Fernão da Orta, was a Spanish Jew from Valencia de Alcántara, who had emigrated to Castelo de Vide in Portugal in 1492. He belonged to the group of Jews who were baptized after Dom Manuel's decree in 1497. The descendants of those converted Jews were called *marranos* (pigs) or *cristãos novos* (New Christians). Garcia da Orta was born in 1501 or 1502. I. S. Révah, *La Famille de Garcia de Orta* (Coimbra: Universitas Conimbricensis, 1960), pp. 1–17. See also Charles R. Boxer, "Two Pioneers of Tropical Medicine: Garcia d'Orta and Nicolás Monardes," *Diamante*, 14 (London, 1964), pp. 6–11, and Augusto da Silva Carvalho, *Garcia D'Orta* (Coimbra: Imprensa da Universidad, 1934), pp. 10–23. Hereafter "Carvalho."

achievements for which he cannot but praise Portuguese valor. "The roundness of the earth has never been known as it is today, especially by the Portuguese."[30] The reduction of the time taken by travel and the possibility of circumnavigating the earth are connected directly to the acquisition of knowledge. "I say that we know more in one day through the Portuguese than we knew through the Romans in hundred years."[31] The fruit of this knowledge is what Orta wishes to discuss; the character of Ruano serves to ask the right questions and so perform the role of Orta's alter ego. In a ventriloquistic fashion, he articulates Orta's desires:

> I have a great desire to know about the medicinal drugs (such as are called the drugs of pharmacy in Portugal), and these other remedies and simples which there are here, as well as all the fruits and pepper [spices]. I would like to learn their names in all the different languages, as also the countries where they grow, and the trees or plants which bear them, and likewise how the Indian physicians use them. Furthermore, I would like to know about some of the other plants and fruits of this land, even if they are not medicinal, and also some of the customs of this country and the things that happen therein.[32]

In a word, Ruano's function is to solicit answers to the questions to which Orta wishes to respond. Ruano is as knowledgeable – about classical Greco-Roman and Arab medicine, and botany, within the Renaissance framework and disciplinary limits – as Orta. He lacks knowledge only of

---

[30] Orta, vol. I, p. 203.   [31] Orta, vol. I, p. 210.   [32] Orta, vol. I, p. 19.

"India," a geographical term that denotes, in Portuguese documents of the period, the entire Asian empire, Africa included. In the manner of a Devil's Advocate, Ruano challenges some of Orta's claims and demands additional explanations. At times, when he feels that Orta exaggerates or omits the whole truth, he even teases him. "You are not just a philosopher as you want to appear, you also want pearls and [precious] stones, just like everybody else."[33] To this friendly provocation, Orta responds briefly, "Yes, I know." His ostentatious transparency in word and deed is in fact a double trick. His scientific motto, "truth is painted naked," is a complex construct of hidden and disclosed facts.[34] In his own "naked" book, he manages to conceal much of himself, his family, his relationships and his religion. Except for a servant woman, Antónia, no one from his fictive or real household, his wife or two daughters, for example, enters the scene. There is no sign of his sisters and relatives, who had had brushes with the Inquisition in Lisbon. Only a few months after Orta's death, Leonel Peres (or Gonçalves), husband of Catarina da Orta, the author's sister, admitted to the inquisitor Aleixo Dias Falcão in Goa that the dead physician had believed that "the Law of Moses was the true Law … that the prophecies were not yet fulfilled. That Christ was not the son of God; that the Jews had not killed him, but he had died of old age, and he was the son of Miriam and Joseph."[35] We know from the Inquisition

---

[33] Orta, vol. II, p. 123.

[34] Orta, vol. I, p. 79. "Porque a verdade se pinta nua."

[35] Carvalho, p. 73. *Reportorio geral de tres mil oitocentos processos, que sam todos os despachados neste Sancto Officio de Goa, & mais partes da India do anno de Mil & quinhentos & secenta & hum, que começou o dito*

records that his marital life was not a happy one and that his wife, Brianda de Solis, refused to pay for a new cloth to cover her husband's corpse.

Long lies were coming from afar. Both Orta and Dom Gaspar use this common proverb in their respective texts, each with a different interpretative twist.[36] Orta uses it to dismiss wrong information about camphor, whereas the archbishop employs it to display the Turk's insulting attitude towards the Christians and the Portuguese. The Turk draws on the proverb to express his doubt and to ridicule the Christian's rendering of the Portuguese victory in Chaul, a small town in the so-called Províncias do Norte. In response to a touching account of the heroism shown by a small Portuguese force in the face of a huge army of the Idalcão (the sultan of Bijapur), an account woven through with miracle and divine protection, we are presented with an ironic and violent reaction on the part of the Turk. He not only disbelieves the story, holding it as "a lie coming from afar," he also readies himself to attack the Christian and avenge the event: "Do you want me to take revenge of your blasphemies with this stick?" The archbishop effectively reverses the meaning of the proverb, showing that the proselytising of Christianity does not abide by the proverbial law. Christianity remains pure and unchanged, whether it comes from afar or

Sancto Officio até o anno Mil & seis centos & vinte & tres, cõ a lista dos Inquisidores que tem sido nelle, & dos autos publicos da Fee, que se tem celebrado na dita CIDADE de GOA. FEITO PELLO LICENCIADO JOÃO Delgado Figueyra do Desembargo de sua Magestade, Promotor & Deputado do dito Sancto Officio. Sendo os Inquisitores os senhores Francisco Borges de Souza & João Fernades de Almeida, ANNO do M. DC.XXIII, Biblioteca Nacional, Lisbon, Reservados, cod. 203.

[36] "De longas vias, longas mentiras," *Desengano*, p. 41; *Orta*, vol. I, p. 154.

not. Unlike camphor, which is liable to arrive in foul or coun-
terfeit form from distant places, Christianity remains incorrup-
tible in transit. According to the archbishop, the healing touch
of salvation travels towards the East, whereas lies – adulterated
spices and drugs, corrupted words, nefarious sins and lewd
religion – waft towards the West.

After the Council of Trent, polemical Christian literature used irony and role reversal as its stock in trade. The
Jesuit students of the Collegio Romano were trained in dis-
putations in which they had to serve as the Devil's advocate.
The Turk in the *Desengano de perdidos* plays just such a role
before his conversion into Disciple. Whenever unable to follow the explanations of his Christian interlocutor, or else
unhappy with them, he hurls insults. "You are a wolf, &
dressed in sheep's skin [and you] want to double-cross
me."[37] Dom Gaspar de Leão Pereira plots the relationship of
his characters in agonistic terms. The Turk is treated all
through the first half of the book as a disorderly child on
whom the Christian inflicts verbal punches and slaps. One
such assault is to install in the Turk's infidel soul a feeling of
temor servil, the servile fear that arises when the eyes of the
soul are directed towards the punishment of Hell. "This fear
causes pain & sadness (*tristeza*) in the soul , & and the desire to
leave the sins, & improve one's life."[38] Fear is in many ways a
major import of Christianity, brought from afar to the local
Asian converts. In exchange for spices, the Portuguese
brought, as their own form of merchandise, the fear of Hell
and sin.

---

[37] *Desengano*, p. 27.   [38] *Desengano*, p. 104.

The teaching of Christian fear was the first and crucial step towards building a colonial Christian community. It was, at least in the beginning, the only cohering principle for the otherwise plural and multicultural society brought about by Portuguese colonial rule. "The first movement of conversion of these people will be fear of torments," the archbishop maintained, since "fear is the origin of wisdom."[39] In the *Desengano de perdidos* the process of ingraining fear into non-Christians is clearly thematized under separate subchapters and shot through with exemplary anecdotes. As central as it was to spiritual conversion and – to use Dom Gaspar's word – healing, fear and its derivatives had also to pass through the body. It is on the matter of the body and the body politic that Orta and the archbishop meet again and, predictably, pull in different directions.

"The taste of flesh"; between corruption and resurrection

Liçenciado Dimas Bosquet, a prominent physician in Portuguese India around the middle of the sixteenth century, commends Garcia da Orta in the opening pages of the *Colóquios* for his long experience in India and knowledge of the remedies and simples that exist "in this country." What Orta endeavoured to do during his thirty years in India was to serve his country (*patria*) and friends, and to search for truth and perfect knowledge. At the same time, Bosquet added that he "cured many different people, not only those who

[39] *Desengano*, p. 100.

accompany viceroys and governors of this oriental India, but also at some courts of the Muslim kings and gentiles, and he communicated with physicians and curious people."[40] In order for everybody to profit from his experience, insisted Bosquet, Orta wrote in Portuguese and in the form of a dialogue, "and this is why he sometimes moves away from medicinal topics and relates some things of this country which are worth knowing."[41]

Wherever Orta's ethnographical digression takes us, we return in the end to the body. It is a body in movement, and the movements of the body that nourish his narrative magnetize all external things, drawing them into its orbit. The classical Galenic-Hippocratic idea of the body as constituted by four humors corresponding to the four elements of the physical world is the basic principle of the sixteenth-century medical profession. Orta belongs to this tradition. Yet, when he needs to show his academic medical learning, he places it in Ruano's lines and repartee. As Orta's doppelgänger, Ruano usually defends or starts with conventional, immobile wisdom or understanding. He also has a penchant for adding short scientific glosses of approval to Orta's experiential demonstrations. "On all the points you have referred to, you have thoroughly satisfied me and much more concerning the first qualities, which are warmth, cold, humidity, dryness."[42]

In contrast to the mechanical and textual framework within which an ordinary European doctor might work out his diagnoses and remedies, Orta presents his own experience, which explodes venerable authorities of all colors and

---

[40] Orta, vol. I, pp. 10–11.   [41] Orta, vol. I, p. 11.   [42] Orta, vol. I, p. 34.

denominations. One reason for this is that the body in Europe and the body in the tropics are not the same. There is nothing revolutionary in Orta's view that different climactic zones endow bodies with different humoral constitutions. What does strike us as exceptional, though, is Orta's unabashedly materialist approach to the body, his refusal to pay lip service to Christian tenets.

By the 1560s, it was common knowledge that there was something "rotten" in the climate of Goa. The male Portuguese body suffered from certain pathologies which were constant menaces to survival. Concupiscence and excessive sexual desire were denounced by the official religious community as a permanent threat to the body and to society. That being said, there was a general obsession with masculine potency, a matter that was viewed as a health concern and was a frequent source of complaints. Orta's treatment of this hot topic never exits the realm of matter-of-fact observation, diagnosis, and remedy. Thus, he might note that the Chinese hold amber to be good for "conversation with women," or that asafoetida is good "for lifting the member."[43] One searches in vain for passages like these in the early nineteenth-century British translation of the *Colóquios*: Sir Clements Markham, the prudish translator, chose either to deliberately misinterpret certain Portuguese phrases or to simply cut out the indecent passages.[44] Orta's straightforward verbal sensualism

---

[43] Orta, vol. I, pp. 52 and 76.
[44] Garcia da Orta, *Colloquies on the Simples & Drugs of India*, new edition (Lisbon, 1895) ed. and annotated by the Conde de Ficalho, trans. with an Introduction and Index by Sir Clements Markham, K.C.B, F.R.S. (London: Henry Sotheran and Co., 1913).

was ironed out because it showed neither lapidary ceremoni-
ousness nor "scientific rigor," two supreme virtues upon
which the British based their self-perception of their role in
the Indian colony.

What Orta proposes to describe through his panoply of
simple and composite remedies are methods to stimulate the
body such that it functions well. Each natural substance is
considered in terms of its origin, qualities or virtues, the history
of its use, as well as the various opinions of the classical and
Arab physicians. "To answer your last question, I say, that I
don't know of any Greek who wrote about *benjuy*. Of the Arabs,
Averoes called it *belenizan* or *bolizan* or *petrozan*. It is warm
and dry in the second degree. It aromatizes and calms down a
humid and week stomach. It makes a good smell in the mouth,
fortifies members and enhances coitus."[45] Good digestion and
good sex are of equal importance to a good physician-
pharmacist experimenting with lesser-known drugs and remedies. Anything that works for the improvement of health is
good, according to Orta, such as the oil massages used by
Ayurvedic practitioners in Malabar (Kerala), bloodletting,
expurgating, sweating, and dieting. The human body in the
tropics is profiled in the *Colóquios* as a porous and open entity
susceptible to humoral changes from without. Heat and humidity in particular accelerate the growth of all natural things: a
sweet-smelling flower turns quickly into a rotten, foetid, reek-
ing fruit. The people are subject to the same regime of accel-
erated decay, in addition to being vulnerable to the "new
illnesses," as yet unknown in Europe.

[45] Orta, vol. I, p. 104.

Just as individuals were prone to catching diseases transmitted through contact between humans, the world at large was at risk from contagion. One such illness, contracted in "very close contact," was syphilis. The theory in vogue, which Orta holds as credible, is that syphilis came from the Spanish Indies, or, as he tells Ruano, "from your Indies."

> Every day there are new illnesses like *morbo napolitano* [Neapolitan disease] (which we call *sarna de Castella* [Castilian scabies]) and God was so merciful that he gave to every country remedies to cure them. Because the one who gives illness, gives remedies for it ... and since we don't know all the remedies for all the illnesses, we bring *ruibarbo* from China, from where we bring *pão* [wood] or *raizes* [roots] to cure Castilian scabies, and *cana fistola* we bring from India, and *manná* from Persia and *guaiacam* from the Western Indies.[46]

This is one of the rare instances in which Orta chooses to invoke divine intervention, which here appears to legitimate and support discovery, travel, and the circulation of goods in various parts of the world. His medical optimism about syphilis may have been enhanced by the fact that the disease seemed curable in its initial stage. The pustules (*buboes*) were not considered ill famed by the "natives of the country," claimed Orta; they called them *fringui*, a name used also to designate Christians and the Portuguese.[47] Writing in the first decade of the seventeenth century, a French visitor to Goa,

---

[46] Orta, vol. I, p. 179.   [47] Orta, vol. II, p. 107.

Pyrard de Laval, gave a more detailed picture. "Concerning syphilis [*vérole*], it is in no way infamous and it was not shameful to have contracted it a few times. They even make a virtue out of it. They cure it without sweating with the *bois de Chine* [China wood]. This illness exists only among Christians and they prefer it to fever or to dysentery."[48]

For Portuguese men, Laval suggested, the contraction of a sexually transmitted disease was a sign of sexual prowess. In the *Colóquios* Orta is especially concerned with the virility of the Portuguese men, and accordingly prescribes a variety of drugs ranging from asafoetida, amber, and benzoin, to opium, *bhang* (hashish), and many others. He also identifies drugs that calm sexual appetite, such as *raíz angélica* (angelic root) or *raíz do Espírito Santo* (root of the Holy Spirit).[49] As bodily virility was closely correlated with mercantile virility, Orta strongly advised those who had plans to engage in speculative imports and exports between Europe and India not to invest in the trading of anti-aphrodisiacs.

For both Orta and Dom Gaspar Leão de Pereira, the new global order, in which people and things circulated and encountered each other in various situations and locations, was fraught with danger. In Orta's opinion, it was the body that had to be fortified and protected, through diet and hygiene and even physical pleasure. The *Colóquios* celebrate tasty fruits like mangoes and durians, and even provide culinary tips.

[48] Pyrard de Laval, *Voyage de Pyrard de Laval aux Indes orientales (1601–1611)* (Paris: Chandeigne, 1998), vol. II, p. 536.

[49] Orta, vol. I, pp. 205, 267.

The richness of the tastes and smells that fascinate Orta and provided pleasure to the Portuguese is precisely what made the archbishop shudder with disgust and anger. The ideal body, as envisaged by Dom Gaspar, is a body closed to exterior experiences and sensations. "From flesh, can one desire anything but delight, what can come out of foolish sensuality but vices, ruled by five boys who are five exterior senses? … The eyes do not want ugly things that frighten them: the ears do not want but gentle and happy voices, & not the thunders that break them; the nose does not want effrontery of stench; the taste [desires] good flavour; the touch [desires all to be] smoothness."[50] The chief culprits of the disorders of flesh, as they were experienced in the tropics (and elsewhere), were the senses, which capture external stimuli. Just like Orta, Dom Gaspar is aware of the fast-changing, hazardous, dense, and odorous texture of Portuguese colonial life. The confusion and over-abundance of perfumes, precious unguents, and mixtures of herbs and water all disorient the senses. Such substances were, moreover, in great demand, and were procured not only from India, "but from the whole universe."[51] The real origin of these olfactory disorders was clearly the East. "These kinds of delights and pleasures, used to be found in the past only among the Orientals, & and now this plague runs throughout the world."[52] The globalization of pleasure, inducted by products discovered outside Europe and then pushed onto the international market by the Portuguese and Spanish monarchies, had changed ancient customs, tastes, and morality. It had also perverted economic and mercantile laws, which ceased to function

---

[50] *Desengano*, p. 158.   [51] *Desengano*, p. 148.   [52] *Desengano*, p. 148.

properly. The Turk remarks in astonishment, for example, that increases in the production of sugar have not made the commodity any less expensive. The Christian responds by saying that when he was a child in Spain an *arroba* of sugar coming from Madeira island fetched 500 *reis*, whereas "now when so much comes from India, & from Brazil loaded on ships, it is valued up to two thousand *reis* per *arroba*."[53]

The skyrocketing price of sugar was due to an increase in demand. According to Dom Gaspar, the cause of this increase is demonic. Because the *Desengano de perdidos* is primarily concerned with psychomachia – the internal battle between vice and virtue, true religion and false religion, as incarnated within the text in the two protagonists, Christian and Turk – the demonic is located in volition. "Since the sin is founded in will, without whose agreement there can be no fault, & no force can move it, the Devil uses skills and manners to bring it down with tricks if he cannot do with force."[54] Thus, the will must continually defend against two enemies – the Devil and "his wife, the flesh."[55]

The best, almost cinematic scenes in which the author depicts the triangulation between the will, the Devil and the flesh are found in the second part of the work, in the wonderfully sensuous allegory of the encounter between Ulysses and the mermaids. It is not by accident that Dom Gaspar chose this classical story for his allegorical psychomachia. The maritime theater in which Ulysses, representing the will, and the mermaids, being "the progeny of the Devil and the flesh," fight out their battle, is the perfect setting for a sixteenth-century Portuguese colonial drama of sin and redemption.

[53] *Desengano*, p. 150.   [54] *Desengano*, p. 157.   [55] *Desengano*, p. 158.

All the topoi of medieval and early modern Christian misogyny are enacted at one point or another. *Serena* in ancient Greek means "attraction and provocation": mermaids are incarnations of the sins of the flesh. To go back to the question of sugar, what seemed to have impressed Dom Gaspar in his childhood is that "in the houses of the devotees of the mermaids, you will find barrels of sugar" and that "the chief confectioner who envelops the evil of the vices with the sugar coating" is the Devil himself.[56] This product of demonic alchemy is mixed with other oriental spices such as musk, amber, and numerous other foods to the point of saturation. The descriptive overflow conveys the disorientation that the soul must feel when faced with too many choice ingredients. The highest moment of the rhetoric arrives, as usual, with a series of tautologies. The mermaids "add taste to taste, food to food, sweetness to sweetness."[57] The result, in Dom Gaspar's sensualist denial, is the vertiginous fusion of all carnal appetites and their effects. The mermaids "add all the instruments to play music to taste."[58] The continuous processing of the information entering the sensory channels creates an effect of synesthesia, which ends up terrorizing both the body and the language. Thus, overexcited men "tremble of cold in the middle of spring" and "turn around on the wheel (*roda viva*) of torments, so many and so contrary that it seems that the furies of Hell persecute them."[59]

The vicious circle of sin and desire is closely related to the availability of goods (*fazenda*). Those who have less, the

[56] *Desengano*, pp. 150, 157.   [57] *Desengano*, p. 149.   [58] *Desengano*, p. 149.
[59] *Desengano*, pp. 146, 162. See also p. 171.

argument goes, desire more, and those who are forbidden to consume certain products consume them abundantly. The example with which Dom Gaspar demonstrates this point brings us to the central aim of the book: It is a refutation or, rather, a vilification of Islam. The case in point involves wine. "Mafamede took away the wine of the word," tutors the Christian in his usual combination of metaphorical and abusive expressions, "so that deceived with this enticement you fall into brutish life."[60] According to Dom Gaspar, contraband wine from Spain was much coveted by the Muslim army of Bijapur, the same army that had besieged Goa not long before the Christian embarked on his journey to the Holy Land. The army had not, however, succeeded in destroying the capital of Portuguese India – perhaps, it is implied, because the Muslim soldiers drank too much!

Dom Gaspar's narrative is constructed in view of two different audiences. He addresses and admonishes directly the Turk and the Muslims, but he lectures the Portuguese Christians at the same time. His statement that "inside of us there is a stable for the beasts, which are beastly appetites" applies universally to all people. The bestiality of the human interior is contrasted with the "movement" of natural reason, which the archbishop tries to create within the soul of the Turk. Right in the middle of the book, he succeeds. The moment at which the Turk's conscience turns and he converts comes at the highpoint of the attack on the mermaids. After the Turk steps over the threshold and becomes a disciple, in fact, the mermaids disappear altogether. This authorial move corresponds to the

[60] *Desengano*, p. 155.

story it depicts. "The poets say finally that the mermaids died of passion, because they were unable to drown Ulysses."[61]

Conversion is death, a certain kind of death. Mermaids die, a Turk dies; the bodily orifices close, and the inward space receives grace. In the archbishop's words, "you feel clarity."[62] At this particular instant in the text, a mask is dropped: it is suddenly revealed that the Turk was born to a Christian father, and sent to work as a boy for a Muslim who converted him to Islam.[63] As for the mermaids, the reader had been advised from the beginning to invest in them merely a poetic interest, the author being sure that "they do not exist in the world."[64] They were conjured up, it seems, for the sole purpose of alerting the Turk to the nefarious workings of his own five senses. As the enemies within, they bewitch the soul, causing it to move against "natural reason"; when they do not succeed, what ensues is painful self-knowledge. "Ay, ay, ay … I am lost, & lost more than anybody," cries the Turk at the moment of his conversion.[65]

Serpents, nuns and soldiers

The importance of confronting one's own five senses, personified as mermaids, in order to know and to control them, seems to have been taken literally in Goa. Creatures resembling mermaids in their astoundingly strange beauty can be seen even today in many Goan churches. One of the oldest, São Pedro, constructed in the early 1540s in the western suburb of the Old Goa, on the bank of the Mandovi river, provides refuge to five breathtaking mermaids.

[61] *Desengano*, p. 160. [62] *Desengano*, p. 173. [63] *Desengano*, p. 173.
[64] *Desengano*, p. 139. [65] *Desengano*, pp. 161, 173.

1 São Pedro, Church in Ribandar (Goa). Pulpit decorated with the wooden statues of *nages* or *naginis* or *nagayakshis* (seventeenth century). These local spirits are traditionally associated with the underworld, with trees and with water. They are worshiped by the Hindus for their power over fertility. These wooden statues can be also interpreted as representing mermaids.

They are made of painted wood, and positioned so as to be holding up the beams of the pulpit box. Dark blue-green scales cover their fish tails, which seem to curve under the weight of the edifice. The upper parts of their identical bodies are skin-colored, with slightly protruding bellies and bulging breasts. The lush, surreal foliage that covers the lower part of the pulpit grows partly out of their arms. A bunch of grapes hangs, like a third breast, from their mouths, the only other "ornament" on the bodies besides their necklaces. Were these wonderful sculptures used to remind the faithful of the transience (albeit a beautiful one) of worldly sensual pleasures? These pulpit cariathides that literally support the place from which the Word was spoken are doubly coded as both accomplices of and distractions from the divine. Although the pulpit in question, like most of the pulpits in Goa, must have been carved in the seventeenth century, it seems to illustrate Dom Gaspar's point. A Christian soul needs to see and know his senses, and, at the same time, reject them under the weight of the divine word.

Attached to these Goan pulpits, such sculpted figures are more than just the European mermaids of Greek mythology. The local wood carvers who produced these creatures smuggled in the forms and images of powerful local divine and demonic agents, the *naga*. The *naga* and *nagini* are male and female divine cobra/serpent kings and queens. Hindu mythology associates them with water and with fertility. They can also inhabit trees and be confounded with tree spirits called *yaksha* and *yakshi*. Most of the cariathides on the Goan pulpits represent a mixture of these elements. They are always located on the base of the pulpit: as a rule, the upper box had mostly a hexagonal plan, unlike rectangular Portuguese models, and often contained sculptures of saints as decorations. When there is a canopy that rises above, it is usually executed in an equally ornamented style, with the Dove of the Holy Spirit hanging from the lotus-shaped rosette in the middle of the round lid.[66]

The church of the Santa Monica monastery in Goa has another pulpit showing full-breasted nymphs. They are wrapped in leaves from the waist down, except for the extreme ends of their tails, which curve up like snakes; more leaves wrap around their necks.

Carved in wood and painted in gold, as were most of the pulpits, altars, and retables that constituted Portuguese colonial splendour, these four intensely feminine *nagini* were seen by generations of nuns. Between 1610 and 1750, some 400 resided in the monastery; the pulpit can be roughly dated to the second part of the seventeenth century. What is striking about these sculpted *nagini* are their faces. With a sober, nun-like expression, they look down in barely perceptible pain onto the church audience. The implicit pain owes to the fact that their hands are upraised in order to support the pulpit box suspended on the southern wall of the church. Above their heads, their hair grows into a lotus flower supporting a (fake) transversal beam of the pulpit. A lotus growing from the inside of the head has special meaning in the Indian *siddha* medical school, which considers it the seventh and last energetic knot (*muticcu*) on the vertebra. We can only speculate as

---

[66] José Pereira, *Baroque Goa: The Architecture of Portuguese India* (New Delhi: Books & Books, 1995), p. 91.

2 Santa Monica, the church of the first monastery for women in Asia, Old Goa. A detail of the decorated pulpit of the church. A female *nagayakshi* (seventeenth century).

to the extent to which the creator of the wooden *nagini* was aware of this fine point in *siddha* medical theory.[67]

---

[67] Brigitte Sébastia, *Les Rondes de saint Antoine: Culte, affliction et possession en Inde du Sud* (Paris: Au lieu d'être éditions, 2007). The nuns, Monicas, were renowned for their syrups and medicinal preparations on the basis of spices they grew in their interior garden. The most beautiful frescoes in their former refectory contain paintings of numerous medicinal plants.

The haunting question that comes to mind when looking at these creatures is how those nuns "read" these bare breasts, placid eyes, and serpentine bodies. Since the pulpit in the church of Santa Monica resides in its "public" part, and the cloistered nuns heard the mass from behind a gilded door, the naked *nagini* were the only female figures associated with the monastery that the lay audience was allowed to see. Like earth spirits, the "Monicas" fought hard to preserve their location and their institution, established in 1610 by Dom Frey Aleixo de Meneses, the archbishop of Goa, in spite of very powerful opponents.[68] Even the king of Portugal was initially opposed to the opening of female convents in India, one reason being that this would do away with both hefty dowries and "white" aristocratic Portuguese women, rare and valuable on the local marriage market. Women from Portugal, some of them endowed by the king, the so-called *órfãs del-Rey*, the King's orphans, were the most coveted. The fear that many such rich marriageable women, young widows in particular, would decide against marriage and use their dowries to enter the monastery infuriated local authorities and exacerbated prevailing misogyny.

Sending *órfãs del-Rey* to Goa was seen as a way of further Portugalizing a society that had grown out of intermarriage between Portuguese men and Asian women.[69] Since the time that Afonso de Albuquerque wrestled this prized

[68] José Nicolau da Fonseca, *An Historical and Archaeological Sketch of the City of Goa* (New Delhi, Madras: Asian Educational Services, 1994 [1879]), pp. 304–11.

[69] Timothy J. Coates, *Degredados e Órfãs: colonização dirigida pela coroa no império protuguês. 1550–1755* (Lisbon: CNCDP, 1998).

string of islands from the sultan of Bijapur in 1510, intermarriage with local women had been encouraged, especially so with "white" Muslim women, as well as other Asian women from the extended Portuguese maritime empire. Just as, for better or worse, the movements of merchants and army ships loaded with spices and other goods connected distant cultural orbits and constellations in Asia and Africa, blood and genes were circulating and intermingling with unprecedented speed.

Staunch opponents of female monasteries in Asia offered yet another, ecological argument. According to them, all women in Asia were under threat of falling into the sin of concupiscence, even if they were white and born in Portugal. The monastic life "was not suitable for the women in India, owing to their great weakness, the great luxury and delights of the land, the intemperance of the climate, and the licentious upbringing of the girls" who grew up in slave households.[70] This argument hints obviously that the monastery would be unable to contain the female sexual energy endemic in the tropics.

Like the immobilized wooden representations of the mermaids/*nagini* of the pulpits, women were either to remain at home, to be locked up and guarded or else to be removed to public institutions. In order to more easily protect women from men and from themselves, Dom Frey Aleixo de Meneses laid the foundations for two other institutions for women, in addition to the Real Convento de Santa Monica: the Recolhimento da Nossa Senhora da Serra and the Recholhimento de Santa Maria

---

[70] Charles R. Boxer, *Mary and Misogyny* (London, Gerald Duckworth and Company, 1975), p. 102. Germano da Silva Correia, *História da Colonização Portuguesa na India* (Lisbon, 1960), vol. II, p. 204.

Madalena. The first admitted respectable widows or abandoned wives and their children. Women whose husbands were away on account of business were allowed to stay here temporarily as paying lodgers. The other *recolhimento* was a shelter for former prostitutes, victims of rape, or those abandoned by their lovers. Such women were called converts, *convertidas*, or repentants, *arrependidas*. Although, in principle, only white women and those not of New Christian origin were eligible to join these institutions, the vast majority of the women and "orphaned" children were classifiable as Euroasians.[71]

Marriageable or married Christian women were seen as best remaining in their "immobile" and "invisible" state, hidden behind doors and veils, circulating as little as possible. Slave girls and non-Christian servants were in a different category, and exposed to proverbial cruelty from men as well as their secluded "respectable" mistresses. Rich prostitutes and unmarried women, the so-called *solteiras* or single women, were also at risk of being immobilized by the colonial administration: they were confined to particular quarters on the outskirts of the city. For Garcia da Orta, any ailing woman, *solteira* or not, had to be succored immediately. Thus, he brings Ruano to a house of a rich *mestiça* and *solteira*, Paula de Andrade, who has been poisoned by her black servant with *datura*, a plant that must have both terrified and titillated Goan men. Stories were told about the workings of this hallucinogenic, stories in which adulterous women fed the drug to

[71] Euroasian in this context means a person of mixed heritages, partly Portuguese and partly Indian, Black African, Chinese, or of any other Asian ethnicity.

their husbands in order to humiliate or kill them. Goan women were generally reputed for their passionate nature, which tended to make them despise all interdictions standing in the way of pleasure and lovemaking. "I confess," says the Christian in the *Desengano de perdidos*, "that today with good reasons we should change the gender, & from Mermaids, *Serenas*, we should make Mermen, *Sereno*: because women have reached such an unfortunate state that they steal from their husbands, sons, & as much as they can, in order to give to their lovers, even when they are black, *cafres*."[72]

Passion for sin and passion for saintliness were closely interwoven in Portuguese colonial society; each was overlaid by the other. Ironically, or perhaps purposely, the Convent of Santa Monica was erected in the part of the town called Ilha do Fogo, the island of fire, notorious for the "lost" (or fallen) women, *mulheres perdidas*, who resided there. The hillock was immediately renamed as Monte de Santa Monica, eventually becoming Monte Santo or Monte Sião (Sion).[73] In a comparable way, the *nagini* mermaids appeared in the Goan pulpits

---

[72] The Arabs employed the word *kafir* to designate "an infidel, and unbeliever in Islam." The Portuguese took it in this sense to designate non-Christian people of color. Henry Yule and Arthur Coke Burnell, *Hobson-Jobson: A Glossary of Colloquial Anglo-Indian Words and Phrases, and of Kindred Terms, Etymological, Historical, Geographical and Discursive* (London: John Murray, 1903; New Delhi: Munshiram Manoharlal Publishers, 1979), pp. 140–2. See also Monsenhor Sebastião Rodolfo Dalgado, *Glossário Luso-Asiático* (Coimbra: Emprensa da Universidade, 1919), p. 170.

[73] Padre M. J. Gabriel de Saldanha, *História de Goa (Política e Arqueológica)* (Nova Goa: Livraria Coelho, 1926; New Delhi: Asian Educational Services, 1990), p. 127.

precisely at the time when, with the majority of "natives" converted and displaying signs of true piousness, Catholicism seemed to have triumphed. Affixed to these pulpits, these creatures could be contemplated in all their silently immobile subalternity.

The mermaids were not the only unruly agents of mundane debauchery upon which Dom Gaspar was making war. Soldado Madrepor is another. We do not have to look far to find the archbishop's literary inspiration for this character. The Braggart Soldier or *miles gloriosus* was a stock character from classical and Renaissance theatre. As comic type, the Soldado Madrepor accepts the blame for all that went awry in the Estado da Índia. He is, in fact, a product of the very economy of the fateful surplus of pleasure and material goods that rendered mermaids the pestiferous companions of the Portuguese Asian empire. The braggard Soldado Madrepor is a "fearful, cowardly, weakling, stupid, vicious, greedy, boastful glutton."[74] It is he who, according to a famous Dutch traveller Jan Huyghen van Linschoten, is found in furtive amorous encounters with "luxurious and unchaste" *mestiças* who poison their husbands with *datura*.[75] "He smells of dishonest women," is Dom Gaspar's opinion.[76] Loitering in and around the capital during the monsoon season (April to September) when the fleet was grounded in Goa, low-class soldiers, joined with some humbler varieties of young *fidalgo*, were targets of

---

[74] *Desengano*, p. 194.

[75] John Huyghen Linschoten, *The Voyage of John Huyghen Linschoten to the East Indies, from the old English Translation of 1598* (New Delhi: Asian Educational Services, 1988), vol. I, p. 209.

[76] *Desengano*, p. 198.

social disapproval as well as charity. Often hungry and home-less, they begged, borrowed or stole to get food. The Santa Casa da Misericórdia and various other confraternities worked daily and hard to nourish, dress, nurse, and bury the most unfortunate of these men, who would die miserably in Goa rather than gloriously on the battlefield.

Unlike the married *mestiças* and mermaids, captured and locked behind doors if not affixed to pulpits, these soldiers were always in motion, moving from patron to patron, from place to place, from the notorious houses of the local *bailaderas* or dancing girls in Cambarjua, on the border with the Goan non-Christian hinterland, to the Muslim courts, where they sold their services for money. The followers of this last course of action were called *renegades*: they sometimes paid their way back to Goa; other times they remained where they were and con-verted to Islam. Their biographies were rarely written because they undermined the official male Portuguese virtues of military prowess, heroism, and Christian faith. The imperatives of empire- and nation-building had destroyed their careers.[77] Dom Gaspar wrote his text precisely at the moment that national aspirations and heroic zeal were at their highest, before Alcácer Quibir (Al Kasr al Kebir) and the death of Dom Sebastião.

Luís Vaz de Camões, a poor, underemployed and underpaid soldier in India, and a friend of Garcia da Orta, praised the valor, courage, boldness, and providential grace of the discoverers under the command of Vasco da Gama.[78] Da

---

[77] Dejaneira Couto, "Quelques observations sur les renégats portugais en Asie au XVIe siècle," *Mare Liberum*, 16 (1998), pp. 57–86.

[78] Camões, *The Lusiads*.

Gama's triumphant but weary soldiers met their own nymphs on the island of love; they were also called mermaids or *Sirenas* (X, 45) and were sent by the pagan gods as reward for the "discovery" of the passage to India. These creatures, ordered by Gods to "fall in love" with da Gama's soldiers, serve also as soothsayers, announcing future Portuguese deeds in Asia. Each one of the "discoverers" had, moreover, to "catch" his nymph. There is a sense of extreme mobility and vigor attached to this small but feisty group of Portuguese men, a sense that seems to defy all odds, natural and supernatural.

The movements of "discovery" and "conquest" were, in the Portuguese case, exclusively maritime ventures. Throughout its course, the whole of the Portuguese Asian empire had been bound and limited to coastal areas. No wonder, then, that the literature of the period is saturated with water, with seas and oceans. No wonder that mermaids, galleys, fleets, and soldiers inhabit the margins of these texts as metaphors, personifications, metonymies, and synecdoche of all the successes and failures of the national enterprise.

The ship of redemption

Surrounded by the sea on one side and by immense continents on the other, the Portuguese Asian empire was not much more than a network of merchant settlements interconnected by Indiamen sailing along what later became known as *carreiras*, or the Crown trade routes.[79] Goa was the biggest territory under Portuguese rule and the closest to a fully

---

[79] Subrahmanyam, *The Portuguese Empire in Asia 1500–1700*, p. 70.

fledged colonial microstate. This precarious geopolitical situation, which worsened in the course of time, transpires both in the *Colóquios* and the *Desengano de perdidos* in the form of a particular sense of insecurity, defiance and pride. In spite of their different and even opposing concerns, the two texts serve as manuals for survival in Asia. The problem that they both tackle is how one is to adjust to, rationalize, understand, interpret, and triumph over the unstable pulse of expatriate life in the tropics. In their own ways, a New Christian physician and an archbishop waged war on colonial and tropical pathologies. "The principal diligence of the wise men to cure infirmities of the soul, and to disillusion the lost [*desenganar os perdidos*]," predicated Dom Gaspar, "is the same as that of the physicians [in curing] the body, and of the judges [in curing] the disorders of the treasury."[80] It is redemption that they each seek for their charges, yet they disagree as to what represent the causes, the prophylaxis and the cure.

Orta's text is the last bulwark and defense of tropical Portuguese society in India as it had evolved during the first half of the century. If the mobility of things, plants, people, and ideas spawned new illnesses, they also pointed towards new remedies. There is a natural equilibrium that remains in spite of movement and the constant reshuffling of elements. For this sedentary doctor, the movement of things is ultimately a matter of language. Under the many layers of names attributed to both real and imaginary objects that the author conjures up in rapid scattered shots throughout the

---

[80] *Desengano*, p. 164.

text, sensuality, the passions, and fantasy alternately surface and sink in the narrative. Orta plays hide and seek with his audience. He trumpets his opinions forcefully, especially when they are safely unexceptional, run-of-the-mill confirmations of political or cultural stereotypes. The deafening noise of the text masks an unexpected critical stance, a vertiginous abyss of things left unsaid, to be read between the lines.

The reader may suspect that the *Colóquios* enclose some hidden Kabbalistic material, especially when Orta quotes transliterated foreign words. "It is called *perla* in Castillian, it is *perola* in Portuguese, and in Latin *unio*; that is for large pearl (*aljofar grande*), because a small one is called *margarita*; in Arab it is *lulu*, so it is in Persian, in other parts of India, *moti*; and in Malabar *mutu*; and in Portuguese and Castillian pearl (*aljofar*)."[81] The tightly packed names in the paragraph, rather than provoking a yearning for the *via mystica*, seem to be contaminated with the thing itself, and the desire to acquire it. As if responding to the demand created through his own verbal magic, Orta dedicates a lengthy passage to providing precise information about where and how to procure the pearl, about the variety of sizes, and differences in price. These were helpful tips to merchants desirous of gaining profit. Yet, just as he seems to decisively succeed in stirring the commercial appetite, Orta will puncture the text with a distancing remark: one of his favorites is the sententious " it is better to be philosopher than merchant."[82] He can distance himself even further with a statement like "it is better to study

---

[81] Orta, vol. II, p. 119.   [82] Orta, vol. II, p. 123.

philosophy than to get rich, but for the one who is needy it is better to get rich."[83] Not at all, says Dom Gaspar.[84]

Material riches are the nerves of the republic, yet they engender the greed that renders the whole world a wheel of torments.[85] The laws of the country, *leys da terra*, "lead the sinners to disturbances and restlessness: just as the Ocean, it cannot stay without storms, the heart of the evil cannot remain still, all life is a torment, & and as soon as one [life] ends, another takes place: because one abyss brings with it another."[86] Leading a nomadic existence in quest of material goods is a new form of idolatry. "Prostrated before the Pagoda of the riches," sinners turn their souls into flesh.[87] This early critique of emerging capitalism is embedded in a Christian version of the theory of limited goods. Unlike immeasurable and everlasting celestial goods, terrestrial goods are limited, and are necessarily wasted when superfluous. Gaspar advocates simply that the investment be made in that which is of "better value," in a source of treasure that is inexhaustible. To carry out this ultimate commercial deal, one needs a galley.

The galley, on which Ulysses executed the stratagem by which he tricked the mermaids, was the only vessel that could sail the ocean of torments and safely reach the harbor of blessedness, *porto de bemaventurança*.[88] It is on this "spiritual galley" that Dom Gaspar urges his audience to embark. No compass is needed, for the galley is "encased in firmness and

---

[83] Orta, vol. I, p. 24.   [84] *Desengano*, pp. 115–19.
[85] The author repeats this image of the wheel of torment over and over. *Desengano*, p. 120.
[86] *Desengano*, p. 110.   [87] *Desengano*, pp. 89, 145.   [88] *Desengano*, p. 177.

certainty"; the only guide it follows is "a navigational map which is the evangelical law, *ley Evangelica*."[89] The banner of the galley, too, is "fixed, and planted into a huge metal ring."[90] This obsessive fixity, immobility, and stillness continues to be metaphorically subverted by diabolical movement. Human will and conscience, subjected to sense perception, are endlessly under the attack of the deadly trinity of flesh, world and devil, *carne, mundo, diabo*.[91] In a parallel fashion, however, conversion, which leads to redemption, is the interior motion of the will that rejects diabolical suggestion and malicious human persuasion.[92] In the end, it is a psychological void that is sought after. "Peace and stillness of the heart are the biggest riches of the world."[93]

At the center of the archbishop's project lies the salvation of the self – the male, Portuguese, Christian self – from the whirlpool of the endlessly moving empirical world. With a reductive rigor, his text peels away a bewildering network of relations that burden the self and threaten its internal coherence. Salvation and redemption, the ultimate diaphanous texture of the soul, are disconnected from nature, temporality, and human sensual experience, "because no merchandise of this world passes into another world … [because] the goods of this life are so false, and corruptible that they do not reach the other [world], but they spoil every rotting body that remains after burial."[94]

---

[89] *Desengano*, p. 187.
[90] *Desengano*, p. 188. The banner is a metaphor for patience.
[91] *Desengano*, p. 83. [92] *Desengano*, p. 83.
[93] *Desengano*, p. 127. [94] *Desengano*, p. 353.

For Dom Gaspar, deterritorialized subjectivity, the nomadic and fragmentary morality of the Portuguese colonial actors, needs to be rooted. Since terrestrial geography provides no stable ground, he offers a map of the otherworldly, holy continent. In its light, the vicissitudes of life become irrelevant in view of the larger picture. War, flesh and the devil can with their torments "soak only the clothes" of the virtuous man.[95] The remedy against the effects of exterior mobility – and here is another point on which Dom Gaspar and Garcia da Orta furtively agree – is primarily linguistic. It is a "force of true words" that the teacher tries to instill into the disciple. This force draws the soul away from the exterior world into the inward space, in which movement and mobility follow different laws. In the third part of the *Desengano de perdidos* especially, the way of perfection and the way of mystical theology and "unitive love" is contrived and formulated as a grammar having parts to be learned by heart, complete with paradigms, parables, comparisons, exempla, and interpretations. Linguistic acts are the points of intersection between the description of the empirical and visible and the naming of hidden, spiritual essentials.[96] This rambling mystical treatise is, after all, articulated as a "scientific language" presupposing unchangeable laws and relations. By following closely the instructions given herein, anybody can reach the goal of redemption in immobility.

Garcia da Orta's health manual has, in spite of surface differences, exactly the same structure. It imposes the same

[95] *Desengano*, p. 111.
[96] Michel de Certeau, *The Mystic Fable: The Sixteenth and Seventeenth Centuries* (Chicago and London: University of Chicago Press, 1992), p. 96.

scientific rigor on its material. It unveils the secrets of nature and of language that enclose meanings and thus control their circulation. However, for the physician who dreamed of traveling and seeing the world, movement turns out to be everything. The more a thing or concept moves, the more it reveals what is hidden within itself. There is nothing spiritual or mystical about these objects, nothing that cannot be reached and experienced by the senses. *Colóquios* is a text without end or conclusion – at the last moment, Orta decided to add a chapter on betel and "some other things," including Persian roses. In the original edition, this chapter appears right after the table of contents. Since nature keeps revealing new remedies, Orta refuses to conclude his treatise. It is precisely here, in the unfinished, in the boundless possibility of *addendum*, that those "heathens" who were willing to follow Orta could glimpse, at least for a moment, their redemption.

Destiny of books and authors

Leaving his book unfinished may have been the strategic ruse of an old, tired physician. He may have worked on or even announced a newer, bigger, improved edition, with even more remedies for the weary and weak bodies of Portuguese men. The reputation of his healing skills and his knowledge of pharmacy may have protected him from that threat for which he had no prophylaxis, namely, the Inquisition. At the *auto-da-fé* in 1580, it was his bones and his book that were declared sick and surgically removed, burned and scattered. Mutilated, translated, and plagiarized, the content of his text nonetheless spilled out into others. Charles de l'Ecluse (Clusius), a Belgian botanist, found the book in Lisbon, translated it into Latin and published it in Antwerp in 1567.[97] After four successive editions, Clusius finally incorporated it into his own botanical compendia.[98] In the meantime, Italian, Spanish, and French translations were printed in Europe. In the year of Orta's death, Cristóvão da Costa, another New Christian physician, came to India and upon returning to Spain published his *Tractado delas drogas, y medicinas de las Indias Orientales, con sus plantas debuxadas al bivo por Christoval Acosta medico y cirujano que las vio ocularmente.*[99] Orta's text was the starting point for this remarkable work on Asian drugs and spices.[100]

[97] Garcia ab Horto, *Aromatum et simplicium aliquot medicamentorum apud Indos nascentium historia* (Antwerp: Officina Plantiniana, 1567), *Aromatum, et simplicium aliquot medicamentorum apud Indos nascentium historia: primum quidem Lusitanica lingua per dialogos conscripta* (Antwerp: Officina Plantiniana, 1574), *Aromatum et simplicium aliquot medicamentorum apud Indos nascentium historia* (Antwerp: Officina Plantiniana, 1579); Carolus Clusius, *Aliquot notae in Garciae Aromatum historiam* (Antwerp: Officina Plantiniana, 1582); Carolus Clusius et al., *Aromatum, et simplicium aliquot medicamentorum apud Indos nascentium historia* (Antwerp: Officina Plantiniana, 1593).

[98] Carolus Clusius, *Rariorum plantarum historia. Quae accesserint, proxima pagina docebit* (Antwerp: Officina Plantiniana, 1601). On Clusius see Florike Egmond, Paul Hoftijzer, and Robert Visser, *Carolus Clusius: Towards a Cultural History of a Renaissance Naturalist* (Amsterdam: Koninklijke Nederlandse Akademie van Wetenschappen, 2007).

[99] Christoval Acosta (Cristóbal or in Portuguese Cristóvão da Costa), *Tractado delas drogas, y medicinas de las Indias Orientales, con sus plantas debuxadas al bivo por Christoval Acosta medico y cirujano que las vio ocularmente* (Brugos, 1578).

[100] Just like Clusius, Acosta discarded the dialogue form of his predecessor and added glosses on the page margins in order to facilitate the reading of the text. There is no more pretension that anything is debated

Ironically, *Colóquios* was so successful and well known that it would become dispersed and absorbed into other botanical works, whose authors barely mention Orta's name. The easy migration of words and meanings from Orta's text into a European spider-web of linguistic fragments was facilitated by the fact that these words were accompanied by the empirical objects themselves, though the objects followed a different rhythm of movement. In contrast, Dom Gaspar's text had itself migrated from European mystical and Christian polemical traditions. Among those identified as providing the basis for his verbal operations are Henrikus Herp (Herphius or Harphius), Alonso de Madrigal el Tostado, and Bernado Perez de Chinchón.[101] Through a twist of fate, the *Desengano de perdidos* was lost for a few centuries; when it was recovered, it became an object of scholarly interest rather than the victim of imitators and literary thieves. The problem lay in the fact that, in his enthusiasm following the battle of Lepanto, Dom Gaspar advanced a series of prophetic passages in his work; he predicted the collapse of Islam and the Ottoman empire, the marriage of Dom Sebastian to a French princess, and so on. By 1581, with Portugal in the hands of the Spanish monarch, all of these prophecies were proved wrong, or "long lies, *longas mentiras*." As a result, the Inquisition condemned the work and added it to the *Indice Espurgatório*.

---

between two fictional or real protagonists. Facts are facts, and when there is a doubt, Acosta clearly spells it out.

[101] See the preface by Eugenio Asensio, "Dom Gaspar de Leão e su 'Desengano de Perdidos,'"in *Desengano*, pp. III–CIX. Bernado Perez de Chinchón, *Confutación del Alcorán y secta mahometana* (Granada, 1555).

Thus, both books reached a dead end, at one point or another – as did their authors. Coming from afar, like nightmares or dreams, these tropical books continue to move us because of their combative attitude, their will to persuade, intimidate, heal, and redeem. As documents of exile and utopia, they reveal as much as they conceal about the powerful drama of mobility that elated and tormented sixteenth-century Portuguese colonial society and culture in India. More than anything, these texts provide a poetic space in which their authors and readers revisited a site of a deep loss produced by the experience and the "discovery" of mobility as constitutive of expatriate life. Both Orta and Dom Gaspar, each in his way, conjured up patterns of gestures, condensed images, and myths from the past in order to revive the feelings of coherence and unity that seemed to be waning. Spices, mermaids, galleys – are these what Aby Warburg called Pathos-formel or "the forms or formulas of emotional style" that are inscribed into works of art? Just how do the snake-like nymphs, the *nagini* carved on the pulpits of Goan churches, correspond to the serpents of the Hopi Indians, or to pagan antiquity? Writers of books, charmers of snakes; each perform the same ritual act of transforming a nomadic, violent, conquering people, a moving people, into sons of the soil, into natives of places rooted in subterranean elements. It is an enterprise doomed to fail, and so it has to be repeated.[102]

---

[102] Aby Warburg, *Images from the Region of the Pueblo Indians of North America* (Ithaca and London: Cornell University Press, 1995). My thanks to Stephen Greenblatt, Pál Nyíri and Ângela Barreto Xavier for suggestions for improving this essay.

3

Theatrical mobility

STEPHEN GREENBLATT

In the twilight of the last millennium I was gripped, like many of my contemporaries, by a powerful sense that something decisive had happened to the world into which I was born. The Cold War, which had conditioned my entire consciousness of the world, from the time I was instructed as a child to hide under the desk and close my eyes in the event of a Russian nuclear strike, had suddenly and unexpectedly come to an end. New nations were springing up everywhere, and the old repressive regimes were being toppled by constitutional democracies. The whole map of the world was being redrawn, and not only in the political sphere. The mapping of the human genome had begun decisively to prove that race, which had seemed so tragically determinative of human destiny, was a sinister set of fantasies based on pseudo-science and vulgar superstition. It turns out that we are all African by descent and that we are virtually all genetically mixed, such tiny differences as actually exist misunderstood, reified, and given fraudulent and twisted explanations.

It is not only race that was revealed to be largely illusory; religious, ethnic, national, and linguistic ideas of purity also seemed to lose their force and to appear now as merely imaginary constructs created by braiding together diverse fantasies and then conveniently forgetting both the act of braiding and the fantastic nature of the braided elements. Giambattista Vico in the early eighteenth century had correctly grasped that central human constructs, including ideas of race and divinity, are all poetic inventions, products of the imagination. And the imagination works through metaphor, personification, magical animation; that is, it works by projecting voices, inventing genealogies, transporting and knitting heterogeneous elements together.

The question was and remains how to respond to this recognition, given the institutional structures and the intellectual tools that we have inherited. The essays in this volume are attempts at answers, to which I wish to add an account of an ongoing project of my own, a project that grew out of my long-standing interest in tracking the peculiar changes that Shakespeare rang on his sources.

This enterprise, which is highly traditional, runs a high risk of the teleological triumphalism that characterized the *translatio* and *figura* models of cultural mobility that I briefly described in the first chapter. One almost inevitably writes as if those sources had a final and perfect form to which they were aspiring – the form that Shakespeare magisterially realized. The problem with this fantasy is not that it exaggerates the great playwright's achievement – it would be difficult ever to do so – but rather that it distorts his own practice. Shakespeare's imagination worked by restless, open-ended appropriation, adaptation, and transformation. He was certainly capable of making stories up on his own, as in *A Midsummer Night's Dream*, but he clearly preferred picking something up ready-made and moving it into his own sphere, as if the phenomenon of mobility itself gave him pleasure. And he never hinted that the mobility would now have to stop: on the contrary, he seems to have deliberately opened his plays to the possibility of ceaseless change.

As a playwright, actor, and theatrical entrepreneur, Shakespeare understood that there was no final form to any of his creations, and he apparently embraced, rather than resisted, the inherent instability of his medium. There was, as Shakespeare's distinguished contemporary Ben Jonson grasped, one way at least partially to stabilize playtexts: to use the medium of print to produce definitive, that is, authorially approved, versions of the plays. But though half of his known plays were published in his lifetime, there is no evidence that Shakespeare interested himself directly in this enterprise or that he concerned himself with establishing definitive versions or that he resented alterations or revisions. On the contrary, the multiple states in which several of his plays exist – including, among others, *Romeo and Juliet*, *Hamlet*, *Othello*, and *King Lear* – suggest that Shakespeare and his company felt comfortable making numerous cuts, additions, and other changes perhaps linked to particular performances, playspaces, and time constraints. This comfort-level, registered intimately in the remarkable openness of the plays to reinterpretation and refashioning, has contributed to the startling longevity of Shakespeare's achievement: the plays lend themselves to continual metamorphosis.

But the question remains: how can one do justice to theatrical mobility, that is, how can one get sufficiently close and inward with its processes? Several years ago I felt I had at least glimpsed a possibility when I first encountered the brilliant work of a contemporary American playwright, Charles Mee. Mee is a cunning recycler who is particularly gifted at registering the original charge of the material he has lifted while moving that material in new and unexpected directions. I had been especially dazzled by a play, *Big Love*, a wild remaking of Aeschylus' *Suppliants* which Mee largely created out of the odd, surviving fragments of lost Greek plays. I was delighted as well by his many other plays, which he generally posts, without copyright protection, on a website (charlesmee.org) that encourages others to feel free to use them in an ongoing process of appropriation and transformation.

I contacted Mee and told him that I would like the opportunity to watch the creation of one of his plays, from its first inception to its actual production. Throughout my career, I explained, I had been studying the creative mobilization of cultural materials in Shakespeare, but it was always at a 400-year distance. I wanted to be able to be close enough to track and understand every move, and I could only hope to do that with a living playwright, someone to whom I could ask questions and from whom I could get direct answers. I added that I had received a grant that would enable me to pay – handsomely, by the standards of a working playwright – for this privilege.

Mee declined. He was not interested in money, he said, and he did not particularly like being watched. But, he added, if I could come up with an idea for a play, he would consider writing something with me. For a Shakespearean, the choice was a fairly obvious one: I proposed that we write a modern version of Shakespeare's lost play, *Cardenio*. This was a play written in collaboration with his younger colleague, John Fletcher, whom Shakespeare near the end of his career seems to have chosen as his successor. Two of their collaborations – *Henry VIII (All Is True)* and *The Two Noble Kinsmen* – survive, but *Cardenio*, performed on several documented occasions in 1613 and registered for print in mid-century, does not. The reason for its disappearance is unclear but entirely unsurprising: only a fraction of sixteenth- and seventeenth-century plays were preserved. Fully half of Shakespeare's plays, including such masterpieces as *Macbeth*, *Antony and Cleopatra*, and *The Tempest*, would in all likelihood have succumbed to oblivion had his friends John Heminges and Henry Condell not edited the first folio in 1623, seven years after the playwright's death.

In 1727 the distinguished editor and sometime playwright Lewis Theobald claimed that he had found the manuscript of the missing Shakespeare-Fletcher play. That manuscript served as the basis, he asserted, for his play *Double Falsehood; or, The Distressed Lovers*, which he successfully produced at Drury Lane. The text of *Double Falsehood* was printed in 1728 and survives, but the precious manuscript or manuscripts on which it was purportedly based became the possession of the Covent Garden Playhouse, which burned down, with all of its books and papers, in 1808. [1]

---

[1] Theobald claimed to have put his hands on more than one manuscript, and in a letter of 1727 to the Countess of Oxford he provides details about one of them: "One of the Manuscript Copies, which I have, is of above Sixty Years Standing, in the Handwriting of Mr. *Downes*, the famous Old Prompter; and, as I am credibly inform'd, was early in the Possession of

Theobald's play confirms what one would in any case expect from the title of the lost work: Shakespeare and Fletcher evidently took their plot from the story of Cardenio as it is episodically recounted in Part One of Cervantes' *Don Quixote*. (Cervantes' great novel, translated into English by Thomas Shelton and published in 1612, must have been a literary sensation in London in 1613, when Shakespeare and Fletcher's play was first performed.) Loosely intertwined with the early adventures of Don Quixote and his servant Sancho Panza, the Cardenio story is a characteristic Renaissance tragicomedy of male friendship and sexual betrayal, the kind of story that had gripped Shakespeare's imagination throughout his career, from the early *Two Gentlemen of Verona* to the late *Two Noble Kinsmen*.

Cardenio and Luscinda grow up together and fall in love. Before they can secure their fathers' consent to their marriage, Cardenio is compelled to leave home to serve in the court of a powerful nobleman with whose son, Don Fernando, he becomes a close friend. Don Fernando, who has seduced the humbly born Dorotea with promises of marriage, now regrets his promise and, to escape Dorotea, goes home with Cardenio. There the irresponsible nobleman promptly falls in love with Luscinda. Having sent his friend Cardenio away on a pretext, Fernando asks Luscinda's parents for their daughter's hand, and, despite her protests, her parents, who are delighted by the socially advantageous

the celebrated Mr. *Betterton*, and by Him design'd to have been usher'd into the World." Quoted in Brean Hammond, introduction to the Arden edition of *Double Falsehood* (forthcoming). I am grateful to Professor Hammond for kindly sharing his draft manuscript with me.

match, peremptorily agree. Luscinda desperately writes to Cardenio, who hurries home, arriving only in time to witness the marriage ceremony from behind a curtain. When he sees his beloved give her hand to the treacherous Fernando, Cardenio rushes away in despair. What he does not see then is that, at the decisive moment, Luscinda faints. A note is discovered in her bodice, declaring her intention to stab herself, whereupon Fernando storms off in a rage. Luscinda flees to a convent.

Unaware of these developments, Cardenio turns his back on civilization and, like Lear on the heath, wanders as a lunatic in the Sierra Morena. Meanwhile, hearing of Fernando's impending marriage, the seduced and abandoned Dorotea decides (like Julia in *Two Gentlemen of Verona*) to go in search of him. Like Julia and any number of other Shakespearean heroines, she dresses herself as a boy, but the expedient does not in Dorotea's case provide safety. Fighting off an attempted rape, she pushes her assailant off a cliff. Then she too flees to the Sierra Morena.

Six months pass. Fernando discovers Luscinda in the convent and abducts her. Cardenio and Dorotea meet in the mountains; Cardenio's hopes (and his sanity) revive when Dorotea tells him that Luscinda has refused Fernando. They arrive with others at an inn, where a priest discovers a story among the innkeeper's possessions and proceeds to read it aloud to the company. The story involves the newlywed Anselmo, who asks his best friend Lothario to attempt to seduce his wife in order to test her virtue. The wife and the friend fall in love and deceive the husband, and the love tangle ends for all in despair and death. In the wake of this storytelling interlude, Fernando and the abducted Luscinda arrive by chance at the same inn. When Dorotea reproaches Fernando for his treatment of her, he is ashamed and agrees to marry her, allowing Cardenio to have Luscinda. There is general rejoicing.

This is the plot that Shakespeare and Fletcher took from *Don Quixote*, but it is not a plot that was immediately ripe for the plucking. In order to render it mobile, the English playwrights had to disentangle it from the exceedingly complex mesh in which Cervantes had interwoven it with the adventures of his chivalry-obsessed knight. The Cardenio plot only emerges in fits and starts, in the interstices of Quixote's encounters after he has arrived in the Sierra Morena and has decided to go mad for the love of Dulcinea.

Cervantes' interruptions of the narrative are characteristically sly, self-conscious and self-reflexive. Having encountered a real madman, Cardenio, Quixote begs him to tell his tale, which he agrees to do on condition that he not, under any circumstances, be interrupted. But the knight of La Mancha is incapable of holding his tongue: just at the point where Cardenio describes Fernando's treacherous interest in Luscinda, Quixote bursts out and is beaten unmercifully by the enraged lunatic, who breaks off his story and runs away. The bruised Quixote sends Sancho to tell Dulcinea about his lovesick madness. On the way, Sancho meets the priest and the barber from his village, who want to find Don Quixote and bring him home. All three head back into the mountains.

The narrative goes on in this vein, the pieces emerging fitfully in a series of accidental encounters, surprises, misunderstandings, revelations, detours, and constant interruptions.

Dressed as a boy, Dorotea's true gender is discovered when she takes off her shoes in order to wash in the stream and discloses her delicate, unmistakably feminine feet. The priest and the barber persuade her to dress as a princess in distress, in order to lure Don Quixote back to his village on the pretext of saving her from a giant. At the inn the priest's reading of the tale of the husband who persuades his best friend to seduce his wife is interrupted by Don Quixote's attack on some wineskins, which he has mistaken for the giant. Nothing is delivered in straightforward narrative sequence, and the two English collaborators must have laughed or groaned as they tried to tease a coherent plot out of Cervantes' deliberately mad tangle.

The only hard evidence that they succeeded in doing so is the title of the lost play – not *Don Quixote* but *Cardenio* – conjoined with Theobald's eighteenth-century adaptation of the manuscript he claimed he had found. All traces of the Knight of La Mancha have disappeared from *Double Falsehood*, along with such narrative interruptions as the cautionary tale read by the priest. What remains is the straightforward and efficient recounting of the trials of Cardenio and Luscinda, rechristened for no particular reason as Julio and Leonora.

When we set out to devise a modern version of *Cardenio*, Charles Mee and I started in the obvious place, with Theobald's *Double Falsehood*, but we immediately ran into a problem: the story seemed relatively difficult to set in motion. The difficulty lay not in the themes of betrayal and madness. Rather, it lay in the motivating premise of an immensely powerful social hierarchy – something far more compelling than wealth alone – that allows Cardenio to be peremptorily called to court, permits his socially superior friend Don Fernando to send him away from his own house, and induces Luscinda's parents to marry her against her wishes. Of course, it would have been possible to use this premise without alteration, if we chose to set the play in the distant past, but Shakespeare's own mobilization of cultural materials depended on his ability to make those materials feel contemporary. Even when, as in *A Comedy of Errors*, he deliberately holds onto something of the original setting – a Mediterranean city in classical antiquity – he contrives to resituate it in his own times and imbue it with his own values.

Mee and I (the phrase "Mee and I" has a comical self-reflexiveness, as if I had split myself) could have found some contemporary equivalent to the hierarchical social code of the Renaissance – in the army perhaps, or in certain extreme business or academic communities. But the task felt artificial and labored, and successful aesthetic mobility thrives on ease or at least on the illusion of ease. Where something immediately clicked for us was not in the principal Cardenio story but rather in the distorted mirror image of that story that the priest in Cervantes reads to Cardenio and Dorotea at the inn.

Anselmo's irrational anxiety about his wife's fidelity and his urgent insistence that his best friend Lothario attempt to seduce her would have been explained by Renaissance physicians as the consequence of severe humoral imbalance. Our own term "neurotic" has a different physiological reference point but serves as a comparably all-purpose way of accounting for behavior that is self-destructive and baffling but seems to follow a perverse logic of its own. For Cervantes, as for Shakespeare, there is a link between this perverse logic and a certain intensity of male friendship: Anselmo and Lothario are mirrored in Valentine and Proteus, Othello and Cassio (or perhaps Iago), Leontes and Polixenes, Palamon and Arcite. There is an erotic charge in all of these friendships – a charge analyzed with astonishing subtlety in Shakespeare's sonnets – but that charge does not serve as an adequate explanation for the compulsive behavior of the hero. That behavior remains perplexing and tantalizing, an invitation to open a set of inquiries about desire, not to bring those inquirites to a halt.

To set Cervantes, Shakespeare and Fletcher, and Theobald in motion and to bring their linked stories into the present, what we needed to do first was to switch the ontology. The fictional story-within-the-story – the tale the priest finds in a book and reads aloud to the company at the inn – became our real story, while the story of the trials of Cardenio became a fictional story or rather, in keeping with the medium, a play-within-the-play. Innumerable adjustments and modifications followed, all deriving ultimately from this initial switch. The Anselmo story in Cervantes had a tragic ending, to set it against the happy conclusion of the Cardenio story: holding onto the overarching genre, we gave the Anselmo story a happy conclusion and had the Cardenio story, as we staged it, break off in misery. And we used Shakespeare's multiple versions of the male friendship-jealousy-betrayal plot as a kind of toolkit, a set of master devices or programs. Hence, for example, displacement of the action to a "green world" (in our case, Umbria); the interplay of contrasting perspectives on the same central problem; certain types of characters performing certain set functions, such as provocation and satirical commentary; alternating rhythms of ensemble scenes and scenes focusing on intimate exchanges; structural equivalents in our own idiom of the soliloquies, asides, and masques that Shakespeare's conventions provided him.

To speak of these devices as a toolkit makes the process of mobilization sound mechanical, and there were indeed some moments in our devising *Cardenio* that involved casting about to find the right-sized piece for the machine we were trying to build. Thus when we sought some contemporary equivalent to those formal rhetorical occasions in which characters in Shakespeare reveal far more about themselves than they intend to, such as Claudius' ceremonious address to his court or Richard III's exhortation to his troops, we thought of the comically disastrous modern genre of the wedding toast. And when we looked for something like the "pleachèd bower" in *Much Ado* or the "box-tree" in *Twelfth Night* that enables crucial moments of overhearing, we seized upon the baby monitor. But once we had established the basic structure of the play – what Renaissance dramatists would have called the "plat" – the writing, the greater part of which was done with astonishing facility by my collaborator, seemed anything but mechanical. On the contrary, it involved something I can only describe as listening to the voices of the characters and transcribing what they had to say. That transcription is an odd effect, I believe, of the cultural mobility that we had triggered: in the particular situation in which these particular characters found themselves, certain things needed to be said, as if they had already been encoded and were now simply unfolding. And conversely, certain things could not be said, even if we tried to make the characters say them.

Here then is the ground plan of our *Cardenio*. In Act One, Anselmo and his bride Camilla have come to Umbria to celebrate their marriage. They were formally married before the play begins, but Anselmo wanted to have a second informal ceremony and a gala wedding party, with his close friends, in the beautiful country house that his Italian-born mother, Luisa, had inherited and where he had spent much time as a child. As the play begins, Anselmo, in the grip of tormenting anxiety, secretly asks his best friend, Will, to attempt to seduce his wife. The marriage party is further complicated by the boorish behavior of the boisterous Edmund (who flirts with the maid, Simonetta), the tensions between Edmund and his wife Sally, and particularly by the extreme unpleasantness of Camilla's sister, Doris.

The group is surprised by the unexpected arrival of Anselmo's parents, Luisa and Alfred, who come enthusiastically bearing a wedding gift: *Cardenio*, a lost play by Shakespeare, which they propose that the wedding party perform. They have brought with them Susana, a college friend of Anselmo and Camilla, who is now a professional actress. Luisa and Alfred, with matchmaking in mind, propose that Susana plays the romantic lead in *Cardenio* opposite Will. But to further his perverse scheme, Anselmo insists instead that Camilla play the lead, and he takes Susana off for an afternoon tour of the countryside. Camilla is understandably baffled and upset by this behavior – her distress is exacerbated by a conversation with Doris – but she is comforted by Will.

Rudi the carpenter, an exuberant, loquacious Albanian refugee, arrives to build the stage for the performance the next day; he is also given a part to play in it. Luisa and Alfred use the baby monitor – which they had installed when Anselmo was a child – to call the group of friends together for a rehearsal. Whatever has begun to happen between Will and Camilla further develops during the love scene they rehearse (a scene borrowed, with some adjustments, from Theobald's *Double Falsehood*). Anselmo and Susana return from their outing, and the group comes together for the wedding feast cooked by Simonetta's husband, Melchiore.

Act Two begins with the dress rehearsal of *Cardenio*. The group begins in a spirit of mockery, but the mockery is silenced by the intensity of the love scene between Will and Camilla. Doris' observation that their kiss was not simply a piece of acting sets off a torrent of accusations. When the others leave, Will and Camilla confess that they have fallen in love with each other. They exit trying to figure out a way out of the excruciating difficulty of their situation. Alone together, Susana and Anselmo also confess that they are drawn to one another. They too are perplexed by how they can possibly resolve the painful tangle – this is, after all, a party to celebrate Anselmo's wedding to Camilla. Edmund flirts with Simonetta but holds himself back. Will and Camilla return, still trying to solve their dilemma: before they exit, they consider staging a scene, via the baby monitor, in which Will will pretend to be attempting to seduce Camilla who will in turn pretend to be virtuously resisting. Rudi enters and, seeing himself alone on the stage, decides to perform a one-man show of the entire *Cardenio*. While he becomes ever more noisily absorbed in his performance, the others all return to watch him. Struck by the resemblance between the play-within-the-play and his own actions – "I am Cardenio!" – Anselmo confesses that he has put Will up to the attempted seduction, and he further confesses that he has fallen in love with Susana. When Susana in turn confesses her own feelings, Camilla forgives them both and agrees to dissolve the marriage. The wedding party, like the marriage it was meant to celebrate, breaks up. The group turns angrily on Doris, who has continued to mock everyone, and then, having driven her away, the couples – Anselmo and Susana, Alfred and Luisa, Edmund and Sally – take their leave. Before he departs, Anselmo asks Will if he would care to stay on at the house for a few days to "console" Camilla. When they are finally left alone on stage, Will and Camilla begin to dance.

This is, in rough outline, where we took the Cervantes/Shakespeare and Fletcher/Theobald materials, or rather where those materials took us. For though we were aware of great latitude in many of our local decisions – Will and Camilla, for example, could actually use the baby monitor trick and get away with the deception; Susana could withhold her admission of love and perhaps only agree to see Anselmo again, if at all, after a long interval– the larger shape seemed to be dictated by the aesthetic inheritance. More precisely, once we made the decision to take the Anselmo story as our main plot and to give that story a comic resolution, Mee and I were carried along by currents whose direction was determined by the meeting of the early seventeenth-century story with our particular twenty-first century sensibilities and values.

The design of the play was given by what the historian Fernand Braudel and the anthropologist Marshall Sahlins have called "the structure of the conjuncture."[2] And consequently the

---

[2] Marshall Sahlins, *Islands of History* (Chicago: University of Chicago Press, 1984), p. xiv.

exhilarating experience of license associated with mobility – the sense that nothing is nailed down, that all options are open, that the world is all before one, where to choose – is set against a powerful experience of limits. If there is far more mobility in culture than one might at first expect, there is also far more constraint, even in circumstances where one imagines almost complete freedom.

I experienced this interplay of freedom and constraint first-hand, in the writing of *Cardenio*, and I have tested it further with an additional experiment. Making contact with theater companies in different parts of the world, I invited them to take the same materials, now including the play Mee and I had written, and rework them into a form that was appropriate for their particular culture. Using the grant money that Mee had declined and specifying that a straight-forward production of our *Cardenio* was not an option, I commissioned translations of the relevant texts (Cervantes was inevitably available in translation already, but Theobald was not, nor, it goes without saying, was our own play). And similarly I commissioned a translation of the new text back into English, so that I could understand something of what was going on, when I traveled to see the production.

The emerging productions have confirmed in remarkable detail the blend of contingency, license, and con-straint that characterized my own experience of cultural mobility. None of the adaptations remotely resembles the other, and none replicates our own play, though all clearly derive from the narrative materials I had provided and all are, in significant ways, versions of the Cardenio story. One example will suffice. For the Japanese version created by the gifted playwright and director Akio Miyazawa, I had ahead of time imagined something in the kabuki style or perhaps in the more farcical mode called kyogan. Conditioned perhaps by Gilbert and Sullivan as well as Roland Barthes, I expected lacquered fans, folding screens, and the delicate sound of the koto harp. What I saw instead was a play called *Motorcycle Don Quixote*, set in a grimy motorcycle repair shop in which the sounds of revving engines mingled with loud American rock music.[3] Cultural projection is not a one-way street.

Miyazawa remarked to me that for him mobility depends on misunderstanding, especially crosscultural misunderstanding. Perhaps that was the principle that led him in his version of the play to undo or reverse, as in a photographic negative, virtually everything that Mee and I had done. His principal couple, Tadao and Machiko, is long married and – despite the difficulties they encounter when Tadao asks his assistant Sakazaki to attempt to seduce his wife – they stay married. They are not both young people, starting out in life and uncertain of their desires, but an old man and a much younger woman. Their difficulties seem to stem in large part from this age difference, or rather from the man's sense of the significance of this difference and his anxieties about it. There is a partial gesture toward resolution – near the end of the play, Tadao abandons his wife and sets out on his motorcycle on a road trip from which he returns after three years claiming to

---

[3] *Motorcycle Don Quixote*, written and directed by Akio Miyazawa, produced by Tadashi Uchino (dramaturg Mika Eglington), performed at the Yokohama Redbrick Warehouse, May 23–29, 2006.

have conquered the "King" against whom he was struggling. But this claim only confirms the fact that he is still living deep inside fantasies that his wife cannot share (or that, in any case, are part of a sense of unreality that haunts and depresses her). They will stay married, it seems, but unhappily so, with the wife soldiering on, in the spirit of the martyred women in *The Three Sisters*.

All other relationships in the play– those between Sakazaki and Machiko, and between Sakazaki and Yuka (Tadao's daughter with his deceased first wife), and between Yuka and her loutish boyfriend, and between Machiko and her former lover Kamiyama, who comes to the shop looking for her – are unresolved and ambiguous. Left ambiguous too is whether Sakazaki (whom Tadao has asked to try to seduce his wife) has actually succeeded, or whether what for a moment appears to be his success is only a fantasy of Tadao's. For the play repeatedly moves, without signal, from reality to fantasy, reality particularly centered on the grimy shop and the depressing marriage, fantasy particularly centered on the story of Cardenio and his unfaithful friend. And it is left unclear even whose fantasy this is: at moments it appears to be the memory trace of a play that Machiko, a former actress, had been in, one in which she had had an unhappy affair with the actor Kamiyama. But at other moments it appears to be Tadao's fantasy, one in which he plays out his fear of abandonment. The ambiguity, which I experienced as perplexing and annoying, seemed to delight the audiences that flocked to see *Motorcycle Don Quixote*.

Working with the same materials and with a translated version of our play in front of him, Miyazawa undid, or reversed, virtually everything that Mee and I had tried to do. This reversal is what he seems to have meant by suggesting that mobility depends upon or is misunderstanding, a misunderstanding manifestly deliberate and willed. *Motorcycle Don Quixote* begins and ends in the same state of frozen anxiety and confusion. At the beginning Machiko looks blank and unresponsive, At the close Tadao claims that he has defeated the King – that is, the enemy or seducer – on his road trip, but it is not at all clear what this claim means and how his wife is supposed to react. Accordingly, she remains blank and unresponsive. The play's setting is not a "green world" but a motorcycle repair shop contiguous with the family's living quarters. Even the road trip offers no escape: the motorcycle roars out from the rather shallow and compressed work- and living-space into a long, wide opening at the back of the stage, visible when the workshop's metal grate is lifted. But a video projection makes it very explicit that what lies outside is a vista of endless crowded highways and heavy traffic. The social world is claustrophobic; there is no Malvolio figure, and the former lover who briefly appears does not stay around long enough to see Machiko or to make any significant impact on any of the characters. There is no real play-within-the play and no "rude mechanicals." Though other characters are glimpsed, there is really only a single plot, a single couple: Tadao and Machiko. Even the assistant enlisted to seduce Machiko does not acquire an independent existence.

In *Motorcycle Don Quixote* virtually nothing happens on stage. Though there are many opportunities for characters to overhear or to spy on one another, such overhearing never happens, or if it does, it makes no impact. The road trip and all other major events (including the possible sexual encounter between Sakazuki and Machiko) happen offstage, and all of the meaningful character development depends on backstory. There is no gambling on love; no trust in happiness; no clarification and no forgiveness. In their place there is only a stoical determination to continue.

In a public discussion after a Sunday matinee I attended in Yokohama, Miyazawa asked me what I made of all the American touches in his production – the rock music, the heavy allusions to *Easy Rider*, and so forth. I said that I regarded them as at once pervasive and superficial, since none of the depicted relationships seemed remotely conceivable to me as an American. The most striking example was the scene at the close in which Tadao, who has abandoned his wife and daughter without support or a word of explanation returns after three years.

TADAO:	I'm home.
MACHIKO:	Welcome back.
TADAO:	What's with your clothes? Is there a ceremony happening today?
MACHIKO:	I'm off to work. I'm earning a living. I need to work to live.
TADAO:	All is fine now. Lucinda was saved and relieved from the King's hands. I did it. I knocked down the King. You follow what I am saying, right? So you've finally forgotten everything.
MACHIKO:	I have to go otherwise I'll be late.

TADAO: Even when I'm home? Come, here, come on, come here.

Machiko goes to the center stage. When Tadao is about to hug her, she escapes from it.

TADAO: What?

MACHIKO: I'm going to work.

Machiko starts walking away.

TADAO: Aren't you pleased that I've come home?

MACHIKO: ... Of course I'm pleased.

TADAO: ...

MACHIKO: But we must carry on with our lives, we must go on living.

Even the recognizable touch of Chekhov, I explained, was not enough to make this moment seem to me anything but strange and incomprehensible. "I understand you," Miyazawa said; "you expect that the wife should embrace her husband and welcome him home, as an American woman would do. But Japanese people do not so easily hug and kiss one another." I had, of course, thought something like the opposite: that no wife I could conceive of would, in those circumstances, welcome her husband back at all. On the stage of the darkened theater in Yokohama, I felt I had been thoroughly initiated into the phenomenon of cultural mobility as misunderstanding.

4

World literature beyond Goethe

REINHARD MEYER-KALKUS

The notion of *Weltliteratur*, or "world literature," which Goethe introduced in 1827, has recently found growing popularity among literary scholars, who increasingly regard world literature as their primary and necessary sphere of competence. World literature, which for Goethe was something that yet lay on the horizon, something to work toward, would today seem to have become a reality.

Berlin can serve as an example of this in the same way that Paris, London, and New York can in other respects. Anyone attempting to write a guide to literary Berlin would no longer be able to limit themselves to German authors but would have to also consider authors working in Arabic, Russian, English, French, Swedish, or other languages, among them the Nobel Prize winner Imre Kertész, writing in his native Hungarian, as well as Syrians, Iranians, and Turks who pen their works in German and who have developed followings in Germany but still remain relatively unknown in their lands of origin.[1]

No longer viable is the old model of literary scholarship in which a single nation or region and its language or

[1] Such as the Turks Aras Ören, Emine Sevgi Özdamar, and Zafer Senocak, or the Lebanese Suleiman Taufiq.

language family is the focus. It is becoming increasingly difficult to relegate authors to a single culture and nation – they
live and write in the spaces between. Those who compose their
works in one of the great languages of global intercourse
(e.g. English, French, Spanish, or Arabic) not only live
between cultures but address readers outside their own lands
of origin, such as the Indians, Pakistanis, and Bengalis in
London, the Chinese in New York, or the North Africans in
France. Many of these have been able to effect a linguistic
change and write in languages that are not their mother
tongue or their "second mother tongue."

Does not the world-literature concept provide transnational literary studies with a category that succeeds in transcending all those discrete philologies defined by a single
language or language family?

Paradoxical to the popularity now enjoyed by
Goethe's term is the fact that its inventor had an understanding of it that differs from our present one. According to
Metzlers Literatur Lexikon from 1990, *Weltliteratur* is the
"total literature of all peoples and times," the "canon of ...
literary works from this total literature that is regarded as
timeless and having universal validity."[2] Goethe had neither
of these meanings in mind. Without offering any conclusive
definition or systematic explanation, in his use of the term

---

[2] Cited in Anne Bohnenkamp, "Rezeption der Rezeption: Goethes Entwurf
einer Weltliteratur im Kontext seiner Zeitschrift 'Über Kunst und
Altertum,'" in *Spuren, Signaturen, Spiegelungen: Zur Goethe-Rezeption
in Europa*, eds. Bernard Beutler and Anke Bosse (Cologne, Weimar,
Vienna, 2000), p. 200.

(mentioned some fifteen times) he brought very clear literary ideas to bear and succeeded in putting these ideas into practice.

I

It was in January 1827 that Goethe first spoke of world literature to his amanuensis Johann Peter Eckermann. At the time he was working on the latest edition of *Über Kunst und Altertum* (*On Art and Antiquity*), a journal that he had been editing since 1816 and which took up much of his energies until his death in 1832. This journal is perhaps the least known of his literary endeavors. It is only recently that it has been viewed as integral to his later work and it is in this context that new interpretive approaches have emerged with regard to the notion of world literature, in particular those of such comparative literature specialists as Hendrik Birus and Anne Bohnenkamp.[3]

In 1827, in the French periodical *Le Globe*, Goethe read a comprehensive review of a Chinese novel from the Ming Dynasty which had just been issued in French translation as *Les deux cousines*,[4] and he subsequently aired his thoughts on world literature with Eckermann:

---

[3] See the annotated edition of the Deutscher Klassiker Verlag, Frankfurt: *Johann Wolfgang Goethe: Sämtliche Werke, Briefe, Tagebücher und Gespräche in vierzig Bänden*, vol. XX: *Ästhetische Schriften 1816–1820*, ed. Hendrik Birus (Frankfurt, 1999); vol. XXI: *Ästhetische Schriften 1821–1824*, ed. Stefan Greif and Andrea Ruhlig (Frankfurt 1998); vol. XXII: *Ästhetische Schriften 1824–1832*, ed. Anne Bohnenkamp (Frankfurt 1999).

[4] *Yü-chiao-li ou Les deux cousines*, translated by Abel Rémusat.

"A Chinese novel?" I said [i.e. Eckermann]. "It must be very exotic." – "Not so exotic as one would suspect," said Goethe. "The people think, act, and feel almost exactly as we do, and one very soon feels them to be kindred souls. With the only difference that everything with them is clearer, purer, and more moral" … "But," I said, "is this certain Chinese novel not then perhaps one of their most exquisite ones?" "By no means," said Goethe; "the Chinese have thousands of them and had them at a time when our ancestors still roamed the forests. I realize more and more," Goethe continued, "that literature is humanity's common heritage and that it arises everywhere and across time in hundreds upon hundreds of people. One person does it a little better than the other and perches at the top a little longer than the others, but that is all … But of course if we Germans are unable to see beyond the narrow confines of our own surroundings, we might very easily end up wallowing in pedantic arrogance. That's why I interest myself in foreign nations, and would advise others to do the same. National literature has not much relevance today, the epoch of world literature is now dawning, and everyone should do what he can to accelerate its arrival."[5]

This last remark is often cited due to its pithiness; but one should not employ it carelessly. Even though Goethe opposed a parochial and limiting preoccupation solely with one's own national literature, it is unclear what he meant precisely by its not having "much relevance today."

---

[5] *Goethe: Sämtliche Werke*, vol. XXII: *Johann Peter Eckermann: Gespräche mit Goethe*, ed. Christoph Michel (Frankfurt 1999), pp. 223 ff.

Christoph Martin Wieland had first used the term *Weltliteratur* twenty years before in a handwritten marginal gloss, defining it as an "ad hoc synonym for learnedness and politesse and being well-read, in combination with cosmopolitan knowledge."[6] Goethe was able to piggyback this definition, for his own use of the word had "little to do with idealistic concepts like *Weltanschauung, Weltgeschichte, Weltseele* or *Weltgeist* [world-view, world history, world soul, world spirit]" as introduced by Kant, Herder, Schelling, and Hegel; rather, it had more to do with *Weltbürger*, or world-citizen (instead of the citizen of a city or state) and world trade (as opposed to domestic trade). He was concerned with transcending the merely private, local, or national; with going beyond self-confinement and self-centeredness; with breaking free of what he called "pedantic arrogance." "Perhaps one will soon attain to the conviction that there is no such thing as patriotic art and patriotic science. Like everything of real value, they both belong to the entire world and can only be promoted through the free and general interaction of all living beings, with an abiding regard for that which remains and is known to us from the past."[7] This he had written as early as 1801.

A venerable hermeneutical method is to ask who or what a statement is directed against – whether spoken or unspoken. Goethe's remark did in fact have a certain polemical edge designed to provoke an exchange. He was disconcerted

---

[6] Hendrik Birus, *Weltliteratur und Littérature comparée*, unpublished manuscript (2002), p. 2.

[7] *Goethe: Sämtliche Werke*, vol. XVIII: *Ästhetische Schriften 1771–1805*, ed. Friedmar Apel (Frankfurt, 1998), p. 809.

by tendencies that he had observed among the Romantics since 1800 and which were still very pronounced two decades later, namely a travesty of what he and Herder in their youth had gotten under way when they sought to discover evidence of *German Style and Art* (*Von deutscher Art und Kunst*), the title of their 1773 publication. In a conscious rejection of the French-influenced court and erudite culture of their time, they collected such things as Alsatian folk songs – or, as Herder termed them, *Nationallieder*, national songs – or adduced what they incorrectly held to be the "German" architecture of the Strasbourg Cathedral,[8] or celebrated pre-modern Germany and towering figures in such dramas as *Götz von Berlichingen* and *Faust*. Lending their talents to these innovative cultural-political endeavors was the early Romantic generation of Wackenroder, Tieck, Novalis, the Schlegels and later Jacob Grimm and nascent German studies (*Germanistik*) – but with clear anti-French and patriotic cum chauvinistic tendencies. During the Napoleonic era their perspectives increasingly narrowed and focused on the Christian-Germanic culture – indeed, on the Catholic Middle Ages. The chief model became "neo-German, religio-patriotic art."[9] Perhaps Goethe so vehemently resisted this Romantic conservatism because he was well aware that his early work had been a seminal catalyst in its development. In opposition to the Romantics, he insisted now

---

[8] According to what we know today, Erwin von Steinbach, the thirteenth-century German architect, was responsible for only one of the façades and cannot be given credit for the entire cathedral.

[9] "Neu-deutsche religiös-patriotische Kunst" was in fact the title of a polemical essay by Goethe's fellow art-lover Heinrich Meyer in *Über Kunst und Altertum*, in *Goethe: Sämtliche Werke*, vol. XX, pp. 105 ff.

on a cosmopolitan broadening of the nation's cultural scope so as to surmount its navel-gazing: "I realize more and more that literature is humanity's common heritage and that it arises everywhere and across time in hundreds upon hundreds of people" – these his words to Eckermann.[10]

As he grew older, Goethe's interest in the contemporary literary output of non-German Europe became all the more lively, in particular for authors such as Lord Byron and Alessandro Manzoni as well as poetry in various languages from various countries and epochs, these being increasingly published during his lifetime. His own poetry bore their imprint. The *West-östliche Divan* (*West-Eastern Divan*, 1819) was an imaginary dialogue with Hafis, the fourteenth-century Persian poet; another dialogue, with Chinese poetry, was the basis for the poem cycle *Chinesisch-deutsche Jahres- und Tageszeiten* (*Chinese-German Book of Seasons and Hours*, 1827). In *Über Kunst und Altertum* there are translations from the Serbian, the Persian, and modern Greek. For Goethe this multilingual poetry was "universal world poetry"; that is, the expression of the poetic faculty that is present in all peoples and which can emerge "wherever the sun shines."[11] But this world

---

[10] And elsewhere, in opposition to the Grimm brothers' Romantic enthusiasm for the folk song, Goethe declared that, "Never in history has a nation been granted the privilege of producing only good and worthy literature." As quoted in Hermann Strobach, *Nachwort zu Volkslieder, gesammelt von Goethe* (Weimar, 1982), p. 76.

[11] *Goethe: Sämtliche Werke*, vol. XXII, pp. 386 ff. As a young man, Goethe had learned from Herder that "the art of poetry is a gift bestowed on the world and its peoples, not the private inheritance of a few refined and cultured gentlemen." From *Dichtung und Wahrheit*, in *Goethe: Sämtliche Werke*, vol. XIV (Frankfurt, 1986), p. 445.

poetry is not the equivalent of world literature. According to him, world poetry first achieves this status when it is translated out of its respective language and made *available* to the world. Comparison has justifiably been drawn with Hegel's *Philosophie der Weltgeschichte* (*Lectures on the Philosophy of World History*). Just as the myriad *Volksgeister*, or national spirits, first attain to self-consciousness through the *Weltgeist*, or world spirit, with this latter only realizing itself through the diverse *Volksgeister*, so too does national poetry (i.e. world poetry) only become part of world literature when it has been translated and widely disseminated so as to transcend its otherwise parochial status – which is also how world literature comes into existence, being the choral sum of the world's voices.

II

Historically, the term "world literature" has scholarly/disciplinary implications that were recently laid bare by Hendrik Birus.[12] It would seem that Goethe developed his concept in dialogue with the founders of *littérature comparée* in France. What with the successes enjoyed by *anatomie comparée* and *morphologie comparée* in the natural sciences and linguistics, as of about 1800 *littérature comparée* had become a fashionable term. Books were appearing with titles like *Mythologie comparée* and *Histoire comparée*. The literary scholar Abel-François Villemain gave a *Cours de littérature comparée* at the Sorbonne in 1827, and the literary critic and historian

---

[12] See Birus, *Weltliteratur und Littérature comparée*.

Jean-Jacques Ampère (1800–1864) published a *Histoire comparative des arts et de la littérature*.[13] *Littérature comparée* did not collect and compare for the mere sake of doing so but aimed rather at a cultural-historical construction of familial relationships across time and space (for example between Nordic-German and Greek literature) and so as to create an artistic philosophy of literature.[14]

Goethe was familiar with these French debates primarily through *Le Globe*, that "*Journal philosophique et littéraire*" established in 1824 which kept him informed not only about literary matters but with respect to discussions in the natural sciences.[15] For him, *Le Globe* was an inexhaustible source of intellectual stimulation. When the periodical ran a review of his own dramatic works translated into French (*Œuvres dramatiques de Goethe*), he translated and excerpted it for *Über Kunst und Altertum*.[16] Conversely, he was also able to read a review of *Über Kunst und Altertum* in *Le Globe*. Goethe had personal links to the major players of the *littérature*

---

[13] This an example of the cross-pollination of perspectives that was central to Goethe's concept of *Weltliteratur*. Goethe had personal contact with the leading actors in the founding of *littérature comparée*, and Ampères even paid him a visit in Weimar.

[14] Ampère, for example, insisted that "literary and artistic philosophy should be an outgrowth of the comparative history of the arts and literature of all the peoples of the world" (as cited in Birus, *Weltliteratur und Littérature comparée*).

[15] On the staff of *Le Globe* were, among others, Jouffroy, Sainte-Beuve, Thiers, and Guizot. During the Bourbon Restoration it was an opposition journal; after the July Revolution of 1830 it became an important mouthpiece of the Saint-Simonians; by 1832 it was defunct.

[16] 1826, *Goethe: Sämtliche Werke*, vol. XXII, pp. 258 ff.

comparée movement, similar to his relationship with the young English literary scholar, translator, and historian Thomas Carlyle, who had written a biography of Schiller and translated tales of the German Romantics.

Here, emerging within the context of the German–French and German–English cultural exchange, was something decisive for the concept of world literature, namely the reciprocal recognition of writers from various lands, which consisted not only in perceiving the other in their particularity and even strangeness, but also a perception of how these others regarded *you*. In familiarizing oneself with other people's perception of one, one would arrive at an altered self-understanding. This was at least the hope that Goethe harbored with respect to the *Weltliteratur* that would emerge in the future. He was astonished to learn that ever since the publication of Madame de Staël's *De L'Allemagne* in France (1813) and England (1814) he had been regarded as a Romantic and his *Faust* was understood to be a Romantic epic.[17] The more he grew accustomed to the foreign perception of himself, the more his opposition to the German Romantics was toned down. Goethe told Eckermann that it was right and proper "that the lively intercourse existing now between the French, English, and Germans allows us to correct one another." This was of very great benefit (15 July 1817).[18] *Weltliteratur* was

---

[17] "Obviously it's the opponents of Classicism who have welcomed my aesthetic maxims and the work based on them" (*Goethe: Sämtliche Werke*, vol. XXII, p. 766).

[18] Cited in Bohnenkamp, "Rezeption," p. 197. In a letter to Carl Jacob Ludwig Iken on 27 September 1827, Goethe wrote, "It is time that the passionate discord between Classicists and Romantics finally be allayed" (ibid., p. 198).

based on such reciprocal perception, on the reception of receptions, on the retransfer of transfers, on translations back into the original culture from translation – all of which can lead to changes in one's own self-understanding.

Goethe's understanding of *Weltliteratur* was neither the archive of everything that had ever been written nor the canon of great works transcending their national cultures, but rather "a form of international literary communication yet to be realized."[19] Its principal players were writers, literary critics, translators, booksellers, newspaper publishers, and all those who participated in the formation of public opinion with regard to other peoples and cultures. The media of this "free intellectual trade" were journals and books, correspondence, and translations, the journeys and encounters of writers as well as an expanding book market. Goethe wrote that, "Nations are growing closer together through express mail and steamer ships as well as through daily, weekly, and monthly periodicals.[20]

[19] Birus, *Weltliteratur und Littérature comparée*, p. 4.
[20] Letter to Carlyle, 8 August 1828, *Goethe: Sämtliche Werke*, vol. XXII, p. 1246. Goethe placed a high value on translation work, especially in Germany, which seemed to him particularly suited to act as an interpreter between cultures. In a review of Thomas Carlyle's English translation of German Romantic tales, which appeared in an 1827 issue of *Über Kunst und Altertum* under the title "German romance," Goethe wrote: "The Germans have long played a seminal role in such mediation and mutual appreciation [of peoples]. Whoever understands and studies the German language now finds himself in a market where all the nations of the world are offering their wares for sale – he plays the role of interpreter while simultaneously enriching himself. Every translator is thus to be respected, for he is the middleman in this universal intellectual commerce; his business is to promote this trade. One may bewail the inadequacy of translations, but it remains one of the worthiest and most important

III

In a review of Thomas Carlyle's English translation of German stories, Goethe described in almost utopian terms this "mediation and mutual appreciation" of the world's literature. One could "not of course expect that thereby a general peace would ensue, but that unavoidable strife would become less grave in its repercussions, that war would become less terrible, that victory would engender less triumphalism ... The characteristics of a nation are like its language and currency – they facilitate human intercourse; in fact, they make it perfectly possible. True toleration will only become universal when a nation's and an individual's particularities go unremarked and people still retain the conviction that that which is truly of value will distinguish itself by belonging to all of mankind."[21]

This liberal belief in progress and education has lately been vehemently criticized. How could one have postulated

enterprises in terms of global intercourse" (ibid., pp. 433 ff.) People have ridiculed this notion of German as the linguistic pivot for *Weltliteratur*, but one should recall that circa 1800 there was indeed a singular plethora of German translations of foreign literature and that in the nineteenth and even into the twentieth century German remained *the* language for many educated Central and Eastern Europeans, for it was thanks to German that they had access to world literature.

[21] *Goethe: Sämtliche Werke*, vol. XXII, p. 1246. And in a similar connection, Goethe said: "For some time now the best poets and aesthetic writers of all nations have aimed at bringing a certain universality into their work. In every particular, whether it be historical, mythological, fables, more or less randomly concocted, one can increasingly perceive the universal shining through the national and personal guise. Such also is the prevailing state in practical life, [this universality] intertwining itself through all earthly crudeness, savagery, cruelty, duplicity, self-interest and dissembling, and spreading its balm" (ibid.).

universal tolerance and peaceableness in an age when European colonialism in North and South America, in Africa and Asia, had never been bloodier? Goethe had in fact been very affected by the Napoleonic era, by the conclusion of the bloody European wars, by the cooling of "national hatreds" and the unification of the "German people in a new and peaceful confederation," as his friend Kanzler Müller wrote in 1832 in the final edition of *Über Kunst und Altertum*.[22] Müller and Goethe believed in the "progress of cosmopolitan education," in its "effect on the smaller and wider circles of receptive contemporaries, even in the most farflung corners of the world."[23]

Goethe's gaze here was certainly trained on what was happening in Europe at the time – in this sense he was Eurocentric;[24] yet this was not perpetrated in any systematic fashion because his reading in foreign languages was naturally limited. If the "good and best from all nations" were able to cooperate, then he was convinced that Europe could serve as a vector for enlightenment and tolerance "to the farthest corners of the world." He alertly registered the fact that communication had been made much easier, that transport was

---

[22] "As in agriculture, trade and shipping, so too in art and science did a cheerfully active life commence to stir and ramify." See Kanzler Müller in his final word on *Über Kunst und Altertum, Goethe: Sämtliche Werke*, vol. XXII, pp. 616 ff.

[23] *Goethe: Sämtliche Werke*, p. 623, note.

[24] See, among others, Doris Bachmann-Medick, *Cultural Misunderstanding in Translation: Multicultural Coexistence and Multicultural Conceptions of World Literature*, Erfurt Electronic Studies in English 7/1996; and for another view, see Bohnenkamp "Rezeption," p. 203.

becoming more rapid, and that there was "expanding activity in the spheres of labor and trade." Thus does "the mind also eventually desire to be swept up in the more or less free exchange of ideas."[25]

Some twenty years later, in 1848, Karl Marx's *Communist Manifesto* would return to this idea of new conditions of transport, communication, and production. Just as the older national and corporative means of production would be replaced by "widespread intercourse and an interdependence of nations," so too would intellectual production undergo a de-nationalization. "The intellectual products of individual nations are becoming property held in common. National one-sidedness and parochialness is becoming increasingly impossible, and out of the many national and local types of literature a *Weltliteratur* is taking shape."[26] Marx saw the utopian implications of the *Weltliteratur* concept and foretold a time when – analogous to production for the world market – a literature would emerge that transcended narrow national bounds; that is, a post-national world literature that would replace "the old needs that were satisfied by national products."

Frequently overlooked are the considerable differences between Goethe's and Marx's notion of *Weltliteratur*. In contrast to Marx, Goethe felt that in the future there

---

[25] See also Goethe's statement: "In an era where the world is criss-crossed by express deliveries of all kinds from all parts of the globe, the thinking literary man finds all kinds of reasons to abandon trifles and have a look around in the big wide world of commerce" *Goethe: Sämtliche Werke*, vol. XXII, p. 280.

[26] Karl Marx, *Manifest der kommunistischen Partei*, ed. Theo Stammen (Munich 1969), p. 52.

would be a variety of nations distinguishing themselves from one another through language, culture and heritage. In fact, these differences were a prerequisite for the emergence of any *Weltliteratur*: "The characteristics of a nation are like its language and currency – they facilitate human intercourse; in fact, they make it perfectly possible."[27] Also to be seen in this light is Goethe's statement to Eckermann that, as already quoted, "National literature has not much relevance today, the epoch of world literature is dawning." This statement was colored by his opposition to the nationally minded Romantics and only involves a single aspect of his attitude toward *Weltliteratur*. He could not imagine *Weltliteratur* without the substratum of diverse national literary cultures. As he declared in June of 1827, poetry was "cosmopolitan and interesting to the degree that it was national."[28] For him *Weltliteratur* did not mean a global literature free of the dross of its cultural heritage, but rather a literature in which all those linguistic, cultural, and personal particularities of the author were mirrored in foreign perspectives – and mirrored in myriad ways. According to Goethe, it was only through the medium of "nationality and personality" that those human universals emerged which served to link up the world's separate literary traditions.[29]

This thesis of an intertwining of *Weltliteratur* and national literature has served to annoy scholars of culture

[27] *Goethe: Sämtliche Werke*, vol. XXII, p. 434.
[28] A report of Graf Kaspar von Sternberg from 15 June 1827, as cited in Bohnenkamp "Rezeption," p. 205.
[29] *Goethe: Sämtliche Werke*, vol. XXII, p. 433.

and literature, who hold the very idea and purpose of national literature to be hopelessly antiquated and would prefer to roundly junk Goethe's notion of *Weltliteratur*. In the final part of this essay I should like to argue that in this enduring era of nation-states Goethe's thesis is not only highly relevant but has real interpretive power – while conceding that there also exist increasingly transnational tendencies encompassing new actors and fields of action that can no longer be harmonized with Goethe's dual notion of national and world literature. Thus, Goethe is the signpost indicating the way beyond his own conceptual legacy.

IV

The paradox of Goethe's conception of *Weltliteratur* is that it was formulated at a moment in history when the discipline of philology was emerging across Europe within the framework of the respective European national cultures. Along with some few loyal followers such as Heinrich Heine and Karl Marx, Goethe also had his opponents, such as the French-hating Wolfgang Menzel, who rebelled against the attempt to "destroy the venerable national literature and replace it with world literature."[30] In the end, Menzel's objection was sustained. In the nineteenth century the concept of *Weltliteratur* faded before the advance of literary scholarship in Germany and other nations, for instance Gottfried Gervinus' *Geschichte der poetischen Nationalliteratur* (*History of Poetic*

---

[30] Wolfgang Menzel, *Die deutsche Literatur*, vol. IV (Stuttgart, 1836), p. 344, as cited in Birus, *Weltliteratur und Littérature comparée*, p. 9.

National Literature, 5 vols., 1835–1842) or William Scherer's *Geschichte der deutschen Literatur* (*History of German Literature*, 1883). In a fragmented country like Germany, literature served as a compensation for the felt trauma of the prevailing political situation. The cultural zenith attained by Germany in the so-called Goethe era was to now have a political sequel in a German nation-state – this at least was the view propagated by Gervinus in his five-volume work.[31] The German philologists were not alone in the nationalist perspective they brought to literature, for similar phenomena could be observed in neighboring countries. Both in and outside of Germany, literature had become an agent of national self-confidence, with its own historical images, founding myths, and the glorification of what Christian Meier has termed a national *Könnenbewusstsein*, or can-do mentality – mostly at the expense of their immediate neighbors.

Goethe's conception of a developing *Weltliteratur* was an accurate diagnosis in the sense of a co-emergence of global literary communication and national literature. It was indeed the changed relationship between peoples and cultures – by dint of translations and reciprocal recognition, through increased intercourse and exchange – that created the initial "matrix for constituting a hitherto unsuspected multiplicity of national literary cultures."[32] Not only were

[31] See Hans Robert Jauss, "Literaturgeschichte als Provokation der Literaturwissenschaft," in *Literaturgeschichte als Provokation* (Frankfurt 1970), pp. 144–207, particularly 148 ff.
[32] Birus, *Weltliteratur und Littérature comparée*, p. 13.

existing national literary cultures discovered and integrated into world literature through translations, criticism, and literary histories, but the new cross-border manufacturing conditions of literature themselves first created the need for a country's own national literary tradition. After Goethe's death, national literary cultures in both Europe and the world multiplied, from the Balkans to Cuba to Vietnam. Perhaps the most eloquent example of such is the development of Czech, Slovenian, Bulgarian, and Romanian literature in the nineteenth century. Writers and philologists from these countries developed their own literary languages in a conscious rejection of long-dominant Western European literature and so as to compete with the literary offerings of their immediate neighbors. In his book *Imagined Communities: Reflections on the Origin and Spread of Nationalism* (1983), Benedict Anderson showed parallel developments in Scandinavia, Latin America, and Asia. The present-day examples of Palestinian, Kurdish, Tartar, and Bosnian literature as well as that of various African countries show that the formation of national literary cultures is by no means a completed process – i.e. cultures with their own poetic language that give expression to a lived experience and are replete with historical images and myths.

V

It is the task of transnational literary studies to examine the various forms of this co-emergence of global literary communication and national literature, placing particular emphasis on the transnational spheres of action that loom ever larger in our present day. Any such transnational viewpoint would not be a mere supplement to the pre-existing and predominantly national literary cultural bequests, but something else. It would change one's perspective on what was hitherto familiar territory. It would, for instance, apprehend German literature as a component part of European literature while also seeing emulation, interaction, rivalry, productive reception, and one-upsmanship vis-à-vis the literature of neighboring countries as constitutive to the entire process – and of course not overlooking the multilingual aspects. The literary reception of German literature in France and England and vice versa since the eighteenth century has been relatively well researched. Now the job is to study how these various spheres of interaction intertwine "polylogically" – as termed by the main representative of *Histoires croisées* in France, Michael Werner.

The focus of any transnational history of literature would not be solely on those epochs where literature served as a vehicle for awakening national consciousness. Also included would be an examination of the preliminary stages and lengthy preparation of the actual constituting of a national literature; that is, not only the emergence and individuation of the various European literary cultures from Latin-dominated scholarly culture but going back even further to the twelfth and thirteenth centuries and the first blossoming of a literature still under the impress of medieval religiosity and a hierarchical society. One must of course be careful not to project later national developments on a certain literature's beginnings.[33]

---

[33] See the historian Kiran Klaus Patel, *Perspektiven einer transnationalen Geschichte: Antrittsvorlesung an der Humboldt-Universität Berlin 2004*, published on the internet.

In such a way could a transnational history of literature help to change our view of the past while at the same time reacting to a present which itself is constantly changing, and responding to phenomena that can no longer be compassed by the terms national literature and world literature. I should like now to conclude with three theses addressing: 1) the scope afforded by cultural mobility in transnational relationship networks, 2) the political sphere, language, and tradition as coordinates of cultural mobility, and 3) the specific task of literary scholarship.

1. Today the world's cultures are being standardized through technology, economics, trade, and political networks. Simultaneously – and surprisingly – we are experiencing a peculiar resistance on the part of nation-states, and in many regions of the world we are even witnessing the resurgence of policies of national self-interest, that is, a re-nationalization. Jürgen Habermas' notion of a continuing "drive toward de-nationalization" that "paves the way economically toward a world society" will for the time being remain a utopia.[34]

What kind of repercussions does this have for the concept of cultural mobility as it is currently being discussed by scholars of cultural studies? Many of them presuppose a teleological development leading to a "changeover

---

[34] See Jürgen Habermas, *Die postnationale Konstellation* (Frankfurt 1998). Nation-states have enjoyed an "astonishing success in the late-modern period of world history" and are still enjoying amazing success in terms of their ability to mobilize popular support. See Patel, *Perspektiven*, pp. 27 ff.

from settledness to movement, from situatedness to a lack thereof, and from a spatial specificity to one of diffuseness."[35] Such a teleology would seem to be the fulfillment of the international tourist's dream, who, with airplane ticket in hand, can at any time meet up with other people in (almost) any part of the world; but it has little relevance for most of the globe's inhabitants, particularly those in the southern hemisphere, who are subject to poverty as well as state regulation and repression.

One cannot say with certainty what sort of cultural developments will be taking place in the coming decades – an increasing homogenization of cultures, as Erich Auerbach and Claude Lévi-Strauss predicted (albeit informed by differing agendas), or increasing differentiation accompanied by unavoidable tension between cultures? We will probably be able to observe both of these conflicting processes, but linked through a growing internal cultural fragmentation – which was far beyond Goethe's purview. As a consequence of migrations and changed lifestyles, strong centrifugal forces below the level of national self-understanding have emerged through religious, ethnic, and other group-identifications; simply call to mind how transregionally acting middle-class groups, strongly regionalized lower-class groups and so-defined religious and ethnic fringe groups live side-by-side in "global cities." Many observers believe that it is precisely the weakening of the nation-state

---

[35] Rüdiger Kunow and Marc Priewe, "Mobilisierte Kulturen: zur Veränderung von Kulturen im Kontext von Internationalisierung und Migration," manuscript (Potsdam, 2004).

through such processes – at the supranational, regional, and local levels – that has led to policies of re-nationalization in many states, even within the European Union.

In any event, the world in which we live is not becoming more simplified; it is not evolving toward a trans-national culture, as surmised by lovers of mobility and motoricity. Rather, we are witness to the painful and frequently tragic tension that exists between de-nationalization and re-nationalization, between de-territorialization and re-territorialization, between the creation and lifting of borders that separate cultures, and we can only hope that their cultural tensions might be contained through a growing awareness that the binding nature of constitutions and international agreements creates scope for political action.

2. When taken together with the attendant existential uncertainty, it would seem that it is precisely the even more potent blend of cultures and migration, of the intertwining of economics and global information technology that creates the need for the clear definition of social groups and for the invocation of political and religious identities that are apparently still intact. This is the only explanation for why people are increasingly clinging to tradition, a phenomenon everywhere to be observed. These traditions are certainly anything but autochthonous and continuous growths – they are often peculiar mixtures of the native and foreign – but one can judiciously assess the scope of cultural mobility only by keeping its counterweights in view – namely the reception of tradition and the nurturing of specific languages as well as the given political context. The idea of cultural mobility is unfortunately often trivialized by overlooking these three

decisive factors: the process of the reinterpretation of tradition, the defining role of language along with its underlying linguistic politics and historical semantics, and the political and social power relations of a given time. I call these "coordinates" of cultural mobility. It would require a whole other article in order to properly elucidate these coordinates. We are not speaking here of fixed and undeviating quantities, but unmistakable is their determining function for all forms of cultural movement. And said coordinates also allow cultural studies to link up once more with approaches from social and political history, disciplines from which it has distanced itself in the last few years, and to its own detriment.

We are of course experiencing how the culture of international media is mixing traditions and languages and virtualizing regions at breakneck speed, as if it could create to its heart's content from an inexhaustible reservoir of cultural building blocks. But one should not overestimate the importance of the media for people's self-understanding, for this is usually nourished by deep-seated sources of meaning and symbolism with which actions and experiences are interpreted.

3. Literary scholars are specialists when it comes to the processes involved in the reinterpretation of traditional linguistic symbols and realms of meaning, whether they be of a literary, religious, national, or ethnic nature. That was what Walter Benjamin, Aby Warburg, Eric Auerbach (all coming from different positions) and others have bequeathed to us as the task of literary and cultural studies, namely to investigate how traditions are reconfigured and remodelled in times of crisis. Every present discovers its own past(s), finding there driving

forces that they use to project themselves into the future. Literature in particular finds its strength in the productive reception of traditions and languages. Literature can be understood as a special system of cultural interpretation, using symbolic forms and transnational realms of meaning to explain people's experiences and actions, thus – in contrast to philosophy and religion, for instance – mobilizing emotion and imagination (an assertion which must here remain at the abstract level). By no means do the symbols of literary interpretive systems come solely from one's own culture; as a rule, they cross borders and circulate internationally. But cultural mobility first attains to a specific historical meaning when one is able to mentally conjoin the topography of the political sphere with the historical semantics of a language and the processes of tradition. That is what we mean when we say that scholars of literature as well as culture are specially trained to contextualize their subjects, placing them within their historical and social milieux to show their functions and meanings. Erich Auerbach called this "historical perspectivism" and viewed it as one of the essential achievements of the humanities in the nineteenth century. Cultural mobility within the context of language, the political sphere, and tradition – that should be the methodological agenda of any transnational literary scholarship.

VI

In December 2004 the Potsdam scholar of Romance languages Ottmar Ette and the Berlin scholar of Arabic studies Friederike Pannewick staged a conference on Arabic-Latin

American literature – "Arabamericas: Literature without a Fixed Abode."[36] Giving the conference an English title was a matter of course, even for a scholar of Romance languages. How else but in English could Arabs, Latin Americans, and Europeans communicate with one another today? A feature of *Weltliteratur* is that only a few languages are on offer as vehicles for international understanding – and German, unfortunately, is being decreasingly found among the chosen few (counter to Goethe's expectations). The conference's subject was the relation between Latin America and Arabic literature, especially from the perspective of Arab immigrants to Latin America and Arabs of the second or third generation who now live between cultures. Their literature would seem to be an example of an odd placelessness and the dissociation between nativity and nationality that characterizes the lives of many writers in today's world. Their literature is situated beyond national and world literature – it is literally "literature without a fixed abode" (Ottmar Ette). But one would indeed be misjudging this placelessness if one failed to recognize how these authors create their own respective places through intertextuality and their relation to tradition. This kind of productive reception of Arabic, Persian, and Turkish literature, or of Spanish, Portugese, and Anglo-American, is what gives any such reception its specific physiognomy. And literary scholars who are trained historically and are familiar with the varying traditions have more to say than simply affirming that here yet again is to be found an example of cultural hybridization and transfer.

[36] Friederike Pannewick and Ottmar Ette (eds.), *Arabamericas – Literary Entanglements of the American Hemisphere and the Arab World* (Berlin, 2007).

The conference would serve as an example of transnational or, more precisely, trans*regional* literary studies, cutting across the philological subdisciplines while still retaining the particular tools of the philologist's trade.

Literary scholars should put their ear to this rail network of the new cultural mobility, even if – as is naturally to be expected – they have their expertise in a certain specific area of literature. They will only be able to make proper use of the changes in this area if they develop a feel for the worldwide literary nexus. Erich Auerbach, the scholar of Romance literature who lived in exile first in Istanbul and then in America, was a founding father of a modern philology of *Weltliteratur*. "In any event … our philological homeland is no longer the Nation but the Earth. Certainly the most precious and indispensable bequest of philology is still the language and culture of a nation; but it first becomes effective upon your separation from it, in your overcoming of it."[37]

(Translated from the original German by Kevin McAleer.)

---

[37] Erich Auerbach, *Philologie der Weltliteratur*, in *Gesammelte Aufsätze zur Romanischen Philologie*, (Bern and Munich, 1967), p. 310. Which is to say: although our perspective is limited by language, culture, and our specific origins, these individual preconditions of our cultural education only gain their complete value when one is prepared to separate oneself from them and indeed surmount them. Auerbach cited a phrase of that medieval personage Hugo von St. Victor: "Pampered is he for whom the fatherland is still sweet; strong, on the other hand, for he who has the entire Earth as his fatherland; and complete and perfect for he who is everywhere in the world homeless" (ibid., p. 310).

5

Cultural mobility between Boston and Berlin: how Germans have read and reread narratives of American slavery

HEIKE PAUL

I

On June 5, 2008 the German left-leaning daily *Die Tageszeitung* published in Berlin ran a cover story with an image of the White House and the headline "Uncle Barack's Cabin" written across it (figure 3). The caption added: "The White House in Washington: Will Barack Obama be the first black president to move in there?" The headline with its allusion to "Uncle Tom," the protagonist of Harriet Beecher Stowe's mid-nineteenth-century sentimental reform novel, caused some controversy, nationally as well as internationally. Many journalists and political commentators considered the reference to the stereotype and racial slur of "Uncle Tom" to be entirely in bad taste, denigrating the presidential candidate of the Democratic Party and, by extension, all African Americans. *Die Tageszeitung* editor Rüdiger Metzger, however, defended the headline as a satirical comment: "*Uncle Toms Cabin* is a book that all Germans know and which they associate with issues of racism. The headline is supposed to make people think about these stereotypes … I'm sure 99 percent of our readers would understand it correctly. As

Onkel Baracks Hütte

3 Front page of the German daily *Die Tageszeitung.*

for the rest, well, tough luck. You can't please everybody."
Local Afro-Germans and civil rights activists in Berlin took
the headline as an opportunity to attack the "acute racism" in
German left-wing circles, and the discussion of the headline
spilled over from Berlin into the pages of the *Washington Post*
as well as other forums and was hotly debated in internet
blogs. American correspondents were astonished by this
German piece of journalism. The Hamburg-based German
weekly *Der Spiegel* offered its English-language audience an
online report on the controversy, ending somewhat apolo-
getically: "Although *Uncle Toms Cabin* is well known in
Germany, ordinary Germans are not always aware of the
controversy surrounding the book."[1]

---

[1] All English-language quotations are taken from this article: David Gordon
Smith, "German Newspaper Slammed for Racist Cover," www.spiegel.de/
international/germany/0,1518,557861,00.html, viewed last on June 9, 2009.

The headline of the Berlin newspaper discloses in exemplary fashion the cultural mobility of American narratives about slavery and their "travels" to Germany. It shows the strange way in which the "peculiar institution" and its literary and popular signifiers are alluded to in German everyday culture and the role Harriet Beecher Stowe's novel *Uncle Tom's Cabin* has played and still plays in this context. Taking American representations and narratives of slavery as my point of departure for studying transatlantic processes of cultural transfer in a broader historical context, I will in what follows discuss, first, the cultural mobility of *Uncle Tom's Cabin*, its wide dissemination, and its diverse reception in Germany as well as the mobility of quite a few of its German readers as nineteenth-century immigrants to America; second, the cultural mobility and increasing commodification of the "Uncle Tom" figure as a nineteenth- and twentieth-century symbol – a symbol not so much of the indictment of the cruelty of slavery but of a nostalgic view of slavery as an idyllic pastoral, which generates quite an "immobile" black stereotype of the happy and docile slave; and third, other white- and black-authored figurations of slavery and the slave (among them Richard Hildreth's *The White Slave*), which I will place next to "Uncle Tom" to analyze the way in which they have or have not been appropriated for a cultural and political critique. Over all, these processes of reception, commodification, and appropriation constitute a valuable source for studying transatlantic cultural mobility. The images, texts, and ideas I will look at in this context bear conflicting implications; they cannot simply be added up in a coherent way as they show the contingency of cultural mobility as well as the polysemic quality of popular texts. They do share, however, the way in which they use the representation of American slavery as a detour to express local concerns while often downplaying the actual process of transfer. Thus, it is crucial to investigate the ideological underpinnings of such transfers and the contexts in which they occur. The study of cultural mobility may reinforce anti-foundational narratives about culture, cultural formations, and cultural change; it may also, however, uncover critical moments in which the "import" and appropriation of culturally mobile images, texts, and ideas can veil precarious investments closer to home.

II

Harriet Beecher Stowe's novel *Uncle Tom's Cabin* qualifies as an early global novel, as a piece of *Weltliteratur*, in Goethe's sense of the term, more than any other nineteenth-century American text, and has done a lot of cultural work in a transatlantic context, to use Jane Tompkins' concept (Tompkins 1985). The novel about the slave Tom, who is sold from his benevolent owner in Kentucky to a cruel slave master "down the river" at whose hands he ultimately dies, has been part of diverse transatlantic negotiations and has left its imprint on social, cultural and political discourses. Legend has it that when Abraham Lincoln met Harriet Beecher Stowe, he called her the "little woman" who had caused the "great war" (cf. Gossett 1985: 314; Hedrick 1994:

viii; Sundquist 1986: 10).[2] Stowe's novel clearly was not only successful but momentous.[3] In the United States, it fueled the protest against slavery and influenced public opinion on a large scale. But the novel left its mark not only in the United States: *Uncle Tom's Cabin* was translated into twenty-six languages immediately after its publication (and into more than forty to date), and was sold and read millions of times. The "Tommania" or "Tommitudes" – as the Uncle Tom craze was referred to in England (Birdoff 1947: 144; anon. in Ammons 1980: 35) – was described by contemporaries as an epidemic which had large parts of Europe in its grip. Harriet Beecher Stowe traveled abroad and was enthusiastically received by crowds of admirers wherever she went (Birdoff 1947: 149). Today, the novel still is regarded by many critics as the "most influential book ever written by an American" (Tompkins 1985: 122) – especially outside the USA: in England, France, Italy, Spain, Russia, and in Germany.[4]

---

[2] As Gossett has it, "[t]here is no direct account of it [a meeting between Lincoln and Stowe, H. P.]" (Gossett 1985: 314), yet it may have taken place in November 1862, when Stowe visited Washington. Nevertheless, "Lincoln probably never read *Uncle Tom's Cabin*" (Gossett 1985: 183).

[3] Cf. Lawrence Buell's discussion of *Uncle Tom's Cabin* as "the great American novel" (Buell 2004: 190–203).

[4] As Leslie Fiedler puts it succinctly: "For better or worse, it was Mrs. Stowe who invented American blacks for the imagination of the whole world" (Fiedler 1979: 26). Yet the repercussions of the text about America's "peculiar institution" in a German context have so far received little scholarly attention; previous transatlantic studies on this topic have focused mainly on England, as does the most recent transnational study *Transatlantic Stowe* (Kohn et al. 2006).

Uncle Tom's Cabin and its circulation in diverse non-American contexts have attracted new attention with the turn to transnationalism in the field of American Studies.[5] Current engagement with the text is not limited to the documentation and philological indexing of the numerous editions and translations in which the book has been published all over the world; rather the novel's effects and its function in different cultural and national contexts are being analyzed. Crucial questions are: why is the book so attractive everywhere and why does it reach such an enormous circulation? What kinds of meanings do Danes, the British, the French, the Spanish, Haitians, Italians, Swedes, Germans, and Russians construct when reading *Uncle Tom's Cabin*? And what kind of cultural transfer occurs?[6]

"[I]t is a live book," writes a contemporary reviewer, "and it talks to its readers as if it were alive. It first awakens their attention, arrests their thoughts, touches their sympathies,

[5] The work of the so-called New Americanists has been important here. Cf. Shelley Fisher-Fishkin's Presidential Address to the American Studies Association, "Crossroads of Cultures: The Transnational Turn in American Studies," in 2004 (Fisher-Fishkin 2005). For an overview of *Uncle Tom's Cabin* scholarship since the 1970s that has re-evaluated the novel in the context of American literary history, see Warren (2004).

[6] Recent studies that respond to these questions are Surwillo (2005) for a Spanish context, Fisch (2004) for a British context, and Brickhouse (2004) for the reception in Haiti. Older studies discuss the reception in France (Lucas 1930), Italy (Woodress 1967) and Russia (Hecht 1948). For the German context, Edith MacLean as early as 1910 took the trouble to document the numerous editions and translations of Stowe's novel in the German states (MacLean 1910); MacLean's text is a valuable (yet not faultless) study on whose meticulous philological research I rely repeatedly in this essay.

rouses their curiosity, and creates such an interest in the story it is telling, that they cannot let it drop until the whole story is told … If it were the story of a Russian Serf, an evicted Milesian, a Manchester weaver, or an Italian State prisoner, the result would be the same" (Anon. in Ammons 1980: 39).

This review illustrates the tendency to read *Uncle Tom's Cabin* as a universal tale of oppression and deliverance already at the time of its publication. Audiences abroad do not perceive it merely as an exotic narrative from a faraway world; rather Stowe's "megaseller" made American slavery tangible as an inhumane system while abstracting from its particularity – the oppression of African Americans and the exploitation of black bodies (cf. Fisher 1983: 283; Fluck 1991: 13 ff.; Reichardt 2001: 100 ff., 105 ff.). Thus, the author manages to create a popular narrative with seemingly universal appeal that speaks to the longings and needs of many[7] – and

---

[7] These longings also seemed to have included the longing for entertainment. Next to the polical agenda, the entertainment qualities of the book with its sentimental and sensationalist strategies have been discussed by many scholars. Sundquist, for instance, describes "the fantasy Stowe's audience eagerly adopted – that slavery was the culture's extreme revelation of lust" (Sundquist 1985: 18). Even Sigmund Freud, many years after the publication of the book, when it had already turned into a book for young readers on the German-language market, comments on the *Angstlust* it produced in a certain kind of young audience, inspiring masochistic fantasies (Freud 1919: 232). Fiedler refers to the novel as a "masochistic masterpiece" with a "pornographic imagination." Stowe, on her part, attributes the enormous success of the book not to her own strategies of representation inviting voyeurism but to a "higher" authority/authorship: she later called it "written by God" (Fielder, 1979: 58; cf. Sundquist 1986: 6).

also makes them act politically. Many incidents and events are attributed to the book's impact: a strike of English maids is stirred by the novel in London; it supposedly gives an impulse to the abolition of Russian serfdom; it fuels discussions of women's liberation and suffrage in Germany; and it mobilizes resistance against a strict Catholic policy in Italy which tries to ban the book that is advertised under the slogan "the new bible from America."[8] American critic Leslie Fiedler points out that Stowe is the child of a revolutionary age, an age which not only produced a novel such as *Uncle Tom's Cabin* but also *The Communist Manifesto* (Fiedler 1979: 37). The European societies at that time are undergoing profound social, economic, and political changes – Wolfram Siemann, for instance, refers to Germany as a "Gesellschaft im Aufbruch" ("society on the move," Siemann 1990) – and Stowe provides them with a narrative whose revolutionary potential is hidden behind a rhetoric of tears and of sentiment (Sundquist 1985: 18).[9]

The success of Stowe's novel is most dramatic in England. When by the end of 1852 the American sales figure stands at 150,000 copies, the English already exceeds a million – and another half million is sold in the colonies (Birdoff

---

[8] Under the title "Onkel Tom in Neapel" ("Uncle Tom in Naples"), the German *Magazin für die Literatur des Auslandes* reports in May 1853 about censored Uncle Tom plays on the Italian stage which for religious and political reasons avoid explicit references to the Bible and instead have the protagonist refer to it simply as "the book."

[9] Tompkins stresses Stowe's radicalism beneath the tears – namely her "world-shaking" vision to completely reorganize society in terms of race and gender relations (Tompkins 1985: 146).

1947: 151; Fisch 2004: 96).[10] In the German states, the novel is immensely popular as well:

> Uncle Tom's Cabin, the book that elicited so many tears and resolutions, has found an enormous circulation in Germany as well. It is dished up to the readers of seven monthlies in monthly portions, and in addition, twenty to thirty translations with or without illustrations have already been published, several of which already in second editions. We would like the book to yield fruit in the interest of humanitarianism. Slaves do not only exist in America; there are more than enough in Germany, only we call them by other names. A slave in America is often treated more humanely and benignly than a poor maid is treated in Germany. (*Die Gartenlaube* 3 [1853]: 32)[11]

[10] Audrey Fisch (2004) has recently investigated "Uncle Tom and Harriet Beecher Stowe in England" and linked the book's success to a number of aspects: dramatic changes in the literary market with regard to production as well as consumption; the way in which stories about (and against slavery) presented their Victorian audiences with thrilling tales (full of violence and illicit sexuality catering to voyeurism but with an intact moral agenda); and the fact that anti-slavery sentiment was becoming increasingly central to British national identity – often in ironic ways: as in those Uncle Tom plays which – modifying Stowe – have the slave at the end escape from the American South to British India, accompanied by loud cheers from the London audience (Birdoff 1947: 154).

[11] "*Onkel Tom's Hütte*, das Buch, das so unendlich viele Thränen und gute Vorsätze hervorgelockt, hat auch in Deutschland eine enorme Verbreitung gefunden. Den Lesern von 7 Monatsschriften wird es in monatlichen Portionen aufgetischt, außerdem sind bereits zwanzig bis dreißig Uebersetzungen mit und ohne Illustrationen erschienen, woran

This review from the gazette *Die Gartenlaube*, a newly launched magazine for the *Bildungsbürger* published in Leipzig, shows that the discussion of Stowe's book leads directly to debates on social inequality in Germany. The sociocritical impetus of the novel's reception even creates a new literary trend in Germany: stories about slavery become fashionable, and in the absence of African Americans Stowe's critique is transferred to other figures (e.g. the German maid) and contexts (e.g. social injustice in the German states). Numerous popular texts try to emulate the book from America and adapt its theme to German conditions. Thus, Harriet Beecher Stowe succeeds James Fenimore Cooper in popularity: only a few decades earlier Johann Wolfgang von Goethe had penned the much-quoted statement that the German writer should "emulate Cooper" and explore the potential of the new world for the production of literature (Goethe 1950 [1827]: 114). Prior to the publication of *Uncle Tom's Cabin*, James Fenimore Cooper had been the most influential and most imitated American author in Germany: his *Leatherstocking Tales* were exceedingly popular and also shaped the German image of America decisively (Rossbacher 1972; Wallace 1986; Wagnleitner 1991: 15). In 1852, German writers start to imitate Harriet Beecher Stowe and thus respond to a demand for popular slave tales that is enormous. In 1910, Edith MacLean compiles

bereits mehrere in neuen Auflagen gedruckt wurden … Wir wollen wünschen, daß das Buch im Interesse der Humanität Früchte trägt. Nicht nur in Amerika giebt es Sclaven, auch in Deutschland hat es deren genug, nur daß sie bei uns unter andern Namen existiren. Ein Sclave in Amerika wird oft menschlicher und freundlicher behandelt, als in Deutschland ein armes Dienstmädchen." All translations from German are mine unless otherwise indicated.

a list of German "re-writings" and counts twenty-three novels and dramas among them, for instance, Friedrich Wilhelm Hackländer's two-volume novel titled *Europäisches Sklavenleben* (*European Slave Life*), published in Stuttgart in 1854, in which the author criticizes feudal social structure by depicting the poverty, bleakness and despair in the lives of those belonging to the lower social classes.

In the German states America is an important topic as German emigration to the United States reaches a historical high in the middle of the nineteenth century. In 1853 alone, a quarter of a million Germans emigrate to the United States – just as Stowe's book is coming across the Atlantic the other way – and many migrants take in *Uncle Tom's Cabin* and take it along – in their luggage as well as in their imagination. The number of German texts about the new world is growing rapidly in these years, be it travel writings, novels, journals, promotional manuals, or immigration guides, and slavery as a new world "curiosity" figures prominently in these texts.[12] Not surprisingly Stowe's novel is frequently referred to as a source of information and as an influence on the traveler's or immigrant's perception of the institution. Take, for instance, the travel account by Moritz Scherzer and Carl Wagner, two travelers who come to the United States in 1853, touring the North and the South. Upon their stay in New Orleans on a sultry day, they attend a slave auction and are shocked by the cruelty of the transactions. Their following night's sleep is uneasy: "The sleep we then tried to abandon ourselves to was not very refreshing;

---

[12] Many of these books have an entire chapter dedicated to the topic of slavery (cf. Busch 1854; Egenter 1857; Fröbel 1857; Griesinger 1858, 1862).

after a few hours ... our heads buzzed with all those horrible scenes from *Uncle Tom's Cabin* ... thus we were extremely glad to be delivered from these dreary apparitions by a bright morning" (Scherzer/Wagner 1857: III 357 ff. [my translation]).[13]

That Stowe's vivid descriptions appear in Scherzer's and Wagner's nightmares shows how pervasive the imagery of the novel was in the German cultural imaginary. The Germans' perceptions and experiences of America were influenced and, it seems, partially even (pre)determined by scenes from the novel, and, like Scherzer and Wagner, a whole generation of German travelers and immigrants measured their impressions of America with and against the book – exactly as they had done with Cooper's *Leatherstocking Tales* prior to 1852, with the result that every German traveler was disappointed when he did not encounter a Native American immediately upon arrival.[14] Yet, the transatlantic re-transport of Stowe's fictional and imaginary world through the eyes of the German beholders also leads to a narrowing of perspective and to misperceptions as "African American" and "slave" seem increasingly to be conflated. German visitors and immigrants equate one with the other and thus, after 1852, are hardly able to imagine African Americans differently from "Uncle Tom," or in other

---

[13] "Der Schlaf, dem wir uns jetzt hinzugeben versuchten, war ein nur wenig stärkender; nachdem uns ein paar Stunden lang alle Schaudermomente aus *Uncle Tom's Cabin* durch den Kopf schwirrten ... wir waren daher herzlich froh, als uns der heitere Morgen von diesen düsteren Erscheinungen erlöste."

[14] Gottfried Duden, for instance, complains that he has arrived in Baltimore and traveled to the "frontier" in Missouri without ever encountering one Native American – contrary to what he expected (Duden 1834 [1829]: 112).

words, other than as slaves. In Stowe's book, Tom dies, and while the light-skinned slave Eliza and her family, the protagonists of Stowe's second plot in the novel, escape slavery and are free in the end, Stowe has them leave America and "return" to Africa as missionaries. In the narrative logic of Stowe's vision there is little room for free blacks in the new world, i.e. for blacks as free Americans, even as it delivers a sharp critique of slavery as an institution. Earlier nineteenth-century German texts about America, mostly travel writing, had portrayed the free African American in the North as a somewhat surprising sight and as a fascinating representative of the new world (Duden 1834 [1829]: 18; Gerstäcker 1849: 45; cf. Paul 2005: 60–70). Most authors stressed that the free blacks in New York or Boston did not meet their expectation of "Africanness" at all but rather appeared to be a "modern" urban presence, and thus they were distinguished quite drastically from African American slaves in the Southern states. This split perspective on blackness in the new world is for the most part eradicated after 1852, and "typically American" for the German visitor now is no longer the free black but the good-humored, docile, and child-like black slave. The cultural mobility of Stowe's novel in the mid-nineteenth century thus – instead of adding complexity and flexibility to the German perception of African Americans – reduces the popular image of black people in America to a single, highly generalized and – above all – static stereotype.[15]

---

[15] For the English context, Douglas A. Lorimer comes to a similar conclusion, namely the paradox that Stowe's novel "aroused English sympathies" for the African American slaves while reinforcing

III

Stowe's narrative strategy of sketching the seemingly "ideal" world of Tom and his family at the beginning of her novel – all of them are well-fed and properly cared-for slaves living in their cozy cabin – before showing the dramatic turn of Tom's fate may have abetted a turn in the German reception of the text that in the last decades of the nineteenth century increasingly leads to a disregard for its actual critique. Given the authoritarian structure of German society in the *Kaiserreich*, in times of social and economic instability many German readers of the novel come to appreciate slavery as a stable, paternalistic social order with duties of care on the part of the slaveholder, an order that seems to contrast with the harsh conditions of early capitalism, industrialization, and urbanization they perceive all around themselves – nothing is wrong, it is argued, with "Uncle Tom" until his good-natured and caring owner runs into debt. It is not slavery itself, so the argument runs, which is the problem, but the profit-oriented trading and mistreatment of slaves at the hands of immoral and brutal owners that give slavery a bad name.[16]

This notion of American slavery as a peaceful rural idyll can easily be traced in German popular culture. It is

stereotypes of difference between black and white "attributed to the influence both of slavery and of race" (Lorimer 1978: 85).

[16] This juxtaposition of a peaceful agrarian plantation system with a cruel industrial society is a dominant current in American pro-slavery thought (cf. Fitzhugh's *Sociology for the South* [1854] and *Cannibals All!* [1857] as well as Wenzel [1982]). Somewhat delayed and less rigidly argued, this kind of argument surfaces in Germany as well.

fueled by the large-scale commodification of *Uncle Tom's Cabin* in the United States and in Europe following the novel's enormous success. The novel is enacted in manifold popular versions on stage, and the so-called "Uncle Tom"-plays are soon followed by all kinds of merchandise: in England, buns à la Uncle Tom are eaten on picnics, and *Uncle Tom's Cabin* wallpapers decorate the dining rooms; in France, the new ladies' fashion à la Eliza is worn on Sunday walks; and in Germany, sheet music allows children to perform Eva's pleasantly pious songs on the piano. This mushrooming of "Uncle Tom" artefacts runs against Stowe's original critique and strongly trivializes if not eradicates the arguments and grounds for abolitionism.

Today, on the city map of Berlin we can still find traces of this "pastoralization": somewhere between the famous boulevard Kurfürstendamm and the forest district Grunewald in the German capital there are a subway stop and a nearby street named "Onkel Toms Hütte" ("Uncle Tom's Cabin") and "Onkel Tom Straße" ("Uncle Tom Street") (figure 4). In the second half of the nineteenth century this area is a popular place for outings among the Berlin population as they discover the Sunday excursion to the forest and the nearby lakes as a pleasurable pastime. In 1884 the city gives permission to build a tavern with a large stable next to such a lake. This rustic inn with its thatched roof is soon called "Onkel Toms Hütte" ("Uncle Tom's Cabin") by the witty Berliners who at this point have been voracious readers of Harriet Beecher Stowe's novel for more than three decades in more than thirty German-language editions. "Onkel Toms Hütte" soon becomes the official name of the beer garden, as

4 Excerpt from a map of Berlin.

the postcard from 1906 shows (figure 5). The name sticks and
is in 1929 (some twenty more editions of Stowe's novel had
been published in Germany by then) extended to the newly
built subway stop and to the adjacent street. From 1929 to 1932,
this neighborhood witnesses a large-scale settlement project.
Bruno Taut, a painter and architect of the Weimar Republic,
who has to flee the Nazis in 1933, builds some apartment
buildings here which are to reflect the state of the art of
modern urban architecture, the new way of life for a population living in a highly industrialized society (Kloß 1982: 29–41).
His urban planning intends to integrate nature into urban
space and to conserve the tree population – thus Taut calls his
project "Onkel Toms Hütte." In the 1960s the original site of
the tavern and the stable is taken over by a riding club, which
takes on "Onkel Toms Hütte" as its name. This example of the

137

Gruss aus „Onkel Toms Hütte"

5 Postcard of a Berlin beer garden.

Berlin neighborhood is not a singular phenomenon: through-out the second half of the nineteenth century, Germans have restaurants in the countryside, garden plots, and beer gardens named after Stowe's novel. There is a double irony at work here: first, we witness the retrospective stylization of slavery as a kind of pre-modern way of life in the American South, in which the home of the African American slave epitomizes a pastoral idyll. Second, this anti-modern, romanticized vision of American slavery makes use of a falsely constructed *American* pastoral rather than having recourse to a powerful *German* romantic legacy closer at hand. In late nineteenth-century German popular culture it is the "imported" and thus geographically as well as historically removed image of the log cabin of a slave that embodies contentment, peacefulness, and German *Gemütlichkeit*.

6 Collector's card of Liebig's Meat Extract.

In a similar fashion, the novel's title scene is used in a series of cards added to the bouillon cubes of meat extract produced and packaged by the famous Liebig Company and sold across the country (figure 6). These collector's cards are reproduced in costly print quality to signal the exclusivity of the product and are a new marketing strategy in order to win customer loyalty. Liebig is a trendsetter in 1872 and runs these collector's series until 1940.[17] The series on *Uncle Tom's Cabin* from 1904 shows an image of the cabin as well as five other, more sensationalist scenes from the novel (including Eliza's escape, Tom's rescue of Evangeline, and Tom's death). A short text on the back of the card summarizes the scene: Uncle

---

[17] Liebig's collector's cards have recently been compiled on a CD (edited by Bernhard Jussen) as a resource for studying popular images of the nineteenth and twentieth centuries.

Tom's home is introduced as "a small log cabin in the South of the North American union." While Aunt Chloe is baking cake, a couple of "wool-headed boys" play and Uncle Tom is practicing writing instructed by his young master George. Liebig's gimmick (contemporaneous with the Berlin beer garden) adds to the kind of "soaping" of American slavery we encounter in these decades in various contexts. It effects a trivialization of slavery and an invalidation of its critique. As another manifestation of the seemingly ubiquitous commodification of "Uncle Tom," the book and the figure, in various popular formats in Germany, the Liebig collector's card signals the notion of a harmonious feudal social order and of the reciprocity of mutually beneficent master–slave relations in slavery. The combination of the innovative cards – in terms of printing technology and marketing strategy – and their anything but modern content presents us with somewhat of a riddle and a paradox that is well captured by the slogan *Vorwärts in die Vergangenheit* ("Forward into the Past"), the title of a book by Wynfrid Kriegleder on German-American text production (Kriegleder 1999). The discrepancy between a claim to modernity and the desire to return to slavery is characteristic of a whole range of race-related German cultural productions of that period.

Therefore, the cultural mobility of "Uncle Tom" and his ubiquity in Germany should not be taken as evidence for a general anti-slavery consensus. On the contrary, the trivialization of the slave cabin as an idyllic beer garden has a different cultural function at a time when Germans, newly united as a nation, are starting out to become colonizers themselves, to rule over black bodies and even to enslave them. In parallel to the downplaying of the cruelty of slavery in the reception of the novel after 1870 and particularly from the 1880s onwards, there is also a remarkable change in the way German commentators approach the African American minority in the United States – those ex-slaves they have formerly pitied. In fact, German writing about the United States in those last decades of the nineteenth century can be read as a projective justification of German colonial intentions and colonizing politics. Thus, a study of the transatlantic cultural mobility of *Uncle Tom's Cabin* has to include the dominant socio-political discourses and ongoing debates at the time – about the United States and about Germany itself. Just as the black minority in the United States, at least on paper, has achieved the status of citizens, they are profoundly and thoroughly stigmatized in the pages of German writing about America. German visitors to the United States tend to articulate their concern about black emancipation and see it as a huge national problem and potential for conflict impossible to contain. German descriptions of African Americans turn more and more derogative and crude. Blacks are now seen primarily as "troublemakers" and as a "foreign element" (Grzybowski 1896: 571). For the majority of authors the "African problem" is the crucial cultural, social, and political problem of the United States, and a solution is not at hand. Never-ending social unrest, violence, and even wars are prophesied. Unanimously, the authors diagnose the impossibility of assimilating African Americans into the American nation. As late as 1911, Hans von Barnekow suggests the deportation of all American blacks to Africa as the only viable solution. Other authors engage in wishful thinking and foresee the "vanishing," i.e. extinction, of the African Americans in the following generations.[18] German observers generally condone the violence against blacks that they witness. After initial reservations, even the brutality of the Ku Klux Klan is seen as a necessary measure: almost every German travel account about America in those decades contains a chapter on lynching which trivializes the cruelties of the Klan actions and declares them to be means of self-defense. Of about 65 texts written by Germans about their American experiences in the period from 1870 to 1914 only three comment critically on racism and on the treatment of blacks as second-class citizens.

This subtext of colonial fantasizing continues beyond the turn of the century and evokes the actual developments in the German colonies in Africa. In the German travel books about America after 1900 fantasies of racial violence play a prominent role. Some authors even conjure up the necessity of destroying and annihilating black people altogether (cf. Gerstenberger 1905; Hintrager 1904). Against the backdrop of the violent conflicts in German Southwest Africa (present-day Namibia) after the turn of the century these texts seem to be an expression of a colonial mind frame and, indirectly, of colonial experiences. Again and again, descriptions of the American South of the United States implicitly connect to developments in the African colony.

---

[18] This "vanishing" is reminiscent of the treatment of another American ethnic group, Native Americans. The topos of the "vanishing race" as a romanticized rendering of Native American expropriation is explicated by Stedman (1982: 173–192).

The shift in the German perception of now free African Americans in the United States corresponds with the retrospective belittlement of American slavery in Germany. The dual recoding creates a "splitting" of images of blacks into two different, yet complementary stereotypes (cf. Hall 1997); it entails, in fact, a demonization of free African Americans in the United States and an infantilization of blacks as slaves taken care of by a paternalistic system of slavery. Thus, we encounter both a displacement and an inversion. Looking at African Americans after 1870 in the spirit of national unity and on the eve of colonial expansion, Germans seem to engage in fantasies and projections that have to do with their own role outside of Germany, their way of interacting and engaging with difference and alterity and, specifically, with black people. German empire-building and German colonialism are, I suggest, part of a crucial subtext for the contemporaneous cultural mobility of "Uncle Tom" and the images of African Americans at that time, a subtext which also offers a rationale and motif for the appropriation itself; this colonialism, as many have argued and shown, cannot be limited to the "hard facts" of German colonial history. Rather, it has to be seen as a set of cultural practices (cf. Honold/Simons 2002; Conrad/Randeria 2002) and thus to be understood as a regime of representation and as a repertoire of fantasies (cf. Flitner 2000; Friedrichsmeyer/Lennox/Zantop 1998).[19] In the general

---

[19] The culture of colonialism is also evidenced by the approximately 100, mostly propagandistic, German films about German colonialism produced up to 1942. Set in Africa, they are, in fact, filmed in Germany with black actors who are living in Germany at the time. The 2002

euphoria for the colonial project in the early 1880s not only
interest groups and politicians articulate and support a colonial agenda in Germany; the German population begins to
identify with the imperial German nation. And, of course, the
construction of national identity rests heavily on figurations
of whiteness and racial superiority. Thus, the denigration of
African Americans in America and the commodification
of American slavery in German popular culture show how
Germans begin to speculate about their own empowerment
vis-à-vis black people and about their own capabilities as
colonial rulers carrying the *white man's burden.* Ironically,
Stowe's narrative about American slavery now plays a crucial
role in the defense of slavery. German respondents no longer
find their own oppression mirrored in the fate of "Uncle
Tom," nor do they carve out analogies between black slaves
and German servants, women, the poor or other victims of
German power asymmetries any more; instead, they begin to
see themselves as agents and as "masters." The inversion of the
evils of slavery and the appreciative, somewhat nostalgic
embracing of the institution are indicative of a dominant
discourse of colonialism in the German imaginary in these
decades. In this ideological climate the continuation or even
"revival" of forms of human bondage and forced labor could
easily be defended and legitimized. The cultural mobility of

documentary *Pagen in der Traumfabrik: Schwarze Komparsen im
deutschen Spielfilm* by Annette von Wangenheim shows the common
stereotypical roles German blacks play in these films (again, either docile
servant or savage demon, but in both cases usually mute/voiceless) and
interviews several of the black actors, some of whom survived National
Socialism in Germany by playing the black servant and thus by fulfilling
accepted role expectations.

Stowe's novel appears once more as double-edged. To sum up: images of American slavery are distilled from the novel of an American writer critical of the institution, they are fashioned and refashioned according to the changing national sensibilities in Germany, and finally, these images are virtually exported again – they are projected onto the German colony on African soil and instrumentalized to make believe that those subjected to German colonial rule in German Southwest Africa are as happy as "Uncle Tom" in his cabin.

This racial backlash seems as anachronistic as the German political agenda itself; yet it can be placed in an international context in which nationalism and race emerged as the new coordinate system of hegemony and white supremacy, as Eric Hobsbawm has pointed out (Hobsbawm 1990). In their reactions to *Uncle Tom's Cabin* and in their demeaning descriptions of African Americans in the new world, the German commentators implicitly and explicitly articulate dreams of colonial power. The absence of German colonies on American soil (a prominent topos in nineteenth-century German literature, both fiction and non-fiction) meets with the idea of becoming a colonial power in Africa.[20]

[20] While the German writers often regret the lack of German colonial success in America, they stress repeatedly that America owes its wealth and well-being to the virtues and labor of the German immigrants: with dedication and modesty they have made America what it is around 1900. One writer even goes so far as to call America "Germany's first colony" (Hopp 1892: vi). At the same time, colonialist conflations make the United States, its people, climate, geography, in the words of one author, "the new Africa of the new world" (Deckert 1892: 270). Again, colonialism and the encounter with blackness make the United States "an imaginary Africa" for the German visitors.

The pastoral turn in the German Stowe reception thus figures as part of a more complex ideological construction to legitimize colonialism and to make it "popular." The longevity of the images of the "happy slave" in Germany is perhaps not surprising in view of the racist ideology of Nazi rule. Just picture this: an African American singer, well-versed in opera, ballads, spirituals, and folk songs, and performing in English, Italian, French, and German, appears in front of a white German audience in the 1950s. He sings a German translation of an American spiritual with the somewhat awkward German title "Heimweh nach Virginia" ("Homesick for Virginia"). The German lyrics of the song translate (back) as follows:

> Homesickness for you, for you, Virginia, burns in my soul, oh you, my home.
> Do you hear the nightingale there in Virginia, where I found a new home as a slave.
> Nothing in the world do I love more than Virginia, where I found my new home as a slave.[21]

The singer touring post-Second World War Germany is Kenneth Spencer. Born in 1913 in Los Angeles as the son of a steel worker, he studies music and moves to Europe after the war. He has guest appearances in several German films, sings with a choir for the German president, Heinrich Lübke, and is very popular with a German audience for whom he gives recitals. The lyrics of his song do not bother German

---

[21] "Heimweh nach Dir, nach Dir, Virginia, brennt in der Seele mir, oh Du, mein Heimatland, / hörst Du die Nachtigall dort in Virginia, wo ich als Sklave eine neue Heimat fand. / Nichts auf der Welt lieb' ich mehr als Virginia, wo ich als Sklave meine neue Heimat fand."

audiences back then as they listen to a black man who expresses his homesickness for Virginia and for slavery.[22] In fact, Spencer appears as a kind of minstrel figure in front of a German audience and conveys the sugar-coated image of slavery that they are quite familiar with. Spencer plays the role of an "authentic" black performer in the context of a, perhaps partially strategic, (self-)commodification/mimicry and producing, once more, a nostalgically tinged version of slavery for a German audience. Spencer's performance demonstrates an anachronistic continuity in the cultural mobility of American slavery which reveals the black slave to be a congealed image frozen in time.

IV

Of course, Harriet Beecher Stowe was not the first and only mid-nineteenth-century American writer critical of slavery. Another prominent white author who turned against this institution was philosopher, philanthropist, and historian Richard Hildreth. In 1836, he anonymously published his *The Slave: Memoirs of Archy Moore* at his own financial risk and with little success. In retrospect, it seems that the time had not been ripe for Hildreth's book. Harriet Beecher Stowe was among the book's few readers and even used it in her own work (Brandstadter 1974). Ultimately, her success led to

---

[22] Spencer's song echoes the early American plantation novelists writing in defense of slavery and often ending their novels with the manumission of a black servant who then prefers to stay with his master and does not want his freedom (cf. Gross/Hardy 1966).

Hildreth's breakthrough as well. In 1852, after the publication of *Uncle Tom's Cabin*, Hildreth ventured an expanded reissue of his novel under the title *The White Slave, or, Memoirs of a Fugitive*. Although *The White Slave* could not compete with Stowe's success, it was by all means popular and also sold in Europe – in Germany, five different editions appeared in short succession. Hildreth's novel is another example I will address from a transatlantic perspective as a curious case of appropriation.

In contrast to Stowe's novel, Hildreth's book draws on the conventions of the African American slave narrative and uses a first-person narrator in order to tell the story of Archie Moore. Archie is the son of a slave who was raped by her owner and grows up on his father's plantation in Kentucky as a slave. The title refers to the fact that Archie, being the son of a white father, is very light-skinned and could pass as a white person, a fact that points to the arbitrariness of racial categories: one drop of "black" blood renders a seemingly white person "black." As a young man, Archie marries the slave Cassie, who is in fact his half sister, and has a son with her, but he is then sold first to Virginia and later to North Carolina. His new master is tyrannical and his actions provoke Archie and his fellow slaves to rebel. Archie flees and goes to sea in order to elude capture. At this point the first version of the novel ends. In the second, expanded, version, Archie returns to the United States after a stay in England in order to redeem his wife and son. In this he succeeds, and the novel ends with Archie's call to all Americans to rebel, be they black or white:

> Yes, my young friends, it is to this destiny that you are called.
> Upon you the decision of this question – no longer to be staved

off by any political temporizing – is devolved. Those who would be free themselves – so it now plainly appears – cannot safely be parties to any scheme of oppression. The dead and the living cannot be chained together. Those chains which you have helped to rivet on the limbs of others, you now find, have imperceptibly been twined about yourselves; and drawn so tightly, too, that even your hearts are no longer to beat freely. Take courage, then, and do as I did. Throw off the chains! And stop not there; others are also to be freed. It seems a doubtful thing; but courage, trust, and perseverance, proof against delay and disappointment, faith and hope, will do it. (Hildreth 1852: 407–8)

In contrast to Stowe's poetics of emotionalism, Hildreth's novel is a militant political manifesto. Hildreth's protagonist, thus, is a nineteenth-century counter-figure to "Uncle Tom" as the author places emphasis on black self-assertion, even recommending violence if necessary.[23] And he creates fear in those of his readers who think they are safe from slavery: the whites. His title, *The White Slave*, is deliberately chosen and refers not only to his light-skinned protagonist.[24] He has his slave trader say: "[B]ut you know, here in the south, we reckon all slaves as 'niggers', whatever their color. Just catch a stray Irish or German girl, and sell her, – a thing

---

[23] Nancy Bentley also contrasts Hildreth's protagonist Archy Moore as a "Europeanized white slave" with Stowe's Tom as a "feminized black slave" (Bentley 1993: 514).

[24] Werner Sollors refers to Hildreth's title as a "cultural oxymoron" (Sollors 1997: 260). Nineteenth-century abolitionist fiction often used a light-skinned character (who could possibly pass as white) to criticize the system of slavery (Sollors 1997: 255–262).

sometimes done, – and she turns a nigger at once, and makes just as good a slave as if there were African blood in her veins" (Hildreth 1852: 337).

This statement must have sounded alarming to the ears of his nineteenth-century German readers, especially those of German immigrants to America. Here an American articulates something which they had already thought about, had dreaded, or even seen. The statement of Hildreth's slave trader articulates the vulnerability of German immigrants in America and the "mobility" of slavery, as it were, as a system which is constantly craving new victims. According to all evidence, these victims could also look/be white and, thus, the color line proved to be a quite contingent demarcation. Louise Weil, daughter of a Swabian minister, writes home from New Orleans with a similar observation:

> I have realized that my view of slavery had been erroneous, as I had been of the opinion that the slaves in the South must always be identifiable either by skin color or by their manners, and in any case by their clothes. But I have seen slaves here in New Orleans with skin as white as is found in Northern Europe only; besides, notably female slaves were walking the streets in dapper garments and attested with the whole of their demeanor to the fact that they were rather civilized, so that often my heart wanted to burst at the sight of them when I took into account what they were and what could still become of them. (Weil 1860: 252 [my translation])[25]

[25] "Gar bald erkannte ich, daß ich mir über die Sklaverei ganz falsche Vorstellungen gemacht hatte, denn ich war seitdem der Meinung gewesen, die Sklaven im Süden müssen immer entweder durch ihre Hautfarbe oder durch ihre Manieren, jedenfalls aber durch ihre

We know of a few historical cases of destitute German immigrants who do not speak English and who are sold into slavery upon their arrival in the US. Instead of the upward mobility those immigrants had hoped for, they experience the direst descent. Rumors of such individual fates spread like wildfire among immigrants and Germans with an interest in America. Next to *Uncle Tom's Cabin*, these immigrant captivity stories circulated widely and were read anxiously by a German audience. The practice of kidnapping newly arrived destitute immigrants is documented in recent historical scholarship (Wilson/Wilson 1998; Talty 2000). Of some fame is the story of Salome Müller, who arrives with her family in New Orleans in March 1818.[26] Her mother has died during the voyage, her father shortly after their arrival in the United States; when relatives send for the two children left behind, the girls have disappeared, one is never heard from again, the other, Salome/Sally, is identified many years later working as a slave in a shop in New Orleans. She herself is of the opinion that she is "yellow" and rightfully the slave of Louis Belmonti. A person who has been on the same ship with her family during the passage recognizes her, tells her that she is white and sues for the restoration of her freedom. A long and

Kleidung, erkenntlich sein. Nun sah ich aber hier [New Orleans] Sklaven mit einer Hautfarbe so weiß wie sie nur im europäischen Norden angetroffen wird; kam noch dazu, daß namentlich weibliche Sklaven in elegantem Anzug einhergingen, und durch ihr ganzes Wesen bezeugten, daß sie ziemlich viel Bildung besitzen, so hätte mir bei ihrem Anblick oft das Herz zerspringen mögen, wenn ich bedachte, was sie waren und was noch vielleicht aus ihnen werden konnte."

[26] The story is also conveyed by George Washington Cable in his *Strange True Stories of Louisiana* (1999 [1888]: 145–191).

complicated court case begins which will take two years: on May 19, 1845 Salome Müller is declared a free person (Wilson/ Wilson 1998: 5–6).[27]

In the German appropriation of Hildreth's novel the issue of "white slavery" becomes a dominant theme. The explicit threat to the incoming immigrants is picked up in many reviews and is at the center of several popular German-American kidnapping tales (or "captivity narratives") which emerged in the 1850s, by popular writers such as Ludwig Gothe or Franz von Elling. The plot of these stories tends to be quite formulaic: penniless German immigrant girl arrives in the United States and looks for a job; out of luck, she is enticed by a seemingly trustworthy gentleman to follow him to the South; upon arrival she is coerced into slavery and ends up as a slave on a Southern plantation; she is saved by a courageous German immigrant (usually someone who remembers her from the passage over and has kept track of her) just as she is attacked by the American plantation owner. Having experienced a downward "fall" instead of upward mobility, the immigrants together return to Germany in the end – disappointed by America and with a gruesome first-hand experience of slavery and a whole range of anti-American sentiments.

The novel *The White Slave* together with most of Hildreth's reform writings soon falls into oblivion, and

---

[27] Carol and Calvin D. Wilson show how these stories of "white slaves" were strategically circulated by African Americans in their writings for abolitionist purposes. The story of Salome/Sally is also mentioned repeatedly in the German texts about America of that time as an awesome vision (cf. Griesinger 1862: 433; Scherzer/Wagner 1857: III 357 ff.).

today the once-popular novel is hardly known – yet it experiences a peculiar comeback after the Second World War. At that time, the new rulers in East Berlin, capital of the German Democratic Republic, are singling out radical literary traditions compatible with their political agenda. In the course of this paradigmatic "invention of tradition," to use Eric Hobsbawm's phrase,[28] they come across Richard Hildreth – his historical writings, his political theory and the only novel he has ever written, which is promptly declared to be *Weltliteratur* ("world literature"). In 1953 *The White Slave* is published as volume 152 in the series "novels of world literature" by Rütten & Loening in East Berlin, under the title *Der weiße Sklave*, flatteringly placed between Goethe, Balzac, Stendhal, and Maupassant. The renowned publishing company has been relocated from Frankfurt to Berlin and is now run by the ruling socialist elite. The latter wants to entertain and educate readers with classical novels and morally elevating narratives – light literature is not published at first as it seems not fit for fostering the proper political education.

The choice of Hildreth's novel is somewhat surprising. It is virtually unknown by the middle of the twentieth century, and no one has ever ranked it among world literature. Even critics who admire Hildreth's merits as a political thinker usually have no love lost for his novel. Why is *The White Slave* so prominently placed on the East German literary market? The novel is considered to be proto-socialist, as Hildreth had been a radical proponent of reforms in the middle of the nineteenth century,

---

[28] The appropriation of Hildreth is an invention not so much in the framework of a national project but in the context of forging a consensus for international socialism.

a fact which Donald E. Emerson reiterates in his Hildreth biography, published in the United States in 1946. Hildreth's *A Theory of Politics* (1854) advocates wide-ranging reforms in nineteenth-century America to bring about the "age of the people" (Hildreth 1984 [1854]: 267). A hundred years later, his words still address current concerns. Hildreth's novel *The White Slave* may be a critical portrayal of American slavery, yet it lends itself to a class critique and evokes the image of the oppressed worker as a victim of capitalist structures, as an industrial slave, a "white slave." On the frontispiece of the East German edition from 1953, a drawing by the well-known East German illustrator Werner Klemke, the iconography of American slavery blends with elements of a typically socialist aesthetics (figure 7). Klemke's white slave, who has broken free from bondage – the chains still dangling from his wrists – does not have any overt African American features and is not recognizable as a light-skinned African American slave. He is a late case of what Sander Gilman has referred to as "blackness without blacks" in a German context: images of blacks circulating in Germany "which bore little resemblance to any contemporary reality" (Gilman 1982: x). The afterword of the GDR edition expatiates the expected reading and focuses on the theme of a divided nation. The historical division of the United States into the slaveholding South and the North, which did not have slavery, is equated with the German division into East and West. The unification of both systems under a humane leadership had been Hildreth's goal in the middle of the nineteenth century. The socialist intellectuals adopt this idea in order to denounce the barbarity of capitalism and propagate the superiority of socialism.

RICHARD HILDRETH

DER WEISSE SKLAVE

RÜTTEN & LOENING
BERLIN

7 Frontispiece of the GDR edition of *The White Slave.*

The White Slave apparently enjoys great popularity in
the GDR. One year after the first a second edition is published –
at a time when second editions are rare in the GDR because of
chronic paper shortages. And in 1979, a third edition is published, then in a series for adolescents called "thrillingly told."[29]

[29] Next to appropriating stories about African American slavery, the
cultural politics of the GDR also took to Native American cultures and
texts as a strategy and source for socialist self-empowerment.

155

The irony inherent in the white slave's transformation from a nineteenth-century African American into a twentieth-century worker becomes obvious when one takes a look at the novel's genesis, which might not have been known to the GDR officials working in the cultural sector. Hildreth, like Stowe a New Englander by birth, is on vacation in the South in the early 1830s and witnesses slavery with his own eyes for the first time. He immediately begins to denounce it publicly. However, his abolitionist novel comes into existence via a transatlantic detour: from April 1831 to February 1832 two French aristocrats visit the United States, the North as well as the South: Alexis de Tocqueville and Gustave de Beaumont. On their tour, which lasts nine months, they cover a distance of more than 10,000 kilometers on foot, and by coach, horse, and steamboat and visit seventeen of the then twenty-four American states. Their original intention has been to inspect the American penal system, but soon they expand their objective and comment on many more aspects of American society, including slavery. Tocqueville becomes famous for his *Democracy in America*, Beaumont writes an abolitionist novel called *Marie, or Slavery in the United States*, and both texts immediately become bestsellers. Richard Hildreth probably meets both aristocrats in Boston, and he is full of praise for their writings. While working on *The White Slave*, Beaumont's *Marie* serves as a model, guiding his own literary efforts (Yellin 1972: 89, 91). Thus, the 1830s novel of a French aristocrat critical of slavery in the United States, yet full of French chauvinism (Lang 2003: 68), seems to have inspired an American abolitionist novel that is appropriated as a literary socialist manifesto by the GDR in the 1950s.

This shows that the paths of cultural mobility can be more labyrinthine than they may appear at first glance. Culturally specific objects can be subject to processes of multiple decontextualizations and recontexualizations across various cultural boundaries. In the present case, the French aristocrat who writes as a cultural outsider about American slavery is imitated by a white American writing about an African American slave whose story, in turn, is "indigenized" as a radical socialist text in the German Democratic Republic. The appropriation of Hildreth's novel, however, was a short-lived affair. The GDR is gone, and the East German Hildreth edition is presently offered at internet auctions for the symbolic sum of one cent. Cultural mobility may be enacted and exploited for political scheming but it is ultimately a highly selective, volatile, and unpredictable process.

V

Notwithstanding the isolated incidents of "white slavery" in the USA, American slavery in the nineteenth century is an institution that thrives on the exploitation of Africans and African Americans. Black resistance countering this exploitation can be found in the voices of those (former) slaves who write harrowing tales about their experiences. These slave narratives point to a hidden side of Stowe's and Hildreth's abolitionist efforts: the white authors' success by far outdoes that of the African American authors, who are for the most part commercially less successful. African American writer Ishmael Reed in *Flight to Canada* (1976), his postmodernist satire on *Uncle Tom's Cabin*, calls Stowe "Naughty Harriet":

she snatches away from the ex-slaves the only thing that they have: the "cultural capital" (Bourdieu 1986) of their tales.[30] Out of these tales Stowe concocted her reform novel and invited transatlantic and crosscultural identification with the African American plight, identification which in a German (and wider European context) often led to an active reception that substituted race and slavery with other forms of oppression. Time and again Stowe's African American contemporaries stressed the fact that it was not appropriate at all (and, in fact, implied a massive belittlement) to compare the conditions of the African American slave to that of the European worker, peasant, maid or any other marginalized group. Black intellectual Frederick Douglass wrote in this regard:

> It is often said by the opponent of the anti-slavery cause, that the condition of the people of Ireland is more deplorable than that of the American slaves. *Far* be it from me to underrate the sufferings of the Irish people. They have been long oppressed; and the same heart that prompts me to plead the cause of the American bondman, makes it impossible for me *not* to sympathize with the oppressed of all lands. Yet I must say that there is no analogy between the two cases. The Irishman is poor, but he is *not* a slave. He *may* be in rags, but he is *not* a slave. He is still the master of his own body, and can say with the poet, "The hand of Douglass is his own" … and poor as may be my opinion of the British Parliament, I cannot believe

[30] Stowe disclosed her African American sources in *A Key to Uncle Tom's Cabin*, published in 1853, and the extent to which she had borrowed from them. She did this not to give credit to the former slaves but to counter criticism of her novel that accused her of exaggerating and overstating the case.

that it will ever sink to such a depth of infamy as to pass a law for the recapture of Fugitive Irishmen! (Douglass 1999: 169 ff.)

William Wells Brown, another black author who had escaped from slavery, spoke out in a similar way. He traveled to Europe in 1849 in order to be safe from his pursuers and to strengthen the abolitionist movement abroad. While a terrific reception was held for Stowe in Liverpool because of her book, which cannibalized Brown's story among others, Brown's arrival in England a couple of years earlier attracted hardly any attention. For the customs officer, William Wells Brown was just a solitary black traveler. Brown recalls how the officer insists on searching his luggage:

> First one article was taken out, and then another, till an Iron Collar that had been worn by a female slave on the banks of the Mississippi was hauled out, and this democratic instrument of torture became the centre of attraction; so much so, that instead of going on with the examination, all hands stopped to look at the "Negro Collar". Several of my countrymen who were standing by were not a little displeased at answers which I gave to questions on the subject of slavery; but they held their peace. The interest created by the appearance of the iron collar closed the examination of my luggage. (Brown 1991: 97f.)

Brown's "souvenir" forestalls any picturesque appropriation and metaphorization of slavery. Little does he know then that the "peculiar institution" as depicted in the pages of Stowe's novel will within just a few years develop into *the* American export hit. Brown stays in Europe until 1854; by then Stowe's novel has fully found its way into European

popular culture, and he is there to witness the commodification and merchandizing it inspires.

Frederick Douglass and William Wells Brown's autobiographical slave narratives are two among the large body of
narratives written by former slaves.[31] Yet, this black textual
production has a limited cultural mobility and hardly reaches
a German audience directly. Frederick Douglass' second autobiography, *My Bondage and My Freedom* (Douglass 1855), is
one of the few texts that actually is translated into German
(Douglass 1860)[32] – it is translated by Ottilie Assing, a German
journalist living in New York and a close friend of Douglass'.[33]
The book does not have the expected success in Germany. By
the early 1860s readers are beginning to be saturated with slave
stories from America, and we are approaching the decades in
which the responses to narratives of American slavery
undergo a marked change. The fact that this was an "authentic"

---

[31] Toni Morrison provocatively asserts that "no slave society in the history
of the world wrote more – or more thoughtfully – about its own
enslavement" (Morrison 1987: 109).

[32] Before Douglass, Olaudah Equiano's slave narrative was published in a
German translation in 1792, and much later Josiah Henson's 1858 slave
narrative was published in German in 1878. Frank Webb's little-known
novel *The Garies and Their Friends* appeared in 1859. No other German-
language editions of African American works could be ascertained.

[33] Maria Diedrich has thoroughly investigated the (love) relationship
between Assing and Douglass (Diedrich 1999). As a German
correspondent, Assing was part of a "transatlantic intellectual network ...
nourished by personal contact, travel, intellectual exchange of letters,
books, and ... journals" (Keil 1997: 139), a network that was prominently
carried on by the generation of the so-called 48ers, German intellectuals
who sought refuge in the United States after the failed revolution in
Germany.

piece written by a former slave himself, a circumstance that for Assing in her preface made all the difference, seemed to matter little, and ironically Douglass' black authorship got lost along the way. MacLean's otherwise impeccable study lists Assing as the author, not as the translator, of the book and calls it a "biography" – apparently falling prey to the literary devices employed by Douglass in his text.[34] MacLean's error is passed on by succeeding generations of historians – even calling Assing's translation of Douglass' autobiography a proslavery text (Woodson 1949: 320; Brenner 1991: 370)! A different kind of cultural mobility is evidenced in this transatlantic misperception that attests to the precariousness of black authorship/authority in the nineteenth century and beyond and, in fact, eradicates it. We can speculate whether narratives of American slavery stopped short in transatlantic travel if the text did not lend itself easily to projective appropriations.[35] Black authors go on spectacularly successful lecture tours outside the United States but usually only to English-language countries where abolitionism is strongest. Neither Douglass nor Brown ever appear before an audience in the German states. Apart from

[34] MacLean writes: "This is the work of a German woman in New York, who tried to write a second *Uncle Tom's Cabin*. She had read the North Star, a paper of which the former slave, Frederick Douglas [sic], was editor, and conceived the idea of writing the story of his life to help the anti-slavery cause as *Uncle Tom* had done" (MacLean 1910: 79 ff.).

[35] At the same time, black authorship certainly cannot be taken for granted at a time when even Stowe's white female authorship is under attack in the German press – nineteenth-century reviewers belittle her "inferior" literary craft, refer to her as a "Blaustrumpf" ("bluestocking") and as a "Frauenzimmer" ("broad") and in general display a wide array of chauvinistic ascriptions.

the success of Stowe's novel, which has reasons that lie beyond her actual subject matter and has not a little to do with a general adaptability of the text, as we have seen, there seems to have been little *genuine* interest in American slavery itself. Douglass' German friend and colleague Ottilie Assing is employed by the German publisher Cotta and writes an America column for his magazine *Morgenblatt für gebildete Leser*. A fervent anti-slavery advocate herself, she seems to overrate the interest on the part of a bourgeois German audience in matters of slavery and abolitionism. She writes profusely and extensively about both; little does she know that many of the articles she sends home are never published. Cotta holds them back – in his view these are not the "hot topics" that German readers want to know about on a weekly basis (cf. Diedrich 1999: 135). That American slavery is, notwithstanding Stowe's success, still a rather marginal theme in the German states in these days and that Germans across the board, after all, do care very little about African Americans themselves has been repeatedly suggested.[36] This explains the German lack of interest in African American texts, and it offers a diagnosis that points us once more to the precariousness of the terms of German engagement with American slavery and of processes of cultural mobility in general. In the appropriation and recontextualization of culturally mobile texts and ideas, new layers of meaning are added, yet other

---

[36] From Volker Depkat (dealing with the America writing in German newspapers in the first half of the nineteenth century) to Alexander Schmidt (focusing on German travel writing during the *Kaiserreich*), several historians have noticed this lack of interest in racial matters.

aspects are erased, silenced and get lost. It is in the German reception of American slavery as depicted in Stowe's novel and through the figure of "Uncle Tom" that black victimhood is addressed; black agency, however, is jeopardized with a lasting effect.[37]

VI

Toni Morrison calls American slavery a "playground for the imagination" (Morrison 1992: 38) which has perversely enriched American literature and culture – and, one can add, many literatures and cultures outside of the United States as well. Narratives of American slavery travel widely and find particular local echoes. In mid-nineteenth-century Germany these echoes include identification with the black slave as well as rewritings of slave narratives that prominently feature German immigrants. In the last decades of the nineteenth century, we encounter popular trends which belittle all matters related to black slavery and which nostalgically imagine a safe haven from modernity in the cabin of a black slave – just as African Americans themselves had left their "slave cabins" for good. After the Second World War images of American slavery reverberate in fantasies of a tradition of international socialist solidarity along the lines of class as imagined by the socialist leaders of the GDR. From a new

---

[37] The German reception of African American literature on a broader scale starts in the 1960s and 70s. Moritz Ege has pointed to a new paradigm of appropriation in these decades, a new kind of "Afroamericanophilia", a phenomenon which I can only mention here in passing (Ege 2007).

historicist perspective we can identify and make sense of these actualizations of the narratives of American slavery in German popular culture, and we can redirect our focus to the various cultural, at times distinct and at times intersecting and overlapping contexts of reception, commodification, and appropriation. The residue of these processes remains with us today – as my opening example has shown – and stories about American slavery and the South apparently continue to intrigue a German audience. In 2008 the first full-length audio book of *Gone with the Wind* was published; it comes on thirty-four CDs and is read by well-known German actor Ulrich Noethen. The CDs' booklet justifies the decision to use Martin Beheim Schwarzbach's 1937 German translation of Mitchell's voluminous novel and to stick with the "negro language" that is rendered in some sort of German vernacular: the book "is a myth, and myths should not be tampered with." The rhetoric of the literary classic – as contingent as it may be, as we have seen in Hildreth's case – is drawn upon to legitimize the project; slavery is, in 2008, not mentioned at any length.

The reception, commodification, and appropriation of narratives of American slavery in a German context point to paradigmatic moments of cultural mobility. They also reveal the absences, biases, and limitations in the process. The tales surrounding *Uncle Tom's Cabin*, *The White Slave* as well as other narratives of American slavery show recurring patterns of localization and "indigenization." As Stephen Greenblatt writes in the introduction to this volume, it is the distinctive capacity of cultures to hide the mobility which drives them. It is therefore of importance to bring to light this mobility (especially in its fleetingness, contingency, and ideological and ironic twists) and the way in which it is discursively situated. Thus, the case studies of instances of cultural mobility are forceful illustrations and evidences of often entangled and complicated ways of exchange and transfer: of people, goods, ideas, and books. Many more stories can be told about transatlantic exchange processes regarding the mobility of representations of American slavery. Cultural mobility in general does not happen only at the periphery of seemingly delimited cultural spaces and identities, it is sometimes obvious and sometimes hidden. Focusing on mobility in the context of cultural studies, we can develop new critical readings of seemingly unequivocal cultural scripts and point to the intricate interwovenness of national discourses.[38]

References

Ammons, Elizabeth, ed. 1980. *Critical Essays on Harriet Beecher Stowe*. Boston.

Bentley, Nancy. 1993. "White Slaves: The Mulatto Hero in Antebellum Fiction." *American Literature* 65.3: 501–22.

Birdoff, Harry. 1947. *The World's Greatest Hit – Uncle Tom's Cabin*. New York.

Bourdieu, Pierre. 1986. "The Forms of Capital." *Handbook for Theory and Research for the Sociology of Education*. Ed. John G. Richardson. New York. 241–58.

Brandstadter, Evan. 1974. "Uncle Tom und Archy Moore: The Antislavery Novel as Ideological Symbol." *American Quarterly* 26.2: 160–75.

[38] I am indebted to Klaus Lösch for critical comments on this essay.

Brenner, Peter. 1991. *Reisen in die Neue Welt. Die Erfahrung Nordamerikas in deutschen Reise- und Auswanderungsberichten des 19. Jahrhunderts.* Tübingen.

Brickhouse, Anna. 2004. "Transamerican Theatre: Pierre Faubert and *L'oncle Tom.*" *Transamerican Literary Relations and the Nineteenth-Century Public Sphere.* Cambridge. 221–50.

Brown, William Wells. 1991. *The Travels of William Wells Brown: Narrative of William W. Brown, Fugitive Slave; The American Fugitive in Europe: Sketches of Places and People Abroad.* Ed. Paul Jefferson. New York.

Buell, Lawrence. 2004. "Harriet Beecher Stowe and the Dream of the Great American Novel." *The Cambridge Companion to Harriet Beecher Stowe.* Ed. Cindy Weinstein. Cambridge. 190–202.

Busch, Moritz. 1854. *Wanderungen zwischen Hudson und Mississippi 1851 und 1852.* Stuttgart.

Cable, George Washington. 1999 [1888]. *Strange True Stories of Louisiana.* Gretna.

Conrad, Sebastian, and Shalini Randeria, eds. 2002. *Jenseits des Eurozentrismus. Postkoloniale Perspektiven in den Geschichts- und Kulturwissenschaften.* Frankfurt/M.

Deckert, Emil. 1892. *Die Neue Welt. Reiseskizzen aus dem Norden und Süden der Vereinigten Staaten sowie aus Kanada und Mexico.* Berlin.

Diedrich, Maria. 1999. *Love across the Color Lines: Ottilie Assing and Frederick Douglass.* New York.

Douglass, Frederick. 1860. *Sclaverei und Freiheit.* Trans. Ottilie Assing. Hamburg.

1999. *Selected Speeches and Writings.* Ed. Philip S. Foner. Chicago.

Duden, Gottfried. 1834 [1829]. *Bericht über eine Reise nach den westlichen Staaten Nordamerikas und einen mehrjährigen Aufenthalt am Missouri (in den Jahren 1824, 25, 26 und 1827), in Bezug auf Auswanderung und Überbevölkerung.* Elberfeld.

Ege, Moritz. 2007. *Schwarz werden. "Afroamerikanophilie" in den 1960er und 1970er Jahren*. Bielefeld.

Egenter, Franz Josef. 1857. *Amerika ohne Schminke: Eine Quellensammlung zur Darstellung des amerikanischen Lebens in der Wirklichkeit*. Zürich.

Fiedler, Leslie. 1979. *The Inadvertant Epic: From* Uncle Toms Cabin *to* Roots. New York.

Fisch, Audrey. 2004. "Uncle Tom and Harriet Beecher Stowe in England." *The Cambridge Companion to Harriet Beecher Stowe*. Ed. Cindy Weinstein. Cambridge. 96–112.

Fisher, Philip. 1983. "Partings and Ruins: Radical Sentimentality in *Uncle Tom's Cabin*." *Amerikastudien/American Studies* 28.3: 279–293.

Fisher-Fishkin, Shelley. 2005. "Crossroads of Cultures: The Transnational Turn in American Studies." *American Quarterly* 57.1: 17–57.

Fitzhugh, George. 1854. *A Sociology for the South, or, The Failure of Free Society*. Richmond.

  1857. *Cannibals All! Or, Slaves without Masters*. Richmond.

Flitner, Michael, ed. 2000. *Der deutsche Tropenwald: Bilder, Mythen, Politik*. Frankfurt am Main.

Fluck, Winfried. 1991. "The Power and Failure of Representation in Harriet Beecher Stowe's *Uncle Tom's Cabin*." *John F. Kennedy-Institute Working Paper* 32: 1–39.

Freud, Sigmund. 1919. "'A Child Is Being Beaten': A Contribution to the Study of the Origin of Sexual Perversions." *The Standard Edition of the Complete Psychological Works of Sigmund Freud*. Vol. XVII: *1917–1919: An Infantile Neurosis and Other Works*. London.

Friedrichsmeyer, Sara; Sara Lennox, and Susanne Zantop, eds. 1998. *The Imperialist Imagination. German Colonialism and Its Legacy*. Ann Arbor.

Fröbel, Julius. 1857. *Aus Amerika: Erfahrungen, Reisen, Studien*. Leipzig.

Gerstäcker, Friedrich. 1849. *Wie ist es denn nun eigentlich in Amerika? Eine kurze Schilderung dessen, was der Auswanderer in Nordamerika zu thun und dafür zu hoffen und zu erwarten hat.* Leipzig.

Gerstenberger, Liborius. 1905. *Vom Steinberg zum Felsengebirg. Ein Ausflug in die neue Welt im Jahre der Weltausstellung von St. Louis 1904.* Würzburg.

Gilman, Sander L. 1982. *On Blackness without Blacks: Essays on the Image of the Black in Germany.* Boston.

Goethe, Johann Wolfgang von. 1950 [1827]. "Stoff und Gehalt." *Schriften zur Literatur. Sämtliche Werke.* Vol. XIV. Munich.

Gossett, Thomas F. 1985. Uncle Tom's Cabin *and American Culture.* Dallas.

Griesinger, Theodor. 1858. *Lebende Bilder aus Amerika.* Stuttgart.

  1862. *Freiheit und Sclaverei unter dem Sternenbanner oder Land und Leute in Amerika.* Stuttgart.

Gross, Seymour L., and John Edward Hardy, eds. 1966. *Images of the Negro in American Literature.* Chicago.

Grzybowski, Paul. 1896. *Amerikanische Skizzen.* 2nd edn. of *Land und Leute in Amerika.* 1894. Berlin.

Hall, Stuart. 1997. *Representation: Cultural Representations and Signifying Practices.* London.

Hecht, David. 1948. "Russian Intelligentsia and American Slavery." *Phylon* 9.3: 265–70.

Hedrick, Joan D. 1994. *Harriet Beecher Stowe: A Life.* New York.

Henson, Josiah. 1878. *Wirkliche Lebensgeschichte des Onkel Tom in Frau Beecher-Stowe's* Onkel Toms Hütte. Trans. Marie Schweikher. Bremen.

Hildreth, Richard. 1852. *The White Slave, or, Memoirs of a Fugitive.* Boston.

  1984 [1854]. *A Theory of Politics: An Inquiry into the Foundations of Governments, and the Causes of Political Revolutions.* New York.

Hintrager, Oskar. 1904. *Wie lebt und arbeitet man in den Vereinigten Staaten? Nordamerikanische Reiseskizzen*. Berlin.

Hobsbawm. Eric J. 1990. *Nations and Nationalism since 1870. Programme, Myth, Reality*. Cambridge.

Honold, Alexander, and Oliver Simons, eds. 2002. *Kolonialismus als Kultur. Literatur, Medien, Wissenschaft in der deutschen Gründerzeit des Fremden*. Tübingen.

Hopp, Ernst Otto. 1892. *Aus Amerika. Erzählungen und Skizzen aus dem amerikanischen Leben*. Berlin and Vienna.

Keil, Hartmut. 1997. "German Immigrants and African-Americans in Mid-Nineteenth Century America." *Enemy Images in American History*. Ed. Ragnhild Fiebig-von Hase and Ursula Lehmkuhl. Providence. 137–58.

Kloß, Klaus-Peter. 1982. *Siedlungen der 20er Jahre: Großsiedlung Britz Hufeisensiedlung, Waldsiedlung Zehlendorf, Onkel-Toms-Hütte, Großsiedlung Siemensstadt, Weiße Stadt, Großsiedlung Schillerpromenade*. Berlin.

Kohn, Denise; Sarah Meer, and Emily B. Todd, eds. 2006. *Transatlantic Stowe: Harriet Beecher Stowe and European Culture*. Iowa City.

Kriegleder, Wynfrid. 1999. *Vorwärts in die Vergangenheit: Das Bild der USA im deutschsprachigen Roman von 1776 bis 1855*. Tübingen.

Lang, Hans-Joachim. 2003. "Der liebenswürdige, aber verschollene Verfasser der Marie, ou l'esclavage aux États-Unis, tableau de moeurs américains: Rückkehr zu einem alten Text." *Cultural Encounters in the New World: Literatur- und kulturwissenschaftliche Beiträge zu kulturellen Begegnungen in der Neuen Welt*. Eds. Harald Zapf and Klaus Lösch. Tübingen. 55–79.

Lorimer, Douglas A. 1978. *Color, Class and the Victorians: English Attitudes to the Negro in the Mid-Nineteenth Century*. New York.

Lucas, E. 1930. *La Littérature anti-esclavagiste au dix-neuvième siècle: Étude sur Madame Beecher Stowe et son influence en France.* Paris.

MacLean, Grace Edith. 1910. *Uncle Tom's Cabin in Germany.* New York.

Morrison, Toni. 1987. "The Site of Memory." *Inventing the Truth: The Art and Craft of Memoir.* Ed. William Zinsser. Boston. 103–24.

——— 1992. *Playing in the Dark: Whiteness and the Literary Imagination.* Cambridge.

Paul, Heike. 2005. *Kulturkontakt und Racial Presences: Afro-Amerikaner und die deutsche Amerika-Literatur 1815–1914.* Heidelberg.

Reed, Ishmael. 1976. *Flight to Canada.* New York.

Reichardt, Ulfried. 2001. *Alterität und Geschichte: Funktionen der Sklavereidarstellung im amerikanischen Roman.* Heidelberg.

Review of *Uncle Tom's Cabin.* 1853. *Die Gartenlaube* 3: 32.

Rossbacher, K. 1972. *Lederstrumpf in Deutschland: Zur Rezeption James Fenimore Coopers beim Leser der Restaurationszeit.* Munich.

Scherzer, Carl, and Moritz Wagner. 1857. *Reisen in Nordamerika in den Jahren 1852 and 1853.* 2nd edn. Leipzig.

Siemann, Wolfram. 1990. *Gesellschaft im Aufbruch. Deutschland 1849–1871.* Frankfurt am Main.

Sollors, Werner. 1997. *Neither Black nor White yet Both: Thematic Explorations of Interracial Literature.* New York.

Stedman, Raymond William. 1982. *Shadows of the Indian: Stereotypes in American Culture.* Norman.

Stowe, Harriet Beecher. 1853. *A Key to Uncle Toms Cabin.* Boston.

——— 1994 [1852]. *Uncle Tom's Cabin.* New York.

Sundquist, Eric J. 1985. "Slavery, Revolution, and the American Renaissance." *The American Renaissance Reconsidered (Selected Papers from the English Institute).* Eds. Walter Benn Michaels and Donald E. Pease. Baltimore. 1–33.

1986. "Introduction." *New Essays on Uncle Tom's Cabin*. Ed. Eric J. Sundquist. Cambridge. 1–43.

Surwillo, Lisa. 2005. "Representing the Slave Trader: *Haley* and the Slave Ship; or, Spain's *Uncle Tom's Cabin*." *PMLA* 120.3: 768–82.

Talty, Stephen. 2000. "Spooked." *Transition* 85: 48–75.

Tompkins, Jane. 1985. *Sensational Designs: The Cultural Work of American Fiction*. New York.

Wagnleitner, Reinhold. 1991. *Coca-Colonisation und Kalter Krieg: Die Kulturmission der USA in Österreich nach dem Zweiten Weltkrieg*. Vienna.

Wallace, J. K. 1986. *Early Cooper and His Audience*. New York.

Warren, Kenneth. 2004. "The Afterlife of *Uncle Tom's Cabin*." *The Cambridge Companion to Harriet Beecher Stowe*. Ed. Cindy Weinstein. Cambridge. 219–234.

Weil, Louise. 1860. *Aus dem schwäbischen Pfarrhaus nach Amerika*. Stuttgart.

Wenzel, Peter. 1982. "Pre-Modern Concepts of Society and Economy in American Pro-Slavery Thought: On the Intellectual Foundations of the Social Philosophy of George Fitzhugh." *Amerikastudien/ American Studies* 27: 157–75.

Wilson, Carol, and Calvin D. Wilson. 1998. "White Slavery: An American Paradox." *Slavery & Abolition* 19.1: 1–23.

Woodress, James. 1967. "*Uncle Tom's Cabin* in Italy." *Essays in American Literature in Honor of Jay B. Hubbell*. Ed. Clarence Gohdes. Durham, N.C.

Woodson, Leroy. 1949. *American Negro Slavery in the Works of Friedrich Strubberg, Friedrich Gerstäcker and Otto Ruppius*. Washington, D.C.

Yellin, Jean Fagan. 1972. *The Intricate Knot: Black Figures in American Literature, 1776–1863*. New York.

6

Struggling for mobility: migration, tourism, and cultural authority in contemporary China

PÁL NYÍRI

In Manhattan's Chinatown, illegal migrants from Fujian Province, on a break from work in Chinese-owned garment workshops, buy telephone cards with Chinese instructions from Chinese vendors in order to call home. Can their experience of mobility, and the way that experience makes them relate to China, be understood in the same framework as that of a middle-class Chinese tourist at a popular "scenic spot" in China? Do these very different situations point to something common in terms of how newfound mobility is affecting subjectivity and its state conditioning in China? In this chapter, I suggest that both individuals have to negotiate their positions as modern Chinese subjects as they cope with contradiction between the expectation of mobility and barriers in front of it. While unifying and mobilizing images of Chinese modernity are transmitted to them through a range of media technologies from telephone cards to tourist brochures, they have to make their way through everyday situations and contradictory local discourses that stand in the way of movement and strip them of their enfranchisement.

Chinatown, Manhattan, March 7, 2001

At the Yidong Shopping Center at 88 East Broadway in Manhattan, Fujianese vendors sell international telephone cards. One vendor stocks fifty-one kinds, many with Chinese text and distinctive design. On one card, called Great Wall, Deng Xiaoping extends his congratulations on the return of Hong Kong to the Motherland.

Phone cards embody the way globalized communication technologies have created unexpected new markets for ethnicity and nationalism, and also the way the mobility of technologies is intertwined with human mobility. International calling is now a largely ethnic business that targets Mexicans, Chinese, or Ukrainians in migrant neighborhoods across the globe. In the United States, at least 40 percent of those working in the prepaid card industry are said to be immigrants (Sachs 2002). The appeal of the marketing is in offering special low rates to particular countries, and even provinces such as Fujian. For low-income migrants, calling family and friends is often the only non-essential spending, and the cards do not require the registration that deters undocumented migrants from getting home phones.

This particular vendor, from Fuzhou, is a woman around twenty-five. She came to America five years ago, following her parents, who had since gone back to China together with her two children. Her situation is typical: at the nearby American East Fuzhou restaurant, the waitress comes from a township to the north of Fuzhou; she has a nine-year-old child back home. She came to the United States to join her husband, an illegal immigrant, but her brother-in-law, who

8 A phone card from East Broadway.

had less money and could not afford passage to America, went to England instead. She phones him every week. Another phone card customer, who like the two women does not have legal residency papers, paid $40,000 – an amount not infrequently mentioned in connection with "illegal immigrants" from China, mostly put together by family or borrowed from usurers – to come to the United States in 1994. He calls his friends in England once every two weeks. He tells them not to come to America, because "the weather is bad and life is bad": he works twelve to thirteen hours every day. Also, if they were caught they would be sent back to China.

Around the corner in Elizabeth Street, the Houyu Overseas Chinese Association of America (Meiguo Houyu Huaqiao Lianyihui) – one of around four dozen organizations in New York founded by migrants from Fujian in the last two decades – celebrates its sixteenth anniversary at Jing Fong restaurant. Outside, the restaurant is inconspicuous, but inside, it displays the latest splendours of modernity one finds in Chinese cities: an escalator leads to two large halls with marble floors and gilt crystal chandeliers. In Chinese newspapers, Jing Fong advertises itself as the largest restaurant in Chinatown. Most of its business comes from Fujianese wedding parties, at which elaborately posed photos are taken and sent back home. Since the 1980s, hundreds of thousands of migrant workers have come to the United States from Fujian, mostly via New York and illegally (see Pieke *et al.* 2004).

Houyu ("Monkey Island"), in Changle Prefecture near Fuzhou, has been one of the major areas sending migrants to the United States. After listening to, in order, the PRC and US national anthems, the Chinese consul-general mounts the stage, decorated with huge American and Chinese flags, to thank the association for its contribution to "homeland construction." The association's secretary-general responds that seeing the "great Fatherland" ever more prosperous and strong is their common desire. Someone reports on the construction of a culture palace in Houyu, for which the association has raised $900,000. After the speeches, the evening continues with a show of "nationalities arts," including Han dancers performing flirtatious pop dances in Uighur costumes. (A major event in China may have the luxury of engaging dancers of various nationalities, but in this small troupe, the majority Han have to perform the roles of the minorities.) For my benefit, the chairman of the Fuzhou United Friendship Association of New York, a construction entrepreneur, points to the stage: "This is the art our Chinese ancestors left to us."

A vice-president of the Fu Tsing American Assocation (representing migrants from Fuqing Prefecture) sits at one of the tables. A former teacher in his mid-thirties, he came to America illegally eleven years ago. "Do you think the bosses around this table all have papers? In America, even millionaires can be without papers!" With officials from the consulate nearby, the vice-president loudly and cheerfully explains that he "does immigration work" (*gao yimin*). This chiefly means handling applications for political asylum. Is there any conflict between doing this kind of work and entertaining official delegations from China? "None whatsoever. It's business. We do our business; they do theirs. Every year, $200 million is sent to China from the Bank of China in New York. And that's only one of ten banks. It goes into building houses, helping relatives, and investment. This is very important for China." The vice-president's boss, the president, has been reported by Fuqing's main official paper, the *Fuqing Ribao*, to have donated around a million yuan to his home area since the eighties, including a contribution to a village Party committee office building (*Fuqing Ribao* 2000). The vice-president says he came to America because here, unlike in the European welfare state system, if you have strength and brains you can get by. His sister lives in the Netherlands; his brother, in France.

Jiuzhaigou National Key Scenic Area, Sichuan Province, September 7, 2003

"Our tour has two names: Natural Scenery Voyage (*ziran fengjing you*) and Ethnic Customs Voyage (*minzu fengqing you*)," our guide, Xiao Ma, has told us. He warned us against patronizing the vendors at our overnight stop on the way, explaining that they were minorities and savages (*yeman*). "If you say you don't like something they might make trouble for you." "Tomorrow evening," he consoled us, "we will learn about the traditions and customs of the Qiang and the Tibetans" in the ordered safety of the scenic spot.[1]

Jiuzhaigou is a nature reserve that comprises a cascade of pools and waterfalls in the Min Mountains in northern Sichuan's Ngawa Tibetan and Qiang Autonomous Prefecture. Designated a National Key Scenic Area in 1982 and entered in UNESCO's World Natural Heritage in 1992, Jiuzhaigou has been one of the "hottest" destinations for Chinese tourists in

---

[1] Kang (2009) writes that Tibetan lamas and worshippers have actually been forced to stay out of a monastery on the route to Jiuzhaigou during peak hours so they don't distract tourists from souvenir shopping after the monastery had been renovated by the reserve administration and contracted out to a business. After the same happened to a temple at Huanglong – a World Natural Heritage site around 50 km from Jiuzhaigou – traditional activities related to the Tibetan pilgrimage, as well as temple fairs, were restricted or banned as "environmentally polluting" and "endangering fire safety," resulting in the decline of pilgrimage by Tibetans. Instead, an International Huanglong Tourism Festival has been organized, showcasing the four nationalities of the region as well as Tibetan lamas.

recent years, with 1.9 million visitors in 2004 (Dombroski 2008). In the Sichuan Tourism Administration's bilingual *Travel Sichuan China* (p. 16), Jiuzhaigou is described as "famed the world over as the Dreamland and the Fairyland." Armed with Deng Xiaoping's authority on its cover, the brochure also endows Jiuzhaigou with epithets (*cheng*) that are designed to project the historic aura and classical style of literati culture and to associate Jiuzhaigou with significant historic sites: "It has been said that 'having been to Huangshan, one no longer looks at mountains; having been to Jiuzhaigou, one no longer looks at waters' and [it has been] called 'the king of China's water views'" ("you 'Huangshan guilai bu kan shan, Jiuzhai guilai bu kan shui' he 'Zhonghua shui jing zhi wang'" zhi cheng, p. 16).

Our group, mostly of mid-level managers from state and private enterprises, spends about five hours inside the park's gate, which looks like a tollgate on a freeway. My colleague and I take a bus up along the cascade, then visit the designated scenic spots one by one as we descend back. At the spots, the walkway broadens into viewing terraces, where tourists take photos. The names of the spots, like Treasured Mirror Cliff, Panda Lake, and Reclining Dragon Lake, have been given by the reserve administration and are displayed and interpreted ("Lotus Basin Waterfall … is like the lotus basin in a Buddhist temple. It is a symbol of luck") on large boards. In the geography of the reserve, they have overwritten the names of the Tibetan villages, which still exist inside the reserve but are not included in the tour.

Instead, we stay overnight in the service area around the entrance, which is far larger than any of the villages. It numbers over 120 hotels, almost all built in the last six years.

9 and 10 The first pages of the Sichuan Tourism Administration's brochure *Travel Sichuan China.*

Our hotel, according to its promotional brochure, features "classic elegance with Tibetan palatial architecture." This means that it is painted with a geometrical pattern of off-white and dark red on the outside – a faint echo of the Potala – and incorporates the same pattern into the design of the spacious lobby, with marble, crystal, and gold finishing. Above the reception counter is the sine qua non of Chinese hotel modernity: four clocks showing the time in the national capital, Beijing (identical to the local time), New York, London, and Tokyo. The staff – like all reserve staff that comes into contact with tourists – is from outside Jiuzhaigou and largely Han Chinese.

After dinner, we are taken to the Ethnic Culture Night, presented by the Jiuzhaigou Nationalities Art Troupe in a concrete arena made up like a giant yurt. At the entrance, a hostess in Tibetan dress places a *hada* on visitors' shoulders: we are reminded that it "has been blessed by the gods and is the Tibetans' way of showing welcome to visitors."

The show, though more elaborate and extravagant, is similar to that at Jing Fong restaurant. The narrators tell us that "minority nationalities" live in harmony in Ngawa, and that their "culture" consists of "solemn and mysterious religious rites, cheerful folk songs and wild folk dancing." Each song and dance is identified as either Tibetan or Qiang, though some are performed in Chinese, including the song entitled "China, I love you." The thrust of the musical representation covers the Oriento-Pop range, from the Soviet- through the Hong Kong-inspired to the largely disco. At one point, the audience is invited, and proceeds, to participate in a drinking ceremony and then to dance with the performers on the stage.

11 A Chinese tourist drapes a hada around a Tibetan performer's shoulders.

Mobility and modernity

Since the PRC embarked on the modernization drive that became the supreme state ideology and social mantra after 1978, Chinese citizens have been challenged to travel in multiple ways (see Rofel 1992). As Liu (1997) has pointed out, a "spatial hierarchy" arose, in which one's "success" as a modern – or "advanced" (*xianjin*), "civilized" (*wenming*), "cultured" (*you wenhua*), "high-quality" (*you suzhi*) – Chinese subject was linked to mobility. At the pinnacle of that hierarchy was international migration to the United States, the country that symbolized global modernity. Migration, only recently seen as treachery, was now reevaluated as an act of patriotic

181

potential: scholarly, official, and popular publications all asserted that "successful" migrants could contribute not only to their own modernization and glory but also to that of the Fatherland (Nyíri 2001). At the other end of the spectrum, recalcitrant rural women who did not jump at the opportunity to go to Saudi Arabia as nurses or to Jordan as seamstresses were chastised in the provincial newspaper for their "backward mentality" (Wang 2004).

From a state that, only recently, prevented foreign travel, China has become one that encourages it but attempts to control its meaning. The public discourse in 1990s China, ranging from academics to the media, equated travel abroad – and, indeed, any travel – with migration in pursuit of individual "development" (*fazhan*) through education or work, but ultimately and optimally through entrepreneurship. Indeed, the master narrative of the "new migrant" is one of what Harvey (1989) termed "flexible accumulation." The "new migrant" is a figure symbolic of a new, globally modern and yet uniquely national – even racial – way of being Chinese, not only by virtue of his connection to more "advanced" nations, but also by the very fact of his mobility. He is successful in the global capitalist economy and rises to a position of economic and even political power in the country that epitomizes modernity and power, the United States. Yet he (or she) is able to do so precisely because of such Chinese moral qualities as hard work and commitment to the family's welfare and the homeland's development (Nyíri 2005). Television programs and newspaper articles are replete with variations on stock phrases celebrating the "national spirit" of "united team players, realistic pioneers, resilient entrepreneurs, courageous trailblazers" (quoted in Pieke *et al.* 2004: 186). In a typical academic article, one author, calling "new migrants" the "precious wealth of the Chinese nation," claims that they account for over one-quarter of "first-rate experts and engineers" in the United States, and at the same time affirms that, as beneficiaries of China's reforms, they "hope to see China stable, prosperous, and strong" (Chen 2004).

For China today, global cities of the West increasingly acquire the meaning of national sites as they come to signify migrant success in a plethora of films, television dramas, and fiction. Beginning with the hugely successful soap opera based on the 1991 novel *A Peking Man in New York*, migrants in these accounts play the roles of both scouts and voyeurs for the nation, providing a continuous peep show but also useful information on foreign localities as backdrops for evolving ways of Chinese life (Sun 2002: 67–111). In these books and films, Tokyo, Moscow, Paris, and New York are above all sites of an unfolding global Chinese modernity. This imagery is carried into the living rooms of Chinese worldwide by a Chinese-language media whose content, thanks to satellite television, overlapping business interests, and cross-borrowing by publishers of Chinese newspapers, is becoming increasingly global (Yang 1997; Zhang Xudong 2001; Nyíri 2005; Parker 2003).

Migrants are expected to live up to this image, becoming successful entrepreneurs with clout in their countries of residence and then using that clout, economic or political, to bring investment, technology, skills, or diplomatic dividends to China. This is exactly what much of the recent literature on "overseas Chinese work" emphasizes. In its *Opinion on*

12 and 13 Two magazines, from Budapest and London.

Implementing New Migrant Work (*Guanyu kaizhan xin yimin gongzuo de yijian*, 1996) the Overseas Chinese Affairs Bureau formulates the task of raising "a core cadre" of new migrants who are "able to actively contribute to accomplishing the country's three great tasks." To this end, it recommends promoting them "in our domestic and foreign media [and] help them increase their fame overseas." The same document calls on Chinese officials to "increase friendship" with and "strengthen guidance" of publishers of overseas Chinese newspapers. The continued connection to the Chinese state is reinforced through festive rituals that imitate those conducted by local governments in China and through the percolation of political-nationalistic symbols such as Deng Xiaoping and the Great Wall down into the mundane.

Until the late nineties, the positive value of mobility lay in its strong association with capital accumulation. Since then, however, a culture of – mainly domestic – leisure travel, once also reviled but now promoted by the state, has rapidly emerged as another attribute of modern urban lifestyle. Mass tourism in China has essentially emerged since 1998, when paid holidays were extended from six days to three weeks and the government made tourism a new "key growth area" of the economy, ordering all regions to promote its growth (Wei 2001: 246). In particular, tourism is an important element of the Great Western Development Programme (Wei 2002), seen not only as aiding economic growth but as helping to bring the "advanced civilization" of Eastern China to the Western and especially the minority regions. In a typical turn of phrase, Ma Ping, writing on the program, argued that "local minority groups, after learning Eastern regions' advanced modes of life, can increase their own quality of life" (Ma 2001: 38, cited in Barabantseva 2005). In this sense, tourism fits into the overall strategy of constructing "socialist material and spiritual civilization," which the 16th Congress of the Chinese Communist Party declared necessary to achieving the goal of a "well-off society."[2] This includes drawing residents of the periphery into the mold of national citizenry. In 2002, the Party's current Secretary-General, Hu Jintao, mentioned the necessity of including the training of tour guides in the national programme of "aid" for Tibet. What this meant was made clear by the declaration of the National Tourism Administration's Party committee, which declared that this task was a "political" one, which was to "contribute to the stability of Tibet and the unity of the peoples … to promote Tibet's economic prosperity and social progress; to resolutely implement a scientific view of development" (CNTA 2005).

As well as civilizing the natives, the state and scholarly commentators of the leisure industry also see tourism as part of an effort to "lead the masses to plan their leisure and cultural lives in a scientific, healthy, and reasonable manner" (Ma 2004: 218–19). The 2001 *Notice on further accelerating the development of the tourism industry* (*Guanyu jin yi bu jiakuai lüyouye fazhan de*

---

[2] This complex ideal can be summarized as one in which development is achieved through both eugenics and productivity, and in which the *petit bourgeois* forms of consumption that stimulate the formation of a productive and modern subject – one endowed with "qualities compatible with the principles of market economy, such as competitiveness, and adaptability to the requirements" of a neoliberal economy (Barabantseva 2009: 235) rather than a willful and wasteful one – prevail. See Anagnost (1997), Flower (2004), Friedman (2004).

tongzhi) calls for "closely connect[ing] the development of tourism with the construction of socialist spiritual civilization; cultivat[ing] superior national culture through tourist activities; strengthen[ing] patriotic education." This project is closely linked to the fact that tourism in China is understood by its managers and promoters squarely as a modern way of consumption whose objects are developed, bounded, approved, and catalogued "scenic spots," each with an incontrovertible canon of cultural references. Between 1 and 7 October 2002 – a holiday week – Chinese citizens purchased 90 million tickets to "scenic spots."[3] Travel as verification of one's knowledge of an accepted canon of scenic spots has its roots in pre-modern Chinese representations of gentry travel, but it has been appropriated by a tourism industry that the party-state continues to control through both ownership and indirect pedagogical practices such as the approval and classification of scenic sites, routes, and tour guide talks. The canon of scenic spots reemerged in a postindustrial era in which the state exhorted its subjects to become modern citizens through consumption. Scenic spots became "themed," enclavic spaces, which were nonetheless far from purely ludic: they are not removed from, but play an important role in, the national body. The master cultural narrative of each spot, enacted in a standardized "nationalities" song-and-dance performance, in the narratives of tour guides, on ticket stubs, and on signs, places the site in the imaginary of the nation. As shown in the two photos below, taken in the town of Songpan in 2003 and 2005 respectively, the

---

[3] Mayakinfo.ru, www.mayakinfo.ru/news.asp?msg=10769, accessed October 15, 2002.

14 and 15 Songpan's North Gate before and after the makeover.

development of a site for tourism involves the creation of public spaces endowed with national symbolism: in this case, the erection of a statue of Tang Princess Wencheng and the Tibetan prince she married as a symbol of "harmony and amity" between the Tibetan and Han people in a Tibetan autonomous prefecture.

The touristic sanitization of nearby Huanglong, Kang (2009) argues, possesses an even clearer national symbolism through the very use of the Chinese name Huanglong (meaning "Yellow Dragon") over the Tibetan one, the designation of the temple closer to the summit as (Chinese) Daoist and the one at the foot as Tibetan Buddhist, and the safe display of the lamas along with minority performers at the tourist show, away from the temple where they could complicate the site's straightforwardly ordered narrative.[4]

Dominant discourses, then, valorize and encourage both international migration and domestic tourism as ways of being modern Chinese citizens. They seek to unify and mobilize migrants and tourists by placing their experiences within an interpretive framework of a national Chinese modernity, transmitted through a range of media technologies: not just print (Anderson 1983) and television or video (Yang 1997; Schein 2005), but also technologies and performances that are adapted to the lives of mobile individuals and therefore more effective, from telephone cards to tourist brochures,

---

[4] Cf. also James Hevia's analysis of Chengde, a World Cultural Heritage site, where the government's presentation of the site as "historic evidence of ... a unitary, multicultural China" "appears to brush uncomfortably against the depoliticizing trust of UNESCO cultural universalism" (Hevia 2001: 224).

from DVDs to theme parks. Standardized participatory rituals of the nation, with "ethnic" songs and dances, "five-thousand-year-old traditional culture" and landscape clips can be reproduced in Jiuzhaigou or New York, or, in the case of the Central Television's Spring Festival Gala, on satellite television as a yearly worldwide master recital of national imagery (Sun 2002: 159–163). The *People's Daily* described this event as a "new folk celebration" that unites 100 million "sons and daughters of China, no matter whether at home or abroad, to the north or south of the Great River," and "without any preaching, with plenty of inspirational force, naturally expresses ... the spirit of the Party's 16th Congress" through its songs and skits (Zhong 2003). The reviewer approvingly analyzed the show as a "ritual" affirming the affective bonds of the Chinese people, structured by the hosts' calls "Embrace your family!", "Thank your friends!", "Greet your neighbours!" and finally "Eulogize the Fatherland!" This provides the cue to the "culmination" of the ritual in the massive performance entitled "Coming together of the nation's soil" (*guotu huiji*), in which soil from all China's provinces, as well as Taiwan, Hong Kong, and Macau, is poured into a ritual *ding* vessel under the solemn guard of army generals. At this point, the song "Love of the Old Soil" (*Guotu qing*) "transports the sons of China and millions of viewers into the great sentiments of our nation, the great goals of our race [*guojia da qing, minzu da yi*], which are unifying the Fatherland, uniting the nation, developing the economy, and making the people happy" (Zhong 2003).

This "indoctritainment" (Sun 2003:191) is clearly inspired by the state discourse celebrating the rebirth of

China as a powerful, harmonious multiethnic nation with a glorious history, but it is produced by quasi-capitalist market mechanisms and popularly consumed. This standardized textual and visual symbolism firmly places migrants within the officially endorsed interpretations of globally mobile Chineseness. The arches and dragon dances in Chinatowns, the displays of red banners and brass plaques from Chinese officials in the offices of Chinese organizations, the congratulatory telegrams from the same officials read out and patriotic pop songs performed at festive events, and the layout and language of new-migrant newspapers communicate, in the same way as tourist brochures and "nationality" shows, not just a homogeneous and timeless ethnic identity but, more specifically, continuity with the Chinese national project (Nyíri 2005). These occasions rehearse the interpretation of movement as a modernizing mission by a global vanguard, a mission that is primarily for the Fatherland's benefit, but one that profits the rest of the world as well.

Mobility and cultural control

When Laura Nader (1997: 720) wrote, "When the use of *social* control becomes less culturally acceptable, especially for the middle class, the use of *cultural* control becomes more central for the mechanics of power," she had Western liberal democracies in mind, but her observation appears to apply to today's China. As the party-state is eager to create capitalism, consumption, and a "middle class" without relinquishing control, cultural control over the processes where the invention of the modern Chinese subject takes place becomes particularly important. As more people begin to move, the state attempts to maintain its authority over the interpretation of their movement through a heavy transnational presence in the migrant public sphere, economic and administrative control of tourism, and a hegemonic televisual discourse that today's Chinese capitalists willingly mediate not just domestically but also in a burgeoning global media.

Domestic tourists are not such heroic figures, but they have much the same tasks of bearing witness to the modern nation through experience and performance. Where migrants are expected to affirm the ethnic aspect of an essential China – drawing together "the Chinese race" though they might no longer be citizens – tourists contribute to reinforcing its territorial aspect, often in minority regions.

The locations onto which mobility is projected, be they global cities of the West or scenic spots, are devoid of agency; along with the locals, they become immobile backdrops to Chinese modernity. In the same vein as Xiao Ma, the guide, warned tourists about the "savagery" of local "minorities" when they appear outside the nationalized cameo of the "cultural performance," Chinese media, and particularly books and soap operas made by or about Chinese migrants overseas, frequently depict "foreigners" (i.e. locals) as colorful and lazy or hapless people unable to cope with modernity and dependent on crafty Chinese entrepreneurs.[5] In the novel *Holy*

---

[5] The nationalist reversal of sexual hierarchies in recent products of Chinese popular culture, in which a feminized West is sexually exploited by a Chinese male, has been noted by several authors; see e.g. Barmé 1999: 255–80.

River, a successful Chinese businessman is the benevolent patron of his secretary, the widow of a Hungarian professor of philosophy who has lost his job, become an alcoholic and committed suicide. At one point, the novel has Hungarian waiters clad in ethnic costume perform a folk dance and deliver a laudatory speech in Chinese for their Chinese boss's birthday (Chen and Chen 1997: 86). Like the "minority culture evening," this scene tames the locals and provides them with a place in a nationalized Chinese cultural universe. The episodes of the soap opera *Into Europe* (Chen 1999) open with glamorous shots of Paris, Rome, or Budapest at night, but the daytime lives of migrants that viewers are invited to follow show a continent that is romantic but slow and lacking in modernity. The New Chinese Migrant embodied by the main hero of the series delivers that modernity. A year after arriving in Paris penniless, he reveals the plan of an ambitious new construction project to the applause of a stunned Parisian audience. "Ladies and gentlemen!" he announces, pointing to the scheme of a building complex with pagoda-style roofs. "What will be different on the new map of Paris two years from now? The beautiful banks of the Seine will be full of Oriental splendour: the Chinatown Investment and Trade Centre!"

The tourist spreads civilization through consumption; the migrant, through production – though the two are, of course, intertwined. The significance of the "new Chinese" showing Paris – the symbolic center of Europe – the road to modernity is not lost on any Chinese viewer brought up on narratives of how imperialist Europe has both humiliated China and forced it to modernize. The Chinese state looms

16 A languid maiden set against a Budapest landmark: the cover of a novel about Chinese in Hungary.

large in the narrative of the film, produced and aired by state broadcasters: the Chinese embassy provides support for the protagonist's project, while funding for it is secured from China.

The struggle to mobilize and immobilize

The discourses of the migrant and the tourist – nearly hegemonic within the media space accessible to residents of and recent migrants from mainland China[6] – communicate that it is essential for the modern Chinese subject to be mobile. Mobility is something that distinguishes him from less modern foreigners or minorities. This idea is frequently rehearsed in private narratives of mobility. In a typical migrant story, the owner of a shipping and customs clearance company recalled her arrival in Hungary in 1990:

> I found out that Hungary was actually an agricultural country with a very backward industry; having only just embarked on reform and opening, goods were very scarce … there were no industrial goods at all, all of them had to be "imported"; so I went home, organized suppliers, and started importing.[7]

Rather than being the ironic behavior of "post-tourists," Chinese tourists' enjoyment of the performative –

---

[6] The first large-scale study of internet filtering in China, entitled "Empirical Analysis of Internet Filtering in China" and conducted by Jonathan Zittrain and Benjamin Edelman in 2002, found tourism to foreign countries – along with Taiwan, Tibet, other political issues, religion, and health – to be one of the topics that the Chinese government regularly blocked web information on (see Iyengar 2004). This may suggest that description of foreign countries is seen as a "sensitive topic," though it may also reflect concern about using tourism as a way of migrating abroad illegally.

[7] "Huaren nüqiyejia Lai Hua" (Lai Hua, Chinese businesswoman), *Shichang* (Budapest), August 12, 2003, p. 11. Originally on Tilos Rádió, August 6, 2003, 9–10 p.m.

photographing the stone stele with the World Heritage inscription or joining in a "minority" tug-of-war, their wariness of the "authentic" everyday life of toured places – the very stuff that Western tourists pursue – seems to stem from the same root: impatience with the "backward," the stationary, and a desire to distance themselves from it. According to a manager from one of the largest travel agencies in Sichuan Province, "Chinese tourists don't want that (seeing 'authentic' village life) because they know it already ... because they lived like that when they were little, or if not they, then their parents or grandparents or great-grandparents."[8]

But the persuasiveness of these hegemonic discourses is undermined by the fact that movement remains formidably difficult for Chinese citizens; sometimes more so than before. Outside the Southeast Asian region, a People's Republic of China passport is among the worst with which to apply for a visa or arrive at a border. The humiliation of being rejected, taken out of the queue, searched, verbally abused, and forced to pay bribes to border guards and customs officers is a recurrent topic in migrants' conversations, and although it is suppressed in media renderings, its consequences are felt. The hero of *Into Europe* arrives in France illegally, with the help of a smuggler. The film interprets this as testimony of his ingenuity and perseverance in the face of a challenge to his mobility; in other words, of his being a true New Chinese Migrant. Migrants acutely perceive the frustration of their movement as yet another attempt by an envious West to frustrate

---

[8] Interview with Zhou Yimin, International Center Manager, China Comfort Travel, Chengdu, September 10, 2003.

the modernization of China. This strikes a chord with the pugnacious nationalistic stories in mainland Chinese – and migrant – media that nurture past humiliations. A Chinese permanent resident of Hungary, returning in a defiant mood from the US Embassy in Budapest where she had applied for a tourist visa, said to me: "If they turn me down I won't go to New York until it has been bombed by China."

This comment is as much a product of the mobilizing discourse of Chinese modernity as of another global narrative, one that strips Chinese migrants of their enfranchisement and equates the cross-border movement of Chinese people and goods with illegality, exploitation, and crime. Headlines from the *Los Angeles Times*, *El Pais*, *Libération*, and the *Guardian* call our attention to Chinese "traffickers" and "sweatshops" in very similar language. Moreover, there are slippages between the imagery of demographic, economic, criminal, and hygienic danger that recreate the classical Yellow Peril imaginary. In *The Art of War*, a Wesley Snipes action thriller from 2000, the discovery of corpses of illegal Asian immigrants in a container is linked to the assassination of the Chinese ambassador preparing to sign a treaty on China's accession to the "United Nations trade charter," creating an implied connection between the threat of demographic and economic domination. The same trope resurfaces in the 2007 Italian-German TV drama *La moglie cinese* (The Chinese wife), based loosely on Roberto Saviano's bestseller *Gomorra*, in which shiploads of Chinese migrants are brought to Italy by the Triads and sold into slavery to the Mafia. This view, in a mirror image of the "leisure culture" campaigns in China, finds it hard to believe that Chinese at their borders could simply be tourists (the metaphor of the tourist being, after all, reserved for the modern Western subject; see Nyíri 2006; Alneng 2002); they are seen to be lying in wait, in the hundreds of thousands, for the opportunity to cross and remain illegally (see Nyíri 2002: 333–334). Those that have done so, the kitchen or garment workers of New York or Prato, put on the brave face of mobile modernity when they visit their home villages in Fujian. But that is preceded by years of struggle against immobilization, first crossing borders, then averting deportation and hiding out in Chinatown basements.

Challenges to domestic tourists' mobility are different: the infrastructure of tourism is such that those who want to move away from approved scenic spots and ways of experiencing may find it difficult. All tour operators and almost all travel agencies in China – except some small ones catering to foreign backpackers – are state-owned, making the travel business one of the least free sectors of the retail economy. The rapid growth of the tourism market and the protection of every tourism development from bankruptcy by some state entity have allowed travel agencies to increase business without differentiating their products. In addition, state actors – a hierarchy of provincial, prefectural and county tourism bureaus with "guidance" from the National Tourism Authority – approve tour routes (*lüyouxian*) and "ethnic tourist villages" (Oakes 1998: 159). These designations do not mean that no organized tours can be conducted to other places in principle, but given their ownership structure, travel agencies strongly rely on them. As a result, most agencies offer exactly the same tour packages, and should one want something other than a package tour – even simply information – they cannot help. Brochures published by tourism administrations offer no more help: they usually provide "suggested itineraries," and some contain lists of flights and trains to and hotels and restaurants of the capital of the province described. What most brochures do not contain is maps or travel information to the scenic spots themselves. They are not intended to help travelers to get to a destination or plan a holiday. They are designed to whet the appetites of tourists, who will then have to turn to a travel agent to organize their visit. But a request for something outside the packages will meet with blank stares. In our case, all travel agencies in Chengdu offered three-day package tours to Jiuzhaigou. But neither travel agency nor hotel staff had heard of any towns on the way to Jiuzhaigou, let alone being aware of public bus services to them. Staff at the Chengdu bus stations were unsure about buses in general, and when asked about Jiuzhaigou, advised us to get a package tour. The provincial tourism administration – which is a purely administrative body without an information service – did the same. Without a guidebook – a genre that, at the time of our visit, was only just becoming popular – or access to a backpacker website, we had only two choices: purchase a tour package or charter a car with a driver.

An extreme example of channeling tourists into a particular experience of a place is on Kuku-Nor, the largest lake in China, which lies in Qinghai Province and is designated a nature reserve. There is only one place to stop on the lake that is accessible from the provincial capital, Xining. This site, called "151" because it lies at a distance of 151 km from Xining, comprises a few hundred meters of the lakeshore and several hotels and restaurants, hermetically surrounded by a fence. It is managed by the quasi-state-owned Qinghai Province Kuku Nor Tourism Development Company and labeled a Provincial-Level Patriotic Education Site. Everyone who wants to see the lake must pay an entrance fee. Local Tibetans who live next to "151" are not allowed to walk to the lakeshore except through the gate, and if they are caught doing so they face a fine. For tourists, accessing the lakeshore outside of the controlled area is difficult: they have to walk around 1 km up to the motorway and then back down through a field between the fence of this site and that next door of what looks like a holiday village construction site. But no one does that: tourists arrive in buses, take a motor boat out to the lake (local fishing boats are prohibited on the lake), take photos, shop, and leave.

Challenges to the cultural control of mobility

Edensor (2001: 64–78) points out that "carefully stage-managed spaces may be transformed by the presence of tourists who adhere to different norms" and by the varying nature of performances staged on them, some of which may be improvisatory, non-conformist, ironic, cynical, or resistant. In China, however, one encounters no such dissent at scenic spots. Fellow travelers in our tour group, and other group tourists we have spoken to, may have been skeptical of the "quality" of sites they were shown or of the truthfulness of superlative and historical claims made about them; they may have complained about the quality of the service; but they did not question or deviate from the basic pattern of sightseeing.

Yet several times, asking tourists whether they had considered traveling alone, we received replies that reflected awareness of the Western hierarchy of "traveler" over "tourist." A young English graduate from Canton in our group told us: "I know that foreigners like to travel alone, with a backpack and so on. And we as young people would like that too." For our guide, too, the attraction of individual travel seemed to lie in its association with the West: "Actually, it is you foreign friends who know what travel really is: take a backpack and go riding. I [too] think it is better to go alone." A middle-aged cadre from Kashgar responded: "When I have time I travel alone, taking buses. That way I can decide how long to spend where. That's the best. But when I am pressed for time I travel with a group."

An increasing number of mostly young Chinese do choose to travel on their own. This is called "self-service travel," *zizhuyou*, to distinguish it from ordinary, group travel. Groups of "jeep safari" enthusiasts with names like Yueye Lianmeng (Cross-Wilderness Federation) and Yezhanpai (Wilderness Warriors) have sprung up across China's large cities. Many "hill cottages" near Peking have bungalow-style accommodation and offer horse riding or bungee jumping. Walsh and Swain (2005) write about young Chinese who drive jeeps to Lugu Lake in Yunnan, stay and eat with local families, and go hiking around the lake.

In the 2000s, books targeting this group emerged. However, it is important that, unlike the mainstream tourism discourse, generated in a "top-down" fashion by the state and state-affiliated large tourism developers, the backpacker discourse first emerged on the internet, in bulletin-board discussions that foster competing information. These tourists engage in an alternative discourse of travel as solitary adventure. As one backpacker wrote in an article entitled "I really hope to be reborn as a bird," "What I like most of all is that feeling of freedom and independence" (Lin 2002b). Seeking authenticity in the Chinese landscape and encounters with ethnic minorities, this tourist counterculture eschews scenic spots, performances, hotel reception counters adorned with four clocks, and seemingly everything else that goes with mainstream tourism in China. One backpacking book (Yizhi 2002) states explicitly that it excludes "scenic spots." Yet although sites of mass tourism, with their development and crowds, seem to stand for everything the authors of these books want to avoid, they – and more surprisingly, participants of online backpacker discussions – do not criticize or satirize these sites and their practices the way their Western counterparts do.[9] Most authors ignore them even when a route they are describing passes right through one; some include them. Thus, writers on the www.lvye.com and www.17lai.com backpacking sites described Jiuzhaigou's nature using standard brochure terms such as "fairytale world" (*tonghua shi-jie*), without reflecting on tourism development there.[10]

---

[9] Consider, for example, this description of Torremolinos on the Spanish coast in the 2002 edition of the popular *Guide du Routard*: "The beaches are beautiful but it is hard to see the sand: all through the summer, scores of buses disgorge the Average Joes of all countries, in flip-flops, sun hats, and T-shirts with holes" (quoted in MIT 2002: 26, fn. 20. See also MIT's discussion of guidebook language there).

[10] www.lvye.org/lyxz07/html/9911/ab01.htm and www.17lai.com/jingddy/ SC/AB/aba_songpan.htm (accessed September 20, 2003).

Despite the efforts of the backpacker discourse to differentiate backpackers from mainstream tourists, it accepts that the imperative of mobility comes from the desire for modernity. Indeed, it describes backpacking as a quintessentially modern lifestyle and, as such, it derives the legitimacy of its pursuits from the imagery of Western modernity, together with North Face fleece jackets, Timberland boots and backpacks. In her account of a trip to India in the popular Shanghai-based *Travel Times*, a female backpacker's joy over the sense of fraternity she experienced with backpackers of other nations leads her to claim that "the backpacker tribe is best able to embody a nation's economic strength and its national quality. The fact that Japanese backpackers are found in every corner of the earth is inseparable from Japan's enormous economic strength" (Lin 2002a). She adds: "When American and Japanese backpackers understood that I was traveling alone and stared at me in admiration – I would not have exchanged that feeling of national pride for anything" (Lin 2002b). The triumphalism of this narrative derives from the liberating experience of experiencing travel abroad on equal terms with Westerners and Japanese. Nonetheless, it is remarkable how much the language of this article echoes the hegemonic, official discourse of Chinese nationalism and modernity that pervades mass tourism.

The superimposition of a leisure-centered view is also affecting the modernity discourse of foreign travel. Chinese tourism abroad has been growing a yearly 20 to 30 percent. Thanks to simplifications of exit procedures and agreements with an increasing number of countries, it has now become

旅游 时报 度假 都市 游览 新闻

上海市旅游协会主办 2002 年 7 月 11 日-7 月 17 日 总第 720 期 统一刊号 CN31-0083

17 The cover of a Shanghai-based magazine.

possible to go on group package tours to most of the world, and to obtain individual tourist visas upon arrival in much of Southeast Asia. Groups travel under the tutelage of travel agents and tour guides who are themselves recent Chinese migrants, steeped in the dominant discourses of mobility and closely linked to those – from travel agencies in China to

204

migrant media personalities – who produce them. Even so, the opening of the world to Chinese leisure travelers, for the first time not limited to the privileged elite – travel to Southeast Asia is now affordable to teachers, lower-level officials, and corporate secretaries from major cities – is an event that will be significant in shaping Chinese views of the world in the years to come.

Some tourists do not hide their disappointment at the lack of "modernity" and "developed" sites, which they interpret as a lack of "tourable" places. Chinese tour guides in Berlin admit that most of their Chinese customers are "a bit disappointed" at the lack of skyscrapers and broad avenues and find Berlin "backward" compared to Shanghai or even Hangzhou. According to one tour guide, what attracts most interest apart from shopping and nightlife is places associated with historical personalities, such as the Marx-Engels monument, but also the site of Hitler's bunker. A Russian tour guide working with Chinese tourists in St. Petersburg echoed her, saying that what her groups wanted to see most were the Smolny and the *Aurora*, sites related to Bolshevik history. Other tourists, however, are more ambivalent. A twenty-nine-year-old employee of a company in a township near Shanghai did not quite know what to make of Budapest: "Western and Eastern views are different. In the East, the newer the better. Here, the older the better ... The modern part is a bit blander, but the historical is very strong. In the last two decades, there doesn't seem to have been much development ..." Some migrants, generally those with more education and those who had spent a longer time in Europe, are also more likely to appreciate the "historic" or "romantic" side of Europe despite its "lack of development." "In Europe, if something is beautiful, everyone protects it," noted a Chinese resident of Budapest. "Historical things are preserved, what's more, preserved in their original state." "Rome, even though it is so expensive, dirty and messy and it is so difficult to park, it has the most tangible spirit of history," admitted another.

Tourists and the mediators who convey the attractions to them may reject, or more precisely refuse to engage with, locally dominant representations of the localities, for example the strongly historical representation of Berlin with Nazism and Communism at its center. In Hanoi, Chinese tour groups visiting the Military Museum are not shown the part of the exhibition that focuses on the war with China. (A Chinese blogger described how a member of her tour group "very patriotically said that we wouldn't look at it even if they took us there." She went on to comment how surprised she was to see American tourists taking photos in front of a U.S. warplane shot down by the Viet Cong: "We Chinese tourists would surely not give in, we would argue [about the war], and the last thing we would do is take a photo as a souvenir!")[11] This lack of attention is linguistically manifested in the wanton misnaming (or renaming) of sites, often with English-sounding names. Thus, in a process similar to the overwriting of Tibetan village names with Chinese names for scenic spots, the Berlin thoroughfare Unter den Linden becomes "Pipal Avenue" in a

[11] Wanshui Yifang (2006) "Yuenan ji xing" (Notes on my trip to Vietnam), November 11, 2006. www.tianya.cn/New/PublicForum/Content.asp? flag=1125:86idWriter=0125:86idArticle=99550125:86strItem=travel (accessed 22 March 2007).

Germany guidebook, and Vietnam's famous Halong Bay is popularized as "Guilin-on-the-sea" (a reference to a famous Chinese landscape). The attempts to name and categorize foreign sites are consistent with the dominant discourse of mobility in that they wish to wrest what Said called "positional superiority" from the West, which has for centuries dictated those categories and defined views. Nonetheless, the "development"- and modernization-centered view of the cultural, which shapes the consumption of domestic scenic spots, is evidently insufficient to deal with experiences abroad. The Chinese tourist encounter with these sites is only beginning, and the production, dissemination, and consumption of tourist canons will be a complex process, with multiple agendas and interpretations. Individual Chinese visitors to Southeast Asia, mostly young urban professionals, are beginning to discover alternative ways of life and imaginings of the world that often have little to do with the sinocentric views of the region they are familiar with.

The Chinese state, as long as it exists in its current form, will, however, persist in its attempts to assert its cultural authority over foreign landscapes. Early in 2004, when PRC Chairman Hu Jintao visited Paris on the occasion of the fortieth anniversary of diplomatic relations between his state and France, the Eiffel Tower turned red and the Champs-Elysées was closed for a "dragon dance" parade. The center of further festivities – to which Nobel Prize-winning Chinese writer Gao Xingjian, who lives in Paris, was not invited – was Euro Disney, decorated in red and gold, the Chinese traditional/ Communist colours. The *International Herald Tribune*'s writer, and probably many Frenchmen and -women, were surprised at the "national, government-sponsored campaign" that marked the first time the Eiffel Tower had been lit in a single color other than its normal golden glow and the first time since the German occupation that the Champs-Elysées had been occupied by a "non-French event" (Smith 2004). But for television audiences in China, the scene was familiar and the symbolism clear. Red lights, street parades, government-sponsored campaign – all these are a must for a successful tourism festival. Though a Nobel laureate, Gao Xingjian is a politically ambivalent figure almost unknown in China: the Eiffel Tower and Euro Disney, by contrast, are well-entrenched symbols of the West. For the duration of the celebrations, the vision of *Into Europe*'s hero came true: Paris became a true and proper scenic spot with Chinese help.

Conclusion

This chapter has argued that a global discourse of Chinese modernity that serves the state's pedagogy (while being produced mostly outside of state structures) subjects citizens of China today to a strong pressure to move. Yet while the experience of modernity that this discourse wishes to impart is appealing, it is frequently frustrated. Internationally, it is frustrated by an emerging global regime of *selective mobilization*, in which mobility (of persons or goods or ideas) is seen as useful and praiseworthy when it fits a particular model of capitalist rationality, and as threatening and illegal in other cases. The Western discourse on Chinese migrants mostly relegates them to the latter category; consequently, Western institutions seek to immobilize them. At home, the Chinese state, too, had long sought to immobilize its own threatening and illegal migrants, the so-called "blind flow" (*mangliu*) of rural–urban migration. Today, while encouraging them to move, the regime confines them to a legally disenfranchised urban underclass. These experiences of frustrated modernity produce a tension in which mobile Chinese subjects must live.

The Western discourse on Chinese migrants, like the Chinese one, suggests their exceptionality. In this case, they are well suited to embody the fear of mass immigration because of their cultural "otherness," the large population, increasing power, and "Communist dictatorship" of their country of provenance, and the appealing mythology of the triads and the "Chinese mafia." Ultimately, both of these discourses derive migratory, economic, or criminal patterns from reified cultural traits (hard work, mutual help, and so on). In essence, the two discourses represent alternative (visions of) globalization, but, in the end, both use the language of "culture" as a foil for competing claims of superiority in hierarchies of modernity and capitalism. Both attempt to discipline mobility by asserting cultural authority over their representation.

For its part, the Chinese state achieves that through the massive imposition of interpretive authority in the public spaces and media of movement both domestically and abroad. This succeeds because the actors who control these spaces are linked to the Chinese state structurally and/or by economic benefits, and because the discourse of pioneers elevates their status. The superimposition of the leisure optic on travel abroad, however, is likely to create public and media spaces that are less firmly linked to state-endorsed interpretations. On the other hand, encounters with Chinese tourists are likely to confuse and discredit "securitized" discourses of Chinese migration in the West. These processes have the potential to impact both Chinese and non-Chinese views of the place of Chinese subjects in the modern world.

References

Alneng, Victor. 2002. "The Modern Does Not Cater for Natives," *Tourist Studies* 2 (2): 119–142.

Anagnost, Ann. 1997. *National Past-Times: Narrative, Representation, and Power in Modern China*. Durham, N.C., and London: Duke University Press.

Anderson, Benedict O'G. 1983. *Imagined Communities*. London: Verso.

Barabantseva, Elena V. 2009. "Development as Localization," *Critical Asian Studies* 41 (2): 225–254.

Barmé, Geremie. 1999. *In the Red*. New York: Columbia University Press.

Chen Dian and Chen Mei. 1997. *Sheng He*. Peking: Wenhua Yishu Chubanshe.

Chen Kemin (dir.). 1999. *Zouru Ouzhou*. 20 episodes. Southeast Fujian Television. Script by A. Hang.

Chen Xiurong. 2004. "Haiwai huaren xin yimin de quanqiuhua yu Zhongguo xibu da kaifa" (The Globalization of New Chinese Migrants Overseas and China's Great Western Development), paper presented at the fifth conference of the International Society for the Study of Chinese Overseas, Copenhagen, May 10–14, 2004.

CNTA Tour Guide Aid Tibet Office (Guojia Lüyouju Daoyou Xuanzang Bangongshi) (2005) "Weile gongtong de fanrong yu fazhan," *Zhongguo Lüyoubao / China Tourism News*, September 5, pp. 1–2.

Dombroski, Kelly. 2008. "The Whole Nine Villages: Local Level Development through Mass Tourism in Tibetan China," in John Connell and Barbara Rugendyke (eds.), *Tourism at the Grassroots: Villagers and Visitors in the Asia Pacific*. Abingdon, Oxon.: Routledge, pp. 98–113.

Edensor, Tim. 2001. "Performing Tourism, Staging Tourism," *Tourist Studies* 1 (1): 59–81.

Flower, John M. 2004. "A Road Is Made: Roads, Temples, and Historical Memory in Ya'an County, Sichuan," *Journal of Asian Studies* 63 (3): 649–685.

Friedman, Sara L. 2004. "Embodying Civility: Civilizing Processes and Symbolic Citizenship in Southeastern China," *Journal of Asian Studies* 63 (3): 687–718.

Fuqing Ribao. 2000. "Juanzhu baiwan yuan xingban jiaxiang gongyi shiye" (Donated Millions to Uplift Homeland's Projects for Common Good), October 30, p. 1.

Harvey, David. 1989. *The Condition of Postmodernity: An Enquiry into the Origins of Cultural Change*. Cambridge, Mass.: Basil Blackwell.

Hevia, James. 2001. "World Heritage, National Culture, and the Restoration of Chengde," *Positions* 9 (1): 219–243.

Iyengar, Jayanthi. 2004. "Digital China Is Booming," *Asia Times Online*, 18 February.

Kang, Xiaofei. 2009. "Two Temples, Three Religions, and a Tourist Attraction: Contesting Sacred Space on China's Ethnic Frontier," *Modern China* 35 (3): 227–255.

Lin Sheng'r (2002a) "Nü beibao du chuang Yindu" (Female Backpacker, Alone, Hits India), *Travel Times* (Shanghai), July 11, 2002, A3.

(2002b) "Zhen xiwang lai shi zuo yi zhi niao" (I Really Hope to Be Reborn as a Bird), *Travel Times* (Shanghai), July 11, 2002, A3.

Liu, Xin. 1997. "Space, Mobility, and Flexibility: Chinese Villagers and Scholars Negotiate Power at Home and Abroad," in Aihwa Ong and Donald Nonini (eds.), *Ungrounded Empires: The Cultural Politics of Modern Chinese Transnationalism*. New York: Routledge, pp. 91–114.

Ma Huidi. 2004. *Renlei meili de jingshen jiayuan (Leisure: The Making of a Beautiful Home for the Human Spirit)*. Peking: Zhongguo Jingji Chubanshe.

Ma Ping. 2001. "Xibu da kaifa dui dangdi minzu guanxi de yingxiang ji duice" (The Impact of Great Western Development on Local Ethnic Relations and Policy Responses), *Minzu wenti yanjiu / Minority Issues Research*, no. 5, pp. 37–42.

MIT (équipe). 2002. *Tourismes 1: Lieux communs*. Paris: Belin.

Nader, Laura. 1997. "Controlling Processes: Tracing the Dynamic Components of Power," *Current Anthropology* 38 (5): 711–737.

Nyíri, Pál. 2001. "Expatriating Is Patriotic? The Discourse on 'New Migrants' in the People's Republic of China and Identity Construction among Recent Migrants from the PRC," *Journal of Ethnic and Migration Studies*, 27 (4): 635–653.

———. 2002. "Afterword," in Pál Nyíri and Igor Saveliev (eds.), *Globalizing Chinese Migration: Trends in Europe and Asia*. Aldershot: Ashgate, pp. 320–337.

———. 2005. "The 'New Migrant': State and Market Constructions of Modernity and Patriotism," in Pál Nyíri and Joana Breidenbach (eds.), *China Inside Out: Contemporary Chinese Nationalism and Transnationalism*. Budapest: Central European University Press, pp. 141–176.

———. 2006. *Scenic Spots: Chinese Tourism, the State, and Cultural Authority*. Seattle and London: University of Washington Press.

Oakes, Tim. 1998. *Tourism and Modernity in China*. London and New York: Routledge.

Parker, David. 2003. "Is There a British Chinese Public Sphere?" in Gary D. and Ming-Yeh T. Rawnsley (eds.), *Political Communications in Greater China*. London and New York: RoutledgeCurzon, pp. 239–260.

Pieke, Frank N., Pál Nyíri, Mette Thunø, and Antonella Ceccagno. 2004. *Transnational Chinese*. Stanford: Stanford University Press.

Rofel, Lisa. 1992. "Rethinking Modernity: Space and Factory Discipline in China," *Cultural Anthropology* 7 (1): 93–114.

Sachs, Susan. 2002. "Immigrants See Path to Riches in Phone Cards," *New York Times*, August 11.

Schein, Louisa. 2005. "Mediated Transnationalism and Other Elusive Objects: Anthropology, Cultural Studies and Questions of Method," in Pál Nyíri and Joana Breidenbach (eds.), *China Inside Out: Contemporary Chinese Nationalism and Transnationalism*. Budapest: Central European University Press, pp. 99–140.

Smith, Craig S. 2004. "Paris Fêtes China with Eiffel Tower and Fanfare," *International Herald Tribune*, 26 January: 3.

Sun, Wanning. 2002. *Leaving China: Media, Migration, and the Transnational Imagination*. Lanham, Boulder, New York, and Oxford: Rowman & Littlefield.

Walsh, Eileen Rose, and Margaret Byrne Swain. 2005. "Creating Modernity by Touring Paradise: Domestic Ethnic Tourism in Yunnan, China," *Journal of Tourism and Recreation Research*, 29 (2): 59–68.

Wang Huan (2004) "Chuguo wugong, jiaobu weihe zheme zhong?" (Going Abroad to Work: Why Are the Steps So Hard?) *Sichuan Ribao*, July 3.

Wei Xiaoan. 2001. *Muji Zhongguo lüyou* (Witnessing China's Tourism). Shijiazhuang: Hebei Jiaoyu Chubanshe.

——— 2002. "Xibu lüyou fazhan zhanlüe" (A Strategy for Tourism Development in the West [of China]), opening speech at the

213

Western Tourism Development Strategy Seminar, Guiyang, April 23. Electronic file courtesy of author.

Yang, Mayfair Mei-hui. 1997. "Mass Media and Transnational Subjectivity in Shanghai: Notes on (Re)cosmopolitanism in a Chinese Metropolis," in Aihwa Ong and Donald M. Nonini (eds.), *Ungrounded Empires*. London: Routledge, pp. 287–322.

Yizhi. 2002. *Zang Di Niupi Shu*. N.P.: Zhongguo Qingnian Chubanshe.

Zhang, Xudong. 2001. "The Making of the Post-Tiananmen Intellectual Field: A Critical Overview," in *Whither China?* Durham, N. C., and London: Duke University Press, pp. 1–78.

Zhong Chengxiang. 2003. "Xin de minsu qingdian, mei de wenhua da can" (A New Folk Celebration, a Beautiful Cultural Feast), *Renmin Ribao*, February 11, p. 14.

7

Performativity and mobility: Middle Eastern traditions on the move

FRIEDERIKE PANNEWICK

This chapter deals with the manifold trajectories of theatrical traditions within the Middle East and far beyond its geographical boundaries. These traditions are in motion, traveling from one period to another, from one place to another. All of the traditions presented in this paper are characterized by a certain degree of "performativity," for they are "enacted" traditions, performed and played out in a certain setting. They consist not only as or in a text, but also onstage; they are performed at a public place at a given time for a certain audience. Through this public enactment these texts gain a unique "life of their own," going beyond the primary textual meaning.

The concept of performativity[1] is based on recent developments in cultural studies since the 1990s, when a modified conception of what constitutes culture emerged. Whereas in textual approaches culture is conceived as "text,"[2] this

---

[1] Cf. the homepage of the Sonderforschungsbereich Kulturen des Performativen at the Free University of Berlin (Prof. Erika Fischer-Lichte), http://sfb-performativ.de; Erika Fischer-Lichte (2004), *Ästhetik des Performativen*, Frankfurt am Main.

[2] Cf. e.g. Doris Bachmann-Medick, ed. (1996), *Kultur als Text: Die anthropologische Wende der Literaturwissenschaft*, Frankfurt am Main.

understanding of culture as "performance" focuses more on the specific event character of cultural settings. Interest no longer gravitates towards deciphering the meaning of single elements within a given culture; rather, acts, occurrences, process of exchange (e.g. between the actors on stage and the audience), transformations, and dynamics are intensely scrutinized. The concept of performativity thus entails a crucial shift: its subject matter is no longer a static work of art that is interpreted but an event and – comparable to cultic acts – the particular experience of this event.

But besides their performative characteristics, the traditions presented in this article touch upon issues related to collective memory. It could be argued that these traditions have proven to be especially effective and durable because of two main reasons: firstly, they gain "power" by having a visible effect on a certain audience or community thanks to their performativity; and secondly, they are part of a commonly shared remembrance of a given community that is reenacted time and again. Therefore, in my own understanding, besides the performative event also the reinterpretation of cultural material, the reenactment of elements out of the collective memory, play an eminent role.

Enacted in many different historical, religious, or social contexts, these long-standing traditions do not remain immutable once exposed to the influence of these diverse enactments – as if this journey would leave them in some pristine original state. Rather, syncretical processes of intermingling and adaptations subliminally transform these traditions. The resulting new and modified form is neither a cultural misunderstanding nor a failed reading. The highly creative procedures of what James Clifford has called "inventive syncretism"[3] do not weaken the expressive power of these traditions at all – on the contrary. These kinds of cultural forms of expression are – like culture itself – *per definitionem* syncretical and "on the move." As Reinhold Göring has put it, culture is "a concept covering the whole range of possibilities of signifying practices, including even those possibilities which are pushed to one side, repressed, neglected, or only existent as a potentiality in a single culture."[4] Therefore, the repressed aspects of a certain culture become apparent in another culture or in realms – such as adolescence, literature, or love – where they are still granted a place. With such an open concept of culture, sensitive to the dynamics of continuous flux, it becomes immediately obvious that culture itself can first emerge out of an interactive process.[5] This process of interaction has to be seen in the context of the "heavy burden" of tradition and collective memory that both influence cultural forms of expression.

[3] "With expanded communication and intercultural influence, people interpret others, and themselves, in a bewildering diversity of idioms – a global condition of what Mikhail Bakhtin called 'heteroglossia.' This ambiguous, multivocal world makes it increasingly hard to conceive of human diversity as inscribed in bounded independent, cultures. Difference is an effect of inventive syncretism." James Clifford (1988), *The Predicament of Culture: Twentieth-Century Ethnography, Literature, and Art*, Cambridge, Mass., pp. 22–3.

[4] Reinhold Göring (1997), *Heterotopia: Lektüren einer interkulturellen Literaturwissenschaft*, Munich, pp. 34 ff.; the translation from German is mine.

[5] Cf. Christian Szyska and Friederike Pannewick (eds.) (2003), *Crossings and Passages in Genre and Culture*, Wiesbaden, pp. 1–9.

In the following I will present two performative traditions which have played an eminent role in the cultural history of the Middle East: the tradition of performative story-telling both in secular and in Islamic contexts and that of the Shiʿite confessional performance called *"taʿziya."* Both are "traveling traditions" in historical time and geographic space, having moved within and beyond the Islamic world; and both are enacted in front of an audience, with the effect they generate based upon the direct interaction between per-formers and audience. Thus, in terms of the concept of per-formativity briefly outlined above, we may understand both as being performative traveling traditions.

The storyteller tradition in the Middle East is espe-cially relevant for the context of this article, as it represents a complex and multilayered example of cultural mobility between Europe and the Middle East. Arab dramatists of the 1960s sought to syncretically combine selected mobile Western forms and techniques with Middle Eastern traditions. This experimental approach was meant to foster both authenticity (*aṣāla*) and modernity (*ḥadātha*) at the same time. One of the most influential factors in the development of a modern exper-imental Arab theatre was the reception of Bertolt Brecht's theatrical approach. In adapting Brecht's concepts of *alien-ation* and *epic theatre*, Arab dramatists reimported so to say a very old indigenous tradition back to the Middle East. This is only one example out of many others in contemporary Arab art showing what Stephen Greenblatt in the introduction of this volume called the intriguing dialectic of persistence and change: a traditional cultural form of expression, on the threshold of oblivion, is being revitalized by its modern

westernized twin. Arab dramatists adapted the narrative political theatre of Brecht within a postcolonial Middle Eastern
context; because of the Eastern origin of storytelling techniques in Brechtian theatre, Arab dramatists could easily adapt
this Western approach without the risk of being suspected of
blind imitation. This way they used so to say their own heritage
(after its detour via Western theatre stages) in order to implement an experimental political theatre much needed in Arab
societies in the 1960s and 1970s.

I Storytelling on the move – from Islamic preaching to political theatre[6]

Storytelling is the Middle East's most famous performative tradition, with *The Arabian Nights* or *Alf layla
wa-layla*[7] being the most popular and renowned example.
The frame story of the young, intelligent Shahrazād and the
cruel ruler Shahriyār points to an element crucial in gaining
an understanding of the function of storytelling. The story
opens with a prefacing address by the world's most famous
storyteller: "Father, I will tell you what is in my mind …
I would like you to marry me to the king Shahriyār, so that

[6] The question as to how far these traditions have been reworked in modern
Arabic theatre productions is dealt with in Friederike Pannewick (1999),
"The Ḥakawātī in Contemporary Arabic Theatre. The Re-Emergence
of an Old Pattern of Communication," in *Myths, Historical Archetypes
and Symbolic Figures in Arabic Literature*, eds. Angelika Neuwirth *et al.*,
Beirut, pp. 337–48.
[7] Cf. for a survey on this form of art: Enno Littmann (1960), art. "Alf Layla
wa-Layla," in *Encyclopedia of Islam*, 2nd edn., vol. I, pp. 358–64.

I may either succeed in saving the people or perish and die like the rest" (tr. Hussein Hadawy). Shahrazād has decided to put her own life at risk in the attempt to bring the suffering of her people to an end. The only weapon she has at her disposal is her knowledge of thousands of stories. Aware of the enormous power storytelling wields, this young woman trusts the narrative potential of her texts and combines it with her own performative talent for the dramatic art. It is this combination that saves her life as well as those of many other innocent girls. The framework story of *Alf layla wa-layla* thus represents a model of the power inscribed in the art of storytelling – a model of literature as live performance that is not only capable of imitating and reflecting reality but indeed of changing it.

The role of storytellers[8] within their respective communities is therefore a crucial one: if their performance of the epic material proves convincing, then they contribute decisively to the production of images of themselves and others. Literature – and particularly the live performance of literature – thus has two aspects: a passive aspect reproducing reality and/or reenacting already well-known stories and figures out

[8] Cf. for the specific techniques in oral epics and narrative poetry Albert B. Lord (1978), *The Singer of Tales*, New York, and Richard Bauman (1986), *Story, Performance, and Event: Contextual Studies of Oral Narrative*, Cambridge; for Arabic storytelling traditions Charles Pellat (1971), art. "Ḥikāya," in *Encyclopedia of Islam*, 2nd edn., vol. III, pp. 367–72; Mia I. Gerhardt (1963), *The Art of Story-telling: A Literary Study of the Thousand and One Nights*, Leiden; Butros Rouhana (1984), *La Narration orale, mode d'expression collective théâtrale*, unpublished dissertation, Paris.

of a society's "cultural archive";[9] and an active aspect forming a certain perception of this same reality. Of course, not every author or storyteller is as fortunate as Shahrazād was. Literature and its performance have not always proven to be a successful means for saving lives or persuading cruel rulers to change their minds. Nonetheless, right up to the present day realizing this awesome potential inherent to the narrative art form has remained one of the foremost goals pursued by Arab artists.[10]

The power and impact of Arabic narrative performance has not gone unnoticed in European intellectual circles. European travelers described their encounters with this genre as early as the eighteenth century:

> Colonel Capper, in his observations on the passage to India through Egypt and across the great Desert, says, that "before any person decides on the merit of these books [of the Nights], he should be eye-witness of the effect they produce on those who best understand them. I have more than once seen the Arabians on the Desert sitting round a fire, listening to these stories with such

---

[9] Walter Benjamin defined the narrator's role as follows: "The story teller takes what he narrates from experience, his own or reported. And in turn he makes it the experience of those who listen to his story." Walter Benjamin (1977), *Gesammelte Schriften*, vol. II, 2, eds. R. Tiedemann and H. Schweppenhäuser, Frankfurt am Main, p. 443.

[10] Cf. e.g. Caton (1990) on this frequently repeated topos of the poet's involvement in society and politics: "The poet has power over men, and poetry is a deeply political act." Steven C. Caton (1990), *Peaks of Yemen I Summon: Poetry as Cultural Practice in a North Yemeni Tribe*, Berkeley, p. 40.

attention and pleasure as totally to forget the fatigue and
hardship with which an instant before they were entirely
overcome."[11]

These observations are typical of other eyewitness accounts of
Arabic narrative performance, underlining just how animat-
edly the audience responds to the storyteller's performance.
Here the European observer clearly perceives storytelling as
a theatrical act, as a live performance that goes beyond the
mere recitation of a written text. A performance – given in a
suitable setting or *mise-en-scène* – furnishes the performer
with a certain creative and individual freedom, a freedom
that may even extend to commenting on religious and political issues: the narrator can use the transmitted text connota-
tively, indirectly declaring his position on events currently
taking place in their respective society. In order to convey
his message, the narrator may also use *rhetorical means*. The
narrator or reciter of a written text sets up a kind of imaginary
auditive stage in the audience's imagination. This way – after
making a "fictitious pact" with them – he is able to stimulate the
listener's power of imagination.

It is precisely this auspicious and dangerous potential residing in a storyteller's rhetorical and performative skills
that attracted the attention of strict Muslim theologians. They
condemned these theatrical elements in the harshest possible
terms. The Ḥanbalite theologian Abū l-Farağ ʿAbd al-Raḥmān
ibn ʿAlī al-Jawzī, born in Baghdad 511/1127 (d. 597/1200), a famous

[11] Richard Hole (1970 [1797]), *Remarks on the Arabian Nights' Entertainments*,
New York, p. 7, quoted from David Pinault (1992), *Story-telling
Techniques in the Arabian Nights*, Leiden, p. 13.

preacher in his own right, is scathing in his criticism of how other religious narrators exploit the potential of dramatic performance:[12]

> When the narrator of the Qur'ān sings, he transforms the psalmodies into songs. The preacher declaims, accompanied by music in verse from *Majnūn Laylā*. So someone applauds, someone else tears his clothes, and all believe that this is all an act of piety! And even though we know very well that these psalmodies, just like the music, provoke emotional upheaval and ecstasy in the soul. And we also know that it is a grave mistake to expose oneself to anything that could cause disorder.[13]

Here Ibn al-Jawzī scolds the audience's emotional outbursts, triggered by – as he would see it – careless religious narrators[14]

---

[12] For biographical details on Ibn al-Jawzī, see Merlin S. Swartz "Introduction" in Ibn al-Jawzī, (1986 [1969]), *Kitāb al-quṣṣāṣ wa'l-mudhakkirīn*, ed. and tr. Swartz, Beirut, pp. 13–45; Henri Laoust (1971), art. "Ibn al-Djawzī," in *Encyclopedia of Islam*, 2nd edn., vol. III, pp. 751–52.

[13] Quoted from Ibn al-Jawzī (1986), *La Pensée vigile*, ed. and tr. Daniel Reig, Paris, p. 134. The English translation is mine. It is important here to point out that the preacher only temporarily acts like a (secular) narrator, for instance when illustrating his sermon with popular, short religious stories. This illustrative addition strengthens the devotional function of his speech/sermon – it does not rupture or suspend his role as preacher. For a comprehensive presentation of Ibn al-Jawzī (including his *rhetorical* skills) cf. Stefan Leder, *Ibn al-Ǧauzī und seine Kompilation wider die Leidenschaft*, Beirut 1984.

[14] The term *qāṣṣ* (pl. *quṣṣāṣ*), is used in Ibn al-Jawzī's work *Kitāb al-quṣṣāṣ wa-l-mudhakkirīn* to designate the teller of religious stories. For a detailed explanation of the etymology of the word and the development of its usage, see Charles Pellat (1978), arts. "Ḳiṣṣa" and "Ḳāṣṣ,", in *Encyclopedia of Islam*, 2nd edn., vol. IV, pp. 185–7 and pp. 733–5.

whose sole aim is to generate cheap effects. The vehemence of his barb demonstrates how widespread this narrative and mimetic practice obviously was amongst narrators of religious stories and popular preachers.[15] Moreover, his detailed criticism demonstrates that, already at this point in time, the art of narration comprised truly dramatic elements which in the eyes of certain theologians lent a narrator's performance dangerous propagandistic potential.

In his work on religious narrators and preachers Ibn al-Jawzī gives a detailed report of these performative practices:

> Abū'l-Ḥusain al-Khayyāṭ reported the following: I passed by Abū ʿAbd Allāh Ghulām Khalīl while he was conducting a meeting in Baghdad during which he got down on all fours. I said to one of the persons present at the meeting: 'Woe unto you! What is the matter with Abū ʿAbd Allāh?' The man replied: 'He is illustrating how ʿAbd ar-Raḥmān b. ʿAwf will cross [the Bridge of] Ṣirāṭ on the Day of Resurrection.' Abū'l-Ḥusain continued: On another occasion I passed by one of his meetings, and he was stretching out his hands while standing in a stooped

---

[15] This practice was particularly predominant in Shiʿite circles, where narrators of religious stories aimed at instigating strong emotional reactions: "The arousal of tears was recommended for inciting revolt, and the qāriʾ or qāriʾa sought, in exchange for a sum of money, to make the audience weep. This practice, as we see with Ibn al-Jawzī sharply condemned by the Sunnis: 'against Shiʿite propagandists (duʿāt the plural of dāʿī) Sunnis oppose their own troupes of preachers (waʿʿāz the plural of wāʿiz) and the tellers of edifying stories (quṣṣāṣ the plural of qaṣṣaṣ).'" Monique Sammoun (1990), L'Expérience radicale dans le théâtre arabe, unpublished dissertation, Paris, pp. 212–13.

posture. So I inquired with one of those present: 'What is the matter with him?' 'He is illustrating how God will cast His protection around his servant on the Day of Resurrection,' was the answer.[16]

A lively insight into Ibn al-Jawzī's own skill in employing and exploiting dramatizing methods to stimulate the imagination of his audiences and so influence their perception and judgment of reality is to be found in an eyewitness account. In 580/1184 Ibn Jubayr attended one of his famous sermons, joining a crowd of thousands of other men:

> Incapable of tempering themselves, they were, overwhelmed by feelings, utterly unrestrained ... He repeated the verses unceasingly and was visibly excited; the tears almost strangled his words, so that he was on the verge of relapsing into silence. Then he stood up suddenly and descended the pulpit with unexpected speed. He had let hearts tremor with convulsions and now left them [the audience] like a cat on a hot tin roof, and their eyes red from crying followed him as he left. Many sobbed loudly, others fell into the dust, prostrate. What an event, how harrowing a sight! ... I would never have believed that a preacher of this world is endowed with the power to control the minds and souls in this way, to play with them as this man had.[17]

---

[16] Ibn al-Jawzī, *Kitāb al-quṣṣāṣ waʾl-mudhakkirīn*, chap. X, § 197, pp. 172–3; Arabic text, ibid., p. 94.

[17] Ibn Jubair, *Riḥlat al-kātib al-adīb al-bāriʿ al-labīb*, ed. W. Wright, 2nd corrected edn. M. J. de Goeje, Leiden and London, 1907, pp. 222 ff.

The storyteller as a political instrument in contemporary Arabic theatre

As we have seen, religious as well as profane storytellers are able to influence their community through the skillful use of the moral, emotional, and aesthetic power of their performance, a power that not only stems from the rational message embedded in the texts they employ but also accrues in the emotional effects generated by a collective experience. The narrator's objective is to reinforce the collective identity of the audience during the actual act of performing. The narrator taps into a key cultural source: how the members of the audience recognize themselves in stories they can directly relate to, thus "feeling at home" in their narrative fabric and reassured by the cultural affiliation and identity. The storyteller actuates and intensifies a latent sense of community based on a shared collective memory. The arousal and possible outbreak of forthright political, religious, and nationalist passions through a theatrical performance has always frightened religious as much as secular authorities.

It is exactly this potential of the storyteller that Arab dramatists picked up on and revived in their theatre productions between the 1960s and 1980s. Ever since the 1960s concepts such as "authenticity of cultural forms" and "politicization of the audience" have become much-quoted *leitmotifs*. Evidently, these concepts of dramatic discourse reflect the social and national developments of the time. Thus, from the late 1960s onwards, the storyteller has increasingly been seen as a critical authority of the collective consciousness.

226

My hypothesis is that the storyteller in theatre has functioned in Arabic literature since the 1960s as a role model of the contemporary Arab intellectual. The function the story-teller is assigned by the author reflects the function the author is assigning himself.

The most important function of the storyteller during the late 1960s and into the 1970s was to politicize the audience.[18] During the 1960s, criticism of monarchy, opportunism and administrative corruption became the favorite subjects of this group of Arab dramatists. The audience expected that Arab theatre demonstrate some sort of commitment to the respective nation's present and future and stimulate the courage of the people to face up to their gloomy situation and effect change. In such a context, the storyteller is to at once activate

---

[18] Angelika Hartmann pointed to the political function of Islamic preaching in the Middle Ages: "In every age, great preachers attempted to arouse the focused sentiments necessary for emotional excitement. Certainly, religious preaching had to be in the service, first and foremost, of exhortation and edification, but this preaching was an ideological instrument of the great and powerful as well as an escape valve for the discontents of the governed. And, let us not forget, it served, in its fashion, as a substitute for the theatre, which did not exist in Islamic civilization before the nineteenth century." Angelika Hartmann, (1987–1988): "Toute époque, de grands prédicateurs se sont entendus à provoquer la partialité des sentiments nécessaires à l'excitation émotive. Certes, la prédication religieuse devait server, au premier chef, à l'exhortation et à l'édification, mais elle a été un instrument de l'idéologie des gouvernants et des puissants ainsi qu'une soupape pour la critique des gouvernés. Et, ne l'oublions pas, elle a servi, à sa façon, de substitut aux pièces de théâtre, que la civilisation islamique n'a pas connues avant le 19ᵉ siècle." "La Prédication islamique au moyen âge: Ibn al-Ğauzī et ses sermons," in *Quaderni di Studi Arabi* 5–6 (1987–1988), pp. 337–45; 337.

the critical mind of the audience while creating and maintaining a certain distance to the story performed on stage. The degree of emotional involvement with the action seen on stage was to be relatively low, for it was believed that this would provide the audience with a perspective facilitating a critical appraisal of the messages conveyed in the story. The affinity of such an approach to Brecht's didactic epic theatre and theory of estrangement is obvious, and Arab dramatists indeed often referred to this concept in their attempt to propagate a so-called authentic style, including grafting it onto the national repertoire and the cultural heritage.[19] But whereas the traditional storyteller's/preacher's (exhortative) function was to reassure the audience by their cultural/religious affiliation and identity, the function of the politicized storyteller in modern Arab theatre is a complex, not to say inconsistent or contradictory one: it is *at the same time* to make people feel "at home" in their common cultural heritage *and* to create a critical *distance* to the events presented on stage. Thus, in the Arab reception of Brecht's concept of theatre additional semantic aspects have been added.[20]

The Syrian dramatist and director Saʿdallāh Wannūs has been especially successful in integrating the storyteller's

[19] Cf. Regina Karachouli (1989), "A Heritage Performed on the Stage: The Contemporary Arabic Theatre," in *Asia Africa Latin America*, special issue no. 22, Berlin, pp. 140–41.
[20] For a discussion of Brecht's multilayered reception in Arab theatre cf. Atef Botros (2006), Die Intellektuellen zwischen dem 'Authentischen' und dem europäischen 'Fremden' – Bertolt Brecht und die Konstruktion eines traditionellen Theaters," in *Der Nahe Osten – ein Teil Europas?* Würzburg, pp. 137–60.

multilayered function into his work. In his play *Muġāmarāt ra's al-mamlūk Jābir* (*The Adventures of Mamlūk Jābir's Head*), written in 1970, a fictitious storyteller is placed amidst his own audience gathered in a coffeehouse. This audience calls for him to relate a story about one of the ancient Arab heroes; he refuses, saying that this is not the right time for heroic stories. Instead he tells the story of the opportunist slave Jābir. The storyteller serves here "as a personification of history and as indicator of what is to be learned from it."[21] The function of the storyteller is to move between the different levels of the action on stage and involve the audience present by directly addressing it. Furthermore, he functions as a chorus when he comments on the events on stage. Such an approach emphasizes a function of the traditional storyteller: while the message he gives is one as an individual artist, it implies – and the implied message is in fact the key trajectory – a political judgment. In this period several Arab authors – in prose, poetry, and theatre – were convinced of literature's potentiality to change reality.[22] Wannūs presents in *The Adventures of Mamlūk Jābir's Head* a self-confident storyteller who teaches the people gathered around him. He provides them with insights and offers advice as to how gain a better understanding of their history and society.

---

[21] Roger Allen (1984), "Arabic Drama in Theory and Practice: The Writings of Saʿdallāh Wannūs, in *Journal of Arabic Literature* 15, pp. 94–113; p. 104.

[22] Even some years later Wannūs stated in an interview: "An author who has lost his belief in the changeability of the world, loses at the same time all motivation for writing." In *al-Ḥurriya* 149 (1986), p. 45.

Here the audience is considered as a cultural and national community. The storyteller's – or the writer's – function is to maintain and strengthen the underlying national and cultural identity. But this identity underwent far-reaching transformations during the late 1970s and the 1980s. The generation of intellectuals who had grown up within the optimistic atmosphere of the 'Arab socialism' of Nasser became rather bewildered and uncertain once Sadat took office. His rapprochement with Israel, culminating in his visits to Jerusalem and Camp David in 1977, the economic policy of opening (*infitāh*) in Egypt, and the abandonment of socialist and pan-Arab ideals, all signaled a massive social and political reorientation (Wannūs mentioned for example in an interview in the 1990s that he was so desperate in 1977 after Sadat's visit to Jerusalem that he tried to commit suicide).

Such developments demanded a fundamental revision of Arab thought and the role literature was seen to play in society. The notion of "committed/engaged" literature (*iltizām al-adab*), from the 1950s up to this point the predominant ideal, now underwent critical revision. To be a responsible and engaged author no longer necessarily meant being directly involved in the current debates and contributing to ideological and political discourses. The literature of the 1970s is characterized by a rupture with former concepts of reality and the value systems they spawned, while the political and national self-assurance so many authors had once felt was now vigorously challenged.

It is my view that, given these circumstances, it is hardly surprising that the seemingly omniscient intellectual power of the storyteller figure is increasingly eroded precisely in this period, the almost sage-like capacity to explain history and interpret present reality called into question. In Wannūs' play *Munamnamāt tārīḥīya/* (*Historical Miniatures*), written in 1992[23], the storyteller figure is in fact replaced by a *muʾarrikh qadīm*, an old historian, whose function has accordingly been reduced to that of a subordinate chronicler without any right to comment on events, let alone offer forthright criticism.

Wannūs is not the only example of this tendency. In the theatrical production of the play *Mudhkkirāt Ayyūb* (*Hiob's Memories*) by the Lebanese actor and director Roger ʿAssāf in 1993, the storyteller is at a complete loss to explain the present predicament. Unable to come to grips with reality on his own, he confines himself to remembering the stories people used to tell him. In this play, the first public critical analysis of the Lebanese Civil War, the audience becomes a witness to the storyteller's vain attempts to arrange the fragmentary stories of the Civil War into some kind of overarching narrative order. The play ends in hopelessness and resignation; the grand narratives the storytellers of former times told are now smashed and pulverized into tiny fragments, History reduced to a seemingly endless set of anecdotes which do not merge into a coherent whole.

---

[23] It is interesting to note that Wannūs decided to stop his literary production on the night after Sadat's visit to Israel in 1977. Only twelve years later, with the publishing of the play *al-Ightiṣāb* (*The Rape*), which reflected on the Palestine question, he raised his literary voice again (German translation in Friederike Pannewick (1993), *Der andere Blick: Eine syrische Stimme zur Palästinafrage*, Berlin. *Historical Miniatures* is the second play after his period of silence (French translation: Saadallah Wannous (1996), *Miniatures, suivi de Rituel pour une métamorphose*, Arles).

II Passion plays on the move in time and place: Iran – India – the Caribbean

My aim in the first section was to demonstrate how the function of the performative tradition of storytelling in both religious and secular contexts has been transformed within the cultural history of the Middle East, from the Islamic Classical Age through to twentieth-century political theatre. We started with a quotation of Shahrazād's famous words on the art of storytelling in the so-called *Arabian Nights* – a masterpiece of Arabic literature that has been received throughout Europe with so much acclaim, even though strictly speaking it is not of "pure" Arab origin but, as we know, contains material gleaned from other sources, mainly India and Persia but also Mesopotamia and Turkish regions.[24] *Alf Layla wa-Layla* is thus not only a telling example of the performative power of storytelling, but also of the enormous mobility of artistic traditions.

The second section is devoted to another traveling performative tradition: the *ta'ziya*,[25] a kind of Shi'ite passion

---

[24] Littmann, art. "Alf Layla wa-Layla."

[25] *Ta'ziya* is a verbal noun from the Arabic verb *'azza*, meaning "to mourn," "console," "express sympathy with." The term *ta'ziya* is mainly used in Iranian contexts, whereas in Arab countries the terms *timthīliyya* or *masraḥiyya*, "dramatization/ theatre play," are more common. The dramatic form of *ta'ziya* arose from the stationary and ambulatory rituals in the first month of the Islamic calendar, *muharram*. Sometimes the term *'āshūrā'* is also used; this refers to the tenth day of *muharram*, when Ḥusayn and his successors were cut off from water in the desert of Karbalā' for ten days and then killed or put into slavery on the tenth day (*'āshūrā'*).

play. If the sources ultimately making up the *Arabian Nights* traveled from South Asia to the Middle East, here it seems as if we have a peregrination of tradition transmitted along very different routes: from Iraq to Iran, on to India, and from there, much later, even to Europe, the US and the Caribbean.

A performative form of ritualized mourning, in Iran this passion play reached its artistic peak as a highly elaborate music drama in the mid-eighteenth century,[26] with a number of European travelers recording eyewitness accounts. But even in our contemporary age, the reactions of Europeans who experience a performance first hand reveal their astonishment and fascination with an art form they have never encountered before:

> I saw in a remote Iranian village one of the strongest things I have ever seen in theatre: a group of 400 villagers, the entire population of the place, sitting under the tree and passing from roars of laughter to outright sobbing – although they knew perfectly well the end of the story – as they saw Hussein in danger of being killed, and then fooling his enemies, and then being martyred. And when he was martyred the theatre form became truth – there was no difference between past and present. An event that was told

---

[26] After the official recognition of Shiʿism as Iran's state religion in the early sixteenth century, "royal patronage ensured that the Muharram festival observances would assume a central position in the cultural and religious identity of the country, and the festival became a unifying force for the nation. When the stationary and ambulatory aspects of the ritual merged in the mid-18th century, taʿziyeh was born as a distinct type of music drama." Peter Chelkowski (2005), "Time Out of Memory: Taʿziyeh, the Total Drama," in *TDR, The Drama Review*, special issue: *From Karbala to New York: Taʿziyeh on the Move*, vol. 49, no. 4, pp. 13–27; p. 16.

as a remembered happening in history, six hundred years ago,[27] actually became a reality at that moment. Nobody could draw the line between the different orders of reality. It was an incarnation: at that particular moment, he was being martyred again in front of these villagers.[28]

This is the eyewitness account given by one of the world's foremost avant-garde theatre directors since the 1950s – Peter Brook. The English artist attended a ta'ziya performance during a visit to Iran in 1979. What is Peter Brook actually describing in this enthusiastic account? A group of people, who all know one another well, come together. They see the presentation of a story that they all know in great detail. Everyone is severely shaken and moved by the events, although shortly before they had still been laughing and joking. The story is part of their religion, their collective memory. Through the martyrdom performance the events of the past become the present: thanks to the religious continuity in the meaning of these events, the levels of reality and fiction become blurred. And what is the impact of this form of presentation? An incarnation – so Brook's impression – of Ḥusayn takes place on the stage, his martyrdom is once more fulfilled in a religious play in front of the eyes of the audience.

---

[27] Sic: the historical date is 680 CE.

[28] Peter Brook (1979), "Leaning on the Moment: A Conversation with Peter Brook," *Parabola* 4, 2 (May), p. 52; cf. Brook (1994), *Das offene Geheimnis: Gedanken über Schauspielerei und Theater*, Frankfurt am Main, pp. 58–67. For further reactions of (earlier) visitors and witnesses to this performance see Peter Chelkowski (1979), "Bibliographical Spectrum," in Chelkowski, ed., *Ta'ziyeh: Ritual and Drama in Iran*, New York, pp. 255–66.

Historical background of the Shiʿite passion play taʿziya

Although this peculiar Shiʿite self-fashioning as a community of victims has been shaped by several hundred years of religiously and politically motivated imagination, it does have a historical foundation. The crucial event in Shiʿite history is the martyrdom of Imam Ḥusayn, grandson of the Prophet, who according to Shiʿite tradition was massacred in 680 CE along with his family on the plain outside of Karbalāʾ near Baghdad by the soldiers of Yazīd, the Caliph.[29]

The Prophet Muḥammad had died in 632 without nominating a definite successor. The group amongst the faithful known today as Shiʿites was of the view that the Prophet had named his son-in-law and cousin ʿAlī as Caliph. However, three respected men from his close circle were nominated successively, before ʿAlī, married to the Prophet's daughter Fāṭima, was first called to rule in 656. He was murdered only four years later. This murder opened the way for Muʿāwiya (reign 661–680) and the Umayyads, who then went on to rule over the faithful until the middle of the eighth century. The

---

[29] The following survey of the historical background has been already presented in an article dealing with the Shiʿite aesthetic representations of martyrdom, Friederike Pannewick (2004), "Passion and Rebellion: Shiʿite Visions of Redemptive Martyrdom," in Pannewick, ed., *Martyrdom in Literature: Visions of Death and Meaningful Suffering in Europe and the Middle East from Antiquity to Modernity*, Wiesbaden, pp. 47–62; cf. further Jamshid Malekpour (2004), *The Islamic Drama: Taʿziyeh*, London and Portland, pp. 20–31.

succession of Muʿāwiya's son Yazīd met with strong resistance from the followers of ʿAlī. According to tradition, in their struggle to avoid rendering allegiance to the Umayyad Caliph Yazīd, the inhabitants of the rebellious city Kufa called upon Ḥusayn for help, who had until then lived a life of scholarly seclusion in Medina. Together with a mere seventy-two followers, Ḥusayn then entered into a battle against several thousand of the Caliph's soldiers. As the expected support from Kufa failed to materialize, Ḥusayn – certain that a bloody defeat was looming – freed his followers from their oath of allegiance and demanded that they flee the imminent massacre. But not one of them was prepared to leave the grandson of the Prophet; all of the men were killed, the women and children abducted, and Ḥusayn's head was sent as a trophy to the capital Damascus, where the Caliph had it put on show in the Umayyad mosque.

These events at the small town of Karbalāʾ near Kufa were subsequently taken to mark the sealing of the religious schism between the dominant Sunni and the group forming around the figure of ʿAlī, the shīʿat ʿAlī. It is difficult for modern historical research to determine the actual course of events, for later interpretations by a variety of Islamic interest groups have obscured the historical facts.

But irrespective of how the historical events are to be evaluated, their integral significance eclipses all other turning-points in the history of the Shiʿite religious community. The martyrdom of Ḥusayn is not only representative of suffering in itself, but it also stands for the deeply human need and endeavor to cope with suffering by lending it a meaning. The crucial step in this search for meaning is, according to Mahmoud Ayoub, the realization that meaning and fulfillment in human life can be attained not *despite of* but *through* suffering and death.[30]

In his study of the history of *taʿziya* Jamshid Malekpour has pointed to the special meaning this dramatic form gained for Iranian Shiʿites. He quotes William S. Haas, who underlines the melancholic and deeply emotional aspects of this religion which coalesce with the ideas of "martyrdom," "purity," and "justice":

> No doubt in the recess of their souls the Persians, at least those of the first centuries after the Islamic conquest, identified themselves with the persecution and martyrdom of Ali and his house. They, too, were a defeated and humiliated people whose rights and deepest convictions had been violated and trodden upon... the great psychological function of the Shia schism was the defence and self-protection against the new religion.[31]

Performative traditions[32]

The Shiʿite passion play is thus a kind of dramatic refiguration of Ḥusayn's martyrdom, the foundational event

---

[30] Mahmoud Ayoub (1978), *Redemptive Suffering in Islām: A Study of the Devotional Aspects of ʿĀshūrāʾ in Twelver Shīʿīsm*, The Hague.

[31] William S. Haas (1946), *Iran*, New York, pp. 133–34, quoted from Malekpour, *The Islamic Drama*, p. 28.

[32] Cf. for performative aspects of *taʿziya*: Chelkowski, ed., *Taʿziyeh*; Navid Kermani (1999), "Katharsis und Verfremdung im schiitischen Passionsspiel," in *Welt des Islams* 39, pp. 31–63; Friederike Pannewick (2000), *Das Wagnis Tradition: Arabische Wege der Theatralität*, Wiesbaden, pp. 186–219; Kamran Scot Aghaie, "The Origins of the Sunnite-Shiʿite Divide and the Emergence of the Taʿziyeh Tradition," in Chelkowski, ed., *From Karbala to New York*, pp. 42–7.

in the history of this confession. Once a year, in the month of *muḥarram*, the Shiʿites celebrate a grand feast during which the martyrdom of Ḥusayn is commemorated. This mourning ritual is evidence of the fascinating degree of cultural mobility in the Middle East. Scholars like Jamshid Malekpour argue that *taʿziya* is not a 'purely Islamic' form, but that Zoroastrian mourning rituals and processions together with oral recitations (often accompanied by music) practiced during the Sassanid era (224–652) were essential for the later development of *taʿziya* as a dramatic form.[33]

Already in the seventh century elegies telling the story of Ḥusayn's tragic death were composed and these evolved over the following two centuries into a set of Shiʿite ritual performances that sought to put on a public display of the Shiʿites' religious legitimacy and so strengthen the sense of solidarity within Shiʿite circles. When in the sixteenth century the Safavids established a Shiʿite state in Iran (1502), *taʿziya* rituals were used for the purposes of power politics, for they were seen as a suitable device for bolstering the Safavid claims to legitimate rule and creating a clear separation from the Sunnites, at that time still the majority branch of Islam in Iran. Colorful and splendid processions developed out of the earlier commemorative ceremonies honoring the Prophet's

---

[33] Malekpour *The Islamic Drama*, pp. 32 ff.; cf. further Yitzhak Nakash (1993), "An Attempt to Trace the Origin of the Rituals in ʿĀshūrāʾ," in *Die Welt des Islams* 33, pp. 161–81; the conception of *taʿziya* as in some respects similar to the Christian passion play is to be found e.g. in Hildegard Müller (1967), *Studien zum persischen Passionsspiel*, Vienna.

grandson. A new genre of pious narratives (gathered in the work *Rawzat al-shuhadā'* by the popular religious orator Ḥusayn Vaʿiz Kashifi) evolved in this period. These narrations and elegies were recited aloud at special gatherings which in turn then gradually evolved into performative mourning rituals known as *razeh khāni*. Numerous travelers from Europe reported enthusiastically about the overwhelming impact generated by the confessional performance. Reports from the seventeenth century describe the inclusion of theatrical elements into the *taʿziya*: impersonations of members of the holy family within public processions. However, a full theatrical form is not reached until the mid-eighteenth century. Since then, during the ten-day festival held in the month *muḥarram*, each day a specific episode is taken from the tale of the passion and presented in scenes.

In the twentieth century this mourning performance initially lost some of its importance in modern Iran and was even prohibited in the early 1930s by Rezā Shah Pahlawi (1925–1941). After the Shah abdicated in 1941 it was once more permitted to openly express religious emotions and this helped the *taʿziya* to flourish anew. More focused interest first emerged, however, in the 1960s, as in the course of engaged research into tradition many intellectuals turned their attention to this form of representation. This "authenticity movement" reached its high point at the *Shiraz Arts Festival* of 1976, where Peter J. Chelkowski organized an international symposium on the *taʿziya*. In a nearby village seven *taʿziya* performances were held, attracting almost 100,000 visitors.

239

Contemporary political configurations of an old performative pattern

It is obvious that *ta'ziya* rituals possess an enormously powerful mass appeal and this potential has been frequently harnessed – and instrumentalized – for political purposes. The Shi'ites regard Ḥusayn as the paradigmatic martyr prepared to sacrifice his life for the sake of the threatened collective. This model of an ideal-type fulfillment of the religiously justified call to *jihād* can be easily applied under the most divergent historical conditions, and has thus been used repeatedly in the varied history of the Shi'ites.[34]

It was the mentors of the "Islamic Revolution" who changed the "Karbalā' paradigm" from an attempt to lend innocent suffering meaning to a call for rebellion and violent resistance against concrete social conditions. The most force-ful figure in this shift was the influential Iranian sociologist 'Alī Shari'atī. He propagated an understanding of the martyr-dom of the Prophet's grandson that regarded the event as a call for struggle, marking a radical break with the tradition, dom-inant since the Safavid dynasty, interpreting this martyrdom as a tragic incident that was to be mourned in passive suffering. Criticizing the quietist "Safavid Shi'a," he countered this with the active "red Shi'a" of 'Alī martyrs, disparagingly labeling the

---

[34] For the political instrumentalization of the "Karbalā' paradigm" in Iran cf. Navid Kermani (2002), "Märtyrertum als Topos politischer Selbstdarstellung in Iran," in *Figurative Politik – Zur Performanz der Macht in der modernen Gesellschaft*, eds. H.-G. Soeffner, D. Tänzler, Opladen, pp. 89–100; Farhad Khosrokhavar (1995), *L'Islamisme et la mort: Le Martyre révolutionaire en Iran*, Paris.

Safavid Shiʿa as a religion for wailers and categorically rejecting the piety of those who solely proclaim their grief by crying, wailing, and flagellating themselves during the processions and assemblies held on religious feast days. Thinkers like Shariʿatī politicized the "Karbala paradigm" and prepared the way for a combative interpretation of martyrdom in the Shiʿa.

Iran – India – Trinidad[35]

This semantic and contextual shift from a quietist mourning ceremony to revolutionary activism, the result of an evolution responding to changing historical conditions over thirteen centuries, is not the only journey the Shiʿite passion play has taken. Having originated and reached its theatrical peak in Iran, the taʿziya, the performative enactment of Ḥusayn's martyrdom within the annual festivities of Āshūrāʾ has also moved across geographical borders, migrating to places as divergent as the Indian subcontinent, France, Italy, the US, and Trinidad.

This movement through large parts of the world has proven to be selective in many ways: it was not always the performance in its entirety that was transmitted; single elements such as gestures, modes of expression, or symbols were

[35] For traditions in Lebanon cf. A. R. Norton, "Ritual, Blood, and Shiite Identity: Ashura in Nabatiyya, Lebanon," in Chelkowski, ed., *From Karbala to New York*, pp. 140–55; Lara Deeb (2006), *An Enchanted Modern: Gender and Public Piety in Shi'i Lebanon*, Princeton and Oxford, pp. 129–64; in Iraq: Kamran Scot Aghaie, ed. (2005), *The Women of Karbala: Ritual Performances and Symbolic Discourse in Modern Shi'i Islam*, Austin; Elisabeth Fernea, "Remembering Taʿziyeh in Iraq," in Chelkowski, ed., *From Karbala to New York*, 130–9.

borrowed and inspired international theatre artists and so found their way into completely new creative environments.[36]

In 2005 *The Drama Review* published a special volume entitled *From Karbala to New York: Ta'ziyeh on the Move*, where all these various adaptations of the Shiʿite mourning performance are extensively studied. The most astonishing journey of this fascinating Shiʿite tradition plots a path from Iran to India and from there to the Caribbean.

One important element within the Shiʿite mourning rituals is the pilgrimage to the tomb of Ḥusayn in Karabalāʾ/ Iraq. This *ziyāra*, alone with the popular tradition of burying the dead at Karabalāʾ's cemetery, could not be performed by Shiʿites living in India because of the great distance from Iraq. The Indian Shiʿites' solution was rather pragmatic: they traveled to Karabalāʾ and brought back soil from this holy site, using it as the ground soil for their own Shiʿite cemeteries on the Indian subcontinent. They called these new cemeteries, which are also used as sites for muḥarram rituals, "Karabalāʾs" and constructed portable replicas of Ḥusayn's mausoleum in Karabalāʾ, known as *taʿziya*.[37] These fancy constructions, whose appearance often differs enormously from Ḥusayn's

---

[36] One example of this phenomenon is the theatre director Peter Brook, who, after experiencing the *taʿziya* in Iran, adapted in his later theatre experiments such as *Orghast* and *Conference of Birds* Middle Eastern mystical traditions, combining them with elements from *taʿziya*; cf. David Williams (1988), *Peter Brook: A Theatrical Casebook*, London, p. xiii.

[37] Cf. Frank J. Korom and Peter Chelkowski (1994), "Community Process and the Performance of Muharram Observances in Trinidad," in *TDR, The Drama Review*, 2, 38, 150–170; Peter Chelkowski, "From the Sun-Scorched Desert of Iran to the Beaches of Trinidad. Taʿziyeh's Journey from Asia to the Caribbean," in Chelkowski, ed., *From Karbala to New York*, pp. 156–69.

actual tomb shrine in Iraq, are a part of the stationary and ambulatory mourning rites that are considered reenactments of his funeral. To participate in these processions with the *ta'ziya* equates spiritually with a pilgrimage to Ḥusayn's real tomb. Researchers like Sadiq Naqvi[38] have observed that not only Muslims but Hindus also actively participate in the muḥarram rites. After the procession comes to an end, the *ta'ziya* constructions are brought to permanent ritual-related buildings, called *ashurkhana* (similar sites are known as *imam-bara, azakhana, ta'ziya-khana*). Naqvi has described this *ashurkhana* as meeting place for people from different castes, for Muslims – Sunnites or Shi'ites – and Hindus.

In his article on the migration of the *ta'ziya* from Asia to the Caribbean Peter Chelkowski states that in "India Hindu rituals and festivals have had a great impact on Muharram ceremonies. The bamboo *pandal* of the goddess Durga, which, like the nakhl, is portable and often quite large, is immersed into water during the ceremony known as *Durga puja*; similarly, the *ta'ziyeh* is immersed in water at the end of the Muharram procession."[39]

This religious syncretism is characteristic for *ta'ziya*, whose fascinating transcultural mobility extended even beyond the Indian subcontinent. The Shi'ite mourning performance

---

[38] Sadiq Naqvi (n.d.), *Qutb Shahi 'Asur Khanas of Hyderabad: Bab-ul-Ilm Society*, Darulshifa and Hyderabad. Cf. Chelkowski, *From Karbala to New York*, p. 164.

[39] Chelkowski *From Karbala to New York*, p. 161; the *nakhl* is a processional bier representing the improvised stretcher on which the body of Ḥusayn was carried to his tomb; in the Caribbean it is known as *tadja*, a phonetic transformation of *ta'ziya*.

was still on the move, on the way to its next station: the Caribbean.

Between 1845 and 1917,[40] thousands of Indians moved to the Caribbean to work there on British sugar plantations. These Indians replaced the African slaves who had farmed these British plantations until their emancipation in 1834. Most of these Indians lived in districts where, according to figures from 1891, approximately 14 percent were Muslims. In their new Caribbean home the Muslim Indians encountered the fancy parades of the main Creole annual celebration, the Carnival – a syncretical tradition featuring both African and Creole elements. Although the number of Shi'ites amongst the Indian Muslim immigrants to Trinidad was very small, they nonetheless introduced their own annual public procession as a way to counterbalance local public Carnival celebrations. In turn, this Caribbean version of an originally Middle Eastern public mourning performance underwent a further metamorphosis, becoming part of annual demonstrations held to support the cause of pan-Indian national unity in Trinidad, once more demonstrating the extraordinary performative power and cultural mobility.

Mobility and performativity of cultural forms of expression

This article has dealt with the *performative power of traveling traditions*, aiming to demonstrate how traditions like

---

[40] The following report is based on Chelkowski, *From Karbala to New York*, pp. 164–169; references are given there.

the Shiʿite mourning performances, performative sermons or storytelling accrue new semantic features through their various journeys in time and space. Not only *taʿziya*, but also the tradition of Middle Eastern storytelling has survived in different religious, political, and artistic contexts, enacted in Arab coffeehouses for instance in Syria, Lebanon, or Morocco until very recently. Both traditions need to therefore be considered as firmly rooted, variously enacted and syncretically extended cultural products of the Middle East.

I have chosen these two examples because both combine aspects of performativity and mobility, and argued that reflecting on these two exemplary aspects represents a key inlet for gaining a better understanding of what culture actually is – a continuous flux, a syncretical and ongoing process of exchange, interactions, and creative overlaps. In Stephen Greenblatt's conception of culture such processes of borrowing are "not evidence of imaginative parsimony, still less a symptom of creative exhaustion." They signal rather a key aspect of cultural mobility:

> This mobility is not the expression of random motion but of *exchange*. A culture is a particular network of negotiations for the exchange of material goods, ideas, and – through institutions like enslavement, adoption, or marriage – people ... Great writers are precisely ... specialists in cultural exchange. The works they create are structures for the accumulation, transformation, representation, and communication of social energies and practices ... They take symbolic materials from one zone of the culture and move them to another, augmenting their emotional force, altering their significance, linking them

with other materials taken from a different zone, changing their place in a larger social design.[41]

I would argue that Arab performative forms are only understandable on the basis of such a conception of culture and art. Arab performative art is a cultural act that cannot be viewed in isolation; rather, we need to approach it as having arisen in and through a complex process of transcultural interaction. Any attempt to interpret this performative art must take such exchange as its starting point.[42]

But this approach has only very recently found resonance in critical studies of Middle Eastern theatre.[43] Essentialist judgments of leading nineteenth-century orientalists like Ernest Renan, but also of influential Arab theatre critics and dramatists like the Egyptian Taufīq al-Ḥakīm (1898–1987), have argued against any capacity of "the Arabs" to develop complex forms of dramatic structure. This line of argumentation has resulted in the history of Arabic theatre being written as a history of absence. Even in Western postwar studies on Arab art and culture, for example, Jacob M. Landau's 1958 work *Studies in the Arab Theater and Cinema* (still, forty-seven years later, the

---

[41] Stephen Greenblatt (1995), "Culture," in *Critical Terms for Literary Study*, 2nd edn., eds. Frank Lentricchia and Thomas McLaughlin, Chicago and London, pp. 225–32; 229 ff.

[42] This process of transcultural interaction is of cause not independent from historical/political and collective constraints limiting individual agency (cf. the chapter "The Storyteller as Political Instrument" in this article). Cf. for a detailed discussion of this approach Pannewick, *Das Wagnis Tradition*. Arabische Wege der Theatralität. Wiesbaden, pp. 301–5.

[43] For example in *The World Encyclopedia of Contemporary Theatre* (1999), vol. IV: *The Arab World*, ed. Don Rubin, London and New York.

authoritative "Anglophone" text on Arab performance art), culturalist judgments are to be found quite often. In the preface to Landau's book, H. A. R. Gibb of the Harvard Center for Middle Eastern Studies has stated bluntly that "drama is not a native Arab art," and that it was only "as a self-confessed imitation of the European theatre that the drama was introduced into the Arab world in the nineteenth century"[44] Consistent with Gibb, Landau develops the idea that "modern theatre" was a "wholly foreign" product "transplanted" to the "virgin soil" of Arab (and mostly Islamic) societies. "There was no regular Arab theatre until the 19th century," Landau asserts, when Napoleon's invasion of North Africa introduced Molière's comedies to Egypt.[45]

One way out of these cultural misinterpretations is to place the debate on Arab theatre forms into the research field concerned with both *performativity* and cultural mobility. For some time now drama and cultural studies have worked on

---

[44] Jacob M. Landau (1958), *Studies in the Arab Theater and Cinema*, Philadelphia, p. ix.

[45] That such a misinterpretation of Arab culture and art is still prevalent in the twenty-first century is revealed by following statement made in the popular American theatre history textbook Oscar G. Brockett and Franklin J. Hildy (2003), *History of Theatre* Boston, p. 69: "In the history of the theatre ... Islam is largely a negative force. It forbade artists to make images of living things because Allah was said to be the only creator of life and to compete with him was considered a mortal sin. Thus, Islamic art remained primarily decorative rather than representational. The prohibitions extended to the theatre, and consequently in those areas where Islam became dominant advanced theatrical forms were stifled." The underlying misunderstanding, stemming from a lack of a clear definition of "theatre" vs. "drama," and dramatic vs. enacted text, is discussed in Pannewick *Das Wagnis Tradition*, pp. 12 ff.

establishing new criteria for understanding contemporary theatre. Theatre is seen as an *event* that happens between the stage and the audience. A literary *text* no longer necessarily stands at the centre of attention; instead, focus is placed on the communication between actors and audience, which is the process of *theatricality* or *performativity*. But besides this important aspect of performativity, the crucial role of the reenacted "cultural archive" to which these performances are always referring back should be taken into consideration.

These criteria allow us not only to grasp avant-garde performances in Europe, but also Arab forms of narrative or ritual performances. In Europe artists experimented with non-European forms of performance, with rituals, dance, and masques; in this way they sought to cast off the prescriptions laid down by conventional Aristotelian drama. Initially in the Arab world European classics were imitated and adapted for the Arab audience. In the course of strengthening anticolonialism, however, artists strove to distance themselves from European drama, as they felt swamped by the colonial influence. Since the 1960s a strong preference has developed for experimenting with Arab traditions such as the storyteller, the shadow play, or ritual portrayals and infusing them with contemporary concerns. Hence, Arab and European performing artists have met, so to say, halfway, each searching for a contemporary understanding of theatre appealing to the public.[46]

---

[46] Cf. Pannewick (2000), "Synkretisches Theater der Moderne – ein Ausblick," in *Das Wagnis Tradition*, pp. 301–5.

Such tendencies are also evident in Singapore, Africa, or Latin America: elements from various periods and cultures are *syncretically* brought together and new, independent forms developed. In the global situation of contemporary art an artistic language has formed that surpasses national or cultural boundaries. In this context culture can no longer be understood as a self-enclosed unity that would need to be clearly distinguished from other such units. For some time now, discussions in anthropology have centered upon an open, dialogical concept of culture. With this new concept of *culture in a continuous flux* important phenomena in Arab culture are only now understandable.[47]

[47] I would like to thank Paul Bowman for his expert and understanding reviewing of this article, and Reinhart Meyer-Kalkus as well as the participants of the Yale Arabic Colloquium and of the Summer Academy at the American University of Beirut (2006) for their productive criticism.

8

A mobility studies manifesto

STEPHEN GREENBLATT

First, *mobility must be taken in a highly literal sense*. Boarding a plane, venturing on a ship, climbing onto the back of a wagon, crowding into a coach, mounting on horseback, or simply setting one foot in front of the other and walking: these are indispensable keys to understanding the fate of cultures. The physical, infrastructural, and institutional conditions of movement – the available routes; the maps; the vehicles; the relative speed; the controls and costs; the limits on what can be transported; the authorizations required; the inns, relay stations and transfer points; the travel facilitators – are all serious objects of analysis. Only when conditions directly related to literal movement are firmly grasped will it be possible fully to understand the metaphorical movements: between center and periphery; faith and skepticism; order and chaos; exteriority and interiority. Almost every one of these metaphorical movements will be understood, on analysis, to involve some kinds of physical movement as well.

Second, *mobility studies should shed light on hidden as well as conspicuous movements* of peoples, objects, images, texts, and ideas. Here again it would be well to begin with the literal sense: moments in which cultural goods are transferred out of sight, concealed inside cunningly designed shells of the familiar or disguised by subtle adjustments of color and form. From here it is possible to move to more metaphorical notions of hiddenness: unconscious, unrecognized, or deliberately distorted mobility, often in response to regimes of censorship or repression. We can also investigate the cultural mechanisms through which certain forms of movement – migration, labor-market border-crossing, smuggling, and the like – are marked as "serious," while others, such as tourism, theater festivals, and (until recently) study abroad, are rendered virtually invisible.

Third, *mobility studies should identify and analyze the "contact zones" where cultural goods are exchanged.* Different societies constitute these zones differently, and their varied structures call forth a range of responses from wonder and delight to avidity and fear. Certain places are characteristically set apart from inter-cultural contact; others are deliberately made open, with the rules suspended that inhibit exchange elsewhere. A specialized group of "mobilizers" – agents, go-betweens, translators, or intermediaries – often emerges to facilitate contact, and this group, along with the institutions that they serve, should form a key part of the analysis.

Fourth, *mobility studies should account in new ways for the tension between individual agency and structural constraint.* This tension cannot be resolved in any abstract theoretical way, for in given historical circumstances structures of power seek to mobilize some individuals and immobilize others. And it is important to note that moments in which individuals feel most completely in control may, under careful scrutiny, prove to be moments of the most intense structural determination, while moments in which the social structure applies the fiercest pressure on the individual may in fact be precisely those moments in which individuals are exercising the most stubborn will to autonomous movement. Mobility studies should be interested, among other things, in the way in which seemingly fixed migration paths are disrupted by the strategic acts of individual agents and by unexpected, unplanned, entirely contingent encounters between different cultures.

Fifth, *mobility studies should analyze the sensation of rootedness*. The paradox here is only apparent: it is impossible to understand mobility without also understanding the glacial weight of what appears bounded and static. Mobility often is perceived as a threat – a force by which traditions, rituals, expressions, beliefs are decentered, thinned out, decontextualized, lost. In response to this perceived threat, many groups and individuals have attempted to wall themselves off from the world or, alternatively, they have resorted to violence.

Cultures are almost always apprehended not as mobile or global or even mixed, but as local. Even self-conscious experiments in cultural mobility, such as the ones we have described in these essays, turn out to produce results that are strikingly enmeshed in particular times and places and local cultures. And the fact that those local cultures may in fact be recent formations, constructed out of elements that an earlier generation would not have recognized, makes very little difference. Indeed one of the characteristic powers of a culture is its ability to hide the mobility that is its enabling condition. Certainly the pleasure, as well as the opacity, of culture has to do with its localness: *this* way of doing something (cooking, speaking, praying, making love, dancing, wearing a headscarf or a necklace, etc.) and not *that*. A study of cultural mobility that ignores the allure (and, on occasion, the entrapment) of the firmly rooted simply misses the point. Theory and descriptive practice have to apprehend how quickly such a sense of the local is often established and also how much resistance to change the local, even when it is of relatively recent and mixed origin, can mount.

INDEX